Language Awareness in the Classroom

Edited by
Carl James and Peter Garrett

Longman
London and New York

P
53
.L35
1991

Longman Group UK Limited,
Longman House, Burnt Mill, Harlow,
Essex CM20 2JE, England
and Associated Companies throughout the world.

Published in the United States of America
by Longman Inc., New York

© Longman Group UK Limited 1991

First published 1992

British Library Cataloguing in Publication Data
Language awareness in the classroom. – (Applied linguistics
and language study).
1. Schools. Curriculum subjects: Language skills.
Teaching
I. James, Carl II. Garrett, Peter III. Series
407.1

ISBN 0–582–06737–5

Library of Congress Cataloging in Publication Data
Language awareness in the classroom/edited by Carl James and Peter
Garrett.
    p.   cm. — (Language awareness in the classroom)
    Includes bibliographical references and index.
    ISBN 0–582–06737–5
    1. Language and languages—Study and teaching. 2. Language
awareness. I. James, Carl. II. Garrett, Peter, 1950–
III. Series.
P53.L35   1991
418′.007—dc20   90–19557
                                                     CIP

Set in 10/12 pt Linotron 202 Ehrhardt

Printed in Malaysia
by Percetakan Mun Sun Sdn. Bhd.,
Shah Alam, Selangor Darul Ehsan

Contents

The Contributors

Jim Anderson
The John Roan School, London

Christopher Brumfit
University of Southampton

Nicholaos Chryshochoos
Completing his PhD at the University of Durham

Romy Clark
Lancaster University

Gillian Donmall
Derbyshire College of Higher Education, Derby

Peter Garrett
University of Wales, Bangor

Hugh Gosden
Teacher in Japan

Brian Heap
UK-based teacher

Nicki Hedge
University of Liverpool

John Holmes
Formerly adviser for the Brazilian ESP project

Janet Hooper
UK-based teacher

Roz Ivanič
Lancaster University

Carl James
University of Wales, Bangor

David Little
Trinity College, Dublin

Diana Masny
University of Ottawa, Canada

Guy Merchant
Sheffield City Polytechnic

Rosamond Mitchell
Southampton University

Howard Nicholas
La Trobe University

Zhou Yan-Ping
University of British Columbia, Canada

Rosinda de Castro Guerra Ramos
National Resource Centre, Brazilian ESP Project, Sao Paulo

Phil Scholfield
University of Wales, Bangor

Mike Scott
University of Liverpool

Lindsay Silvester
Portsmouth Polytechnic

David Singleton
Trinity College, Dublin

Tony Tinkel
UK based teacher

Elizabeth Toncheva
Formerly of Institute for Foreign Students, Sofia, Bulgaria.
Currently Principal, Surrey Language Centre

Tony Wright
Formerly Christ Church College, Canterbury. Now College of
St. Mark and St. John, Plymouth

General Editor's Preface

One of the objectives of the *Applied Linguistics and Language Study Series* is to offer to its audiences reasoned discussions of a state of the art kind to enable networks of interested practitioners to form and ideas to coalesce, especially internationally across institutional and disciplinary boundaries. By its very diversity, the study of Language and its applications needs such taking stock more frequently than many disciplines. We need to formulate where we are and what opportunities exist in our different areas for research and practice.

This latest contribution to the Series edited by Carl James and Peter Garrett is one such formulation, and in an applied linguistics field which has already gathered to itself workers in just the multiplicity of institutions and branches I refer to. A glance at the contributors to this specially collected volume of original papers will show this to be so: teachers from different countries and different levels within diverse educational systems, academic researchers in education, linguistics and psychology, practitioners with interests in curriculum design, evaluation or in learner performance, all are represented here. Readers of this book can look forward, then, to a conspectus. Not, however, to a doctrine; the editors make this very plain. The *British Association of Applied Linguistics* Seminar which gave rise to the book was clearly an occasion of challenges, of issues and of positions, and these debates are well represented in the book. Indeed, the editors' introductory and closing Chapters, while identifying commonalities, does capture very well the unevenness of the terrain.

A preferred definition suggests why this might be so. *'Language awareness is a person's sensitivity to and conscious perception of the nature of language and its role in human life'* clearly needs unpacking. What is meant by *language*? Are we referring to the breadth of communicative competence or the narrower focus on lexico-grammatical and phonological form? Readers will need to know and not just for academic reasons. Current educational debates in the United Kingdom and Australia, as well as in many other countries, show that in the minds of educationalists and in particular of politicians concerned with education, the definition is crucial and has the most intimate implications for preferred educational practices.

If *language* is difficult to define, then *awareness* is likely to stimulate even greater debate. Is it, for example, to be defined primarily cognitively, in terms of some heightened perception of salience, or social-psychologically in terms of some ensuing attitude or evaluative judgement, or, indeed, sociologically, in terms of connections to be made between language choice and our understanding of the nature and function of social institutions? The 'alternative' growth of a *critical* language awareness movement emphasises how, for some, awareness on its own can never be enough, it has to be awareness *about* and awareness *for*. At first blush, it seems a tall order to connect a Freirean *conscientizacao* with the reported beneficial cognitive effects of bilingualism, yet it may be that the effects of the socially neutral consciousness-raising techniques of some current SLA research might be enhanced if the techniques were informed by such a socially critical dimension. Above all, this need to deconstruct the metaphor is itself inherent in the quotation, speaking as it does about *sensitivity* and *perception* as well as *role*. Nonetheless, as one might say, awareness about awareness is not sufficient either. Like the writers of the papers in this valuable collection we need not only to define terms but to translate them into action. We need to ask not only questions about what but also questions about why, whom and what for.

Translating concepts into action is probably the hardest task of all, and it is one which this volume has at its heart. How can one relate being aware about language to improvements in language performance? Is this indeed a viable and researchable question? How can one relate awareness about language to a greater understanding of the determining role of language in social life? Does being more aware about language translate into ameliorating many of the interpersonal conflicts that have language issues at their root? How can one relate the teaching about language awareness (if, again, *teaching* is what one does) to learning? What is the role of learning strategy to awareness gains? How can one construct curricula which have language awareness at their heart without disturbing the traditional boundaries between academic subjects? Can one have language awareness *across* the curriculum? If so, what are the implications for teacher pre-service and in-service education? If the scope of what language is held to be is constrained in educational contexts often by what it is thought can be formally evaluated, how much more is this so with a notably subjective set of terms like *sensitivity* to, and *heightened awareness* and *appreciation* of language? How one goes about the formative and summative evaluation of awareness is an inescapable question. As this collection amply makes plain, these issues and more are indeed crucial, raising significant questions of how coherence and progression can be designed for, achieved and measured.

To pose such questions baldly ought not to imply however incapacity for useful action. As the editors show in this collection, there is already in place a substantial body of writing and an established range of organisational networks wherein the debates can take place. It is part of the attraction of the theme that it does offer a forum for this interdisciplinary discussion and critical appraisal. Moreover, it is a forum which has avoided debilitating exclusiveness. Like all good collaborative applied linguistic research, the issues here forge relationships among a variety of types of folk, many of which figure in these pages. So, who gets the benefits? It is part of the purpose of this volume to suggest an answer.

Language Awareness in the Classroom, in the understanding of the editors, is an attempt to represent a 'meeting of minds'. That may sound too definite for some. Perhaps a forum for discussion and action might characterise the state of play better. Whichever readers prefer, it is plain that the five sections with their papers offer a catholicity of view around some central questioning themes, all admirably topical for a problem-based discipline like applied linguistics. Moreover, these are themes which could not have greater immediacy. As I write this Preface, for example, issues of language and its definition and its impact upon the curriculum and on people's social and working lives top the charts in a variety of countries and in relation to a rich variety of audiences: children and the National Curriculum in the UK, migrant workers and award restructuring in Australia, minority peoples and their languages vis a vis majority language users in the USA, to name only a fraction. If a topic like language awareness can encourage the making contingent and relevant of such apparent disparity, then we owe the editors a debt, but not only them, also their contributors and in turn their co-workers and their audiences.

Professor Christopher N Candlin
General Editor

Acknowledgements

The Publishers are grateful to the National Council for Language Education (NCLE) for permission to reproduce copyright material on pages 29–33 from C. Brumfit's chapter in the report on language in teacher education (1988).

We regret we are unable to trace the copyright holder of the extract from The Happy Mean from the Green-O-Pine Guide to Family Health and Fitness and would appreciate any help that would enable us to do so.

APPLIED LINGUISTICS AND LANGUAGE STUDY

General Editor

Professor Christopher N. Candlin, Macquarie University

Error Analysis
*Perspectives on second
language acquisition*
JACK C. RICHARDS (ED.)

Stylistics and the Teaching of
Literature
HENRY WIDDOWSON

Language Tests at School
A pragmatic approach
JOHN W. OLLER JNR

Contrastive Analysis
CARL JAMES

Language and Communication
JACK C. RICHARDS AND
RICHARD W. SCHMIDT (EDS)

Learning to Write: First Language/
Second Language
AVIVA FREDMAN, IAN PRINGLE
AND JANICE YALDEN (EDS)

Strategies in Interlanguage
Communication
CLAUS FAERCH AND GABRIELE
KASPER (EDS)

Reading in a Foreign Language
J. CHARLES ALDERSON AND A.H.
URQUHART (EDS)

Discourse and Learning
PHILIP RILEY (ED)

An Introduction to Discourse
Analysis
New edition
MALCOLM COULTHARD

Computers in English Language
Teaching and Research
GEOFFREY LEECH AND
CHRISTOPHER N. CANDLIN (EDS)

Bilingualism in Education
*Aspects of theory, research and
practice*
JIM CUMMINS AND MERRILL
SWAIN

Second Language Grammar:
Learning and Teaching
WILLIAM E. RUTHERFORD

The Classroom and the Language
Learner
*Ethnography and second-language
classroom research*
LEO VAN LIER

Vocabulary and Language Teaching
RONALD CARTER AND MICHAEL
McCARTHY (EDS)

Observation in the Language
Classroom
DICK ALLWRIGHT

Listening to Spoken English
Second Edition
Gillian Brown

Listening in Language Learning
MICHAEL ROST

An Introduction to Second Language
Acquisition Research
DIANE LARSEN-FREEMAN AND
MICHAEL H. LONG

Language and Discrimination
*A study of communication
in multi-ethnic workplaces*
CELIA ROBERTS, TOM JUPP AND
EVELYN DAVIES

Translation and Translating:
Theory and Practice
ROGER T. BELL

Section One: Introduction

1 The scope of Language Awareness

Carl James and Peter Garrett

1 Competing definitions – or complementary perspectives?

Language Awareness (LA) is a term that crops up more and more in a widening range of academic and pedagogical contexts, and this growing frequency of use has brought with it a proliferation of senses of the label. This, in its turn, has led to an increased lack of clarity and consensus regarding its meaning. At times, there is no doubt what the user is referring to; at others it is used somewhat vaguely, perhaps in passing, and one is not really sure what the user has in mind.

A major motivation for the Bangor British Association for Applied Linguistics (BAAL)/LA Seminar was to assemble representatives of some of the various branches of LA each with its own understanding of the term and invite them to explore common ground and areas of difference in terms of definitions, objectives and means to achieve these objectives. This would be a first step towards delineating the different fields of LA and beginning to find answers to the burning questions: What meanings does LA usually have? Why the variety? What meanings were uppermost in people's minds at the seminar?

A fair starting point for answering these questions is the pioneering work of Hawkins (1981, 1984), which has formed the foundation of what is increasingly referred to as the 'British Language Awareness Movement'. He argued for the implementation of LA by means of programmes of study about language, beginning in primary school and continuing into secondary school to bridge the gap between the mother tongue (MT) and foreign languages (FLs). It was initially and essentially a response to the notoriously dismal achievements in two areas of British education: foreign language learning and school-leavers' illiteracy. For example, according to the survey *Modern Languages in Comprehensive Schools* (1977), written by Her Majesty's Inspectorate (HMI), two out of every three pupils starting a foreign language in the first year of secondary education opted to drop it as soon as the opportunity arose. And in the case of low achievement in MT literacy, Gardner (1968) claimed that one in four school-leavers were 'functionally illiterate'.

Hawkins (1984: 4) defines LA in terms of its objectives, thus offering a utilitarian definition. Awareness of language is intended to bridge the transition from primary to secondary education language work; to provide a meeting place and common vocabulary for the different fields of language education (MT English, FL, English as a Second Language, Community Languages); to prepare the way for child-care courses in the fourth and fifth years of secondary education; to facilitate discussion of linguistic diversity (on the assumption that discussion and the greater awareness it engenders are the best weapons against prejudice); to develop listening skills (as a prerequisite for efficient foreign language study), along with confidence in reading and motivation for writing. Activities relying on pair work and often involving data collecting are to feature prominently in such pro-grammes, since in this way pupils will be encouraged to ask questions about language.

The National Council for Language in Education (NCLE) Working Party on Language Awareness agreed on the following simpler albeit pleonastic definition: '*Language Awareness is a person's sensitivity to and conscious awareness of the nature of language and its role in human life*' (Donmall, 1985: 7).

The NCLE Report sees LA programmes developing such sensi-tivity and awareness within the following three broad parameters: a cognitive parameter (e.g. developing awareness of pattern in language), an affective parameter (e.g. forming attitudes) and a social parameter (e.g. improving pupils' effectiveness as citizens or consumers) (ibid.). Such programmes are seen as taking a variety of forms, and serving a variety of objectives: making explicit pupils' intuitive knowledge of their MT; strengthening language skills and increasing the effectiveness of communication in the MT or FL; placing in a positive light the linguistic diversity increasingly prevalent in classrooms; fostering better relations between ethnic groups in and beyond school, especially at the workplace; helping pupils to overcome disadvantages incurred by discrepancies between the home and school language; introducing pupils to the concepts and techniques of basic linguistics; imparting an understanding of the value of language as part of human life.

Most of the papers in this volume can be comfortably accommodated within this broad field of LA. Both the definitions we have cited (by Hawkins and by Donmall) allow for considerable flexibility in the papers, some of them focusing more on pupils, programmes and materials (see, for example, Anderson (Paper 10), Donmall (Paper

8), Heap (Paper 18), Little and Singleton (Paper 9), Tinkel (Paper 7) and others focusing more on teachers' views and expectations (Brumfit (Paper 2), Merchant (Paper 4), Mitchell and Hooper (Paper 3)), and teaching methodology (Wright (Paper 5)).

There has also been some extension of the above field to tertiary education – i.e. to students rather than, or as well as, pupils, native as well as non-native speakers. So again we are not referring to the specialist courses offered in linguistics departments but to something more utilitarian. This dimension is explored in this volume by Clark and Ivanič (Paper 13), Hedge and Gosden (Paper 14), Scholfield (Paper 17), Silvester (Paper 16), Wright (Paper 5). It is noteworthy that LA work has been most vigorously implemented in ESP (English for Special Purposes) programmes abroad (Holmes and Ramos (Paper 15), Scott (Paper 20)). Somewhat different perspectives on LA appear in the articles by Chryshochoos (Paper 12) and Toncheva (Paper 11), which look more specifically at FL learners' awareness of themselves in the learning process, suggesting a vital link between learners and their optimal syllabus definable in terms of a self-generated awareness-based needs analysis. Toncheva's paper is 'observational' while Chrysochoos' is experimental. Masny (Paper 21) takes a comparative turn, looking at what second language learners' language judgements are based on at different levels of language development. She shares some common ground with Nicholas, who sees different forms of language awareness as a means of distinguishing between first and second language acquisition and between younger and older child second language acquisition.

Clearly then, the range of the papers in this collection reflects the above-mentioned breadth of definition, and this is undoubtedly attributable in part to the imprecision inherent in the expression 'Language Awareness' itself. To begin with 'awareness', this is bound up with 'knowledge' of various types, and calls to mind immediately the competence/performance dichotomy in, e.g. Chomsky (1968), recycled for 'applied' consumers in terms of learning and acquisition (e.g. Krashen, 1981).

In some cases (e.g. Tinkel (Paper 7), Silvester (Paper 16)), where LA work is conducted with groups sharing a MT, LA focuses on making pupils or students more aware (by which is meant conscious), through exploration, of the intuitions they hold about their MT, on turning their implicit knowledge into explicit knowledge. In this type of self-discovery interpretation, we might see LA as based around and providing a means to bridge the *consciousness gap* within the individual. Insofar as LA and consciousness raising (CR) are terms often used interchangeably, this is CR in Rutherford's sense of 'raising to consciousness', of guiding the learner's attention to particular aspects of language, thereby increasing the degree of explicitness:

> The role of C-R is . . . one in which data that are crucial for the learner's testing of hypotheses, and for his forming generalizations, are made available to him in a somewhat controlled and principled fashion.
>
> (Rutherford, 1987: 18)

For others (e.g. Merchant (Paper 4), where LA work is with groups not sharing a MT, there is more focus on making each pupil aware not only of his or her OWN implicit knowledge but also of each other's (new or old) explicit knowledge. There is a concentration on learning about all the languages present in the LA group, on their differences and what is common to them. This, then, is the LA of multilingual and multicultural classrooms. In this second type of LA, the dominant perspective is that of sharing each other's explicit knowledge about their own languages and the aim now is to bridge a different kind of gap, which methodologists might refer to as a *knowledge gap*, or even an *information gap*, which so often divides the conceptual worlds of pupils within the same class. Such a gap – as we know from Teaching English as a Foreign Language (TEFL) methodologies (cf. Prabhu, 1987) – creates a natural context for talking about language. Here CR/LA can be seen in terms of increasing (raising) the amount of conscious knowledge in each individual through new and explicit input, from teachers or, better still, from one's peers, via the perceptive teacher's mediation.

Somewhere between (or is it alongside?) the above types comes the LA aimed more at foreign language learners, where the focus is on both making the learners aware of their MT intuitions, and increasing their explicit knowledge of what happens in the FL. This suggests scope for a new type of Contrastive Analysis (CA), not CA of the classical sort done by linguists and then made over to textbook writers, but CA done by pupils as FL learners themselves, to gain linguistic awareness of the contrasts and similarities holding between the structures of the MT and the FL. This new role for CA seems unfortunately to have gone unnoticed by Rutherford.

A further aspect of the term LA itself which allows for a great deal of breadth is the word 'language' and the fact that it can be used in either a generic sense (i.e. languages in general) or a specific sense (i.e. a particular language). The relative proportions of already-possessed implicit knowledge raised to consciousness on the one hand, and new explicit knowledge (or input) on the other, will be dependent in part on which of these senses of 'language' is dominant.

In the sort of LA where 'language' is meant generically (say, 'multicultural LA'), each pupil is likely to experience far more new explicit input in comparison to the degree of implicit knowledge raised to consciousness, than a pupil in the specific-language LA, working with the MT, where most work will involve raising intuitions to consciousness. In addition, course content seems likely to vary far more in the former, since it will (ideally) depend greatly on the language backgrounds of the particular pupils. Whether one considers it desirable to call these by different names – e.g. Mother Tongue Awareness; Awareness of Languages; Foreign Language Awareness, Language Awareness, Awareness of Language, Consciousness Raising – for the sake of drawing clear distinctions, is another question. In any event, all of the above would or could involve at the very least thinking about language, and probably also learning to talk about it. At least, both involve coming to terms with language. Whether this talk is to be conducted in a standard 'received' metalanguage, or in a non-technical one, is a further issue to be resolved some day. If 'talking about language' implies linguistics, the question arises whether LA is just another name for linguistics. Perhaps LA is to linguistics what nature study is to biology.

Within what we have referred to as the British Language Awareness Movement, there is considerable emphasis on reflecting on and talking about language, and a clear implication that the teaching of languages involves talking about language in an illuminating way. This requires the establishment of a common, acceptable and adequate metalanguage that is accessible to both teachers and learners (see, for example, Department of Education and Science DES, 1988a). Holmes and Ramos (Paper 15) provide learners with a checklist of reading and summarising strategies, which they make use of in work sessions when they take stock of their awareness of why they 'choose' to work in the way they do. This, then, is a means of gaining and sharing LA, and, equally importantly, it is a source of evidence in learners for this variety of LA. However, it is stimulating to discover that, outside Britain, LA has even been seen in terms of the acquisition of implicit knowledge rather than explicit knowledge, the evidence for which is observed not in metalinguistic performance, but solely in linguistic performance (e.g. Nicholas (Paper 6)). LA in this sense goes beyond the above-quoted definition from the NCLE Report (Donmall, 1985: 7), since there is nothing in that definition that explicitly includes talking about language.

What is clear from the picture we have painted so far of LA is that any attempt at defining LA has to take account of the variety of purposes of LA in the minds of those using the term. It is to these purposes that we now turn.

2 The goals of Language Awareness work

In this section we shall attempt to add some clarity to the question of goals. In doing so, we shall first return to the question of the likely benefits that would accrue from the widespread adoption of LA programmes in schools. We shall begin with the question 'Who is likely to benefit from educational reforms that introduce LA work into schools and colleges?' and then we deal with the question 'How might pupils and students benefit from such a modification in the curriculum?' In other words, what dimensions of the individual (and, by extension, of society) are likely to be affected through such a provision? We feel that until these questions are fully addressed, it is speculative and even futile to consider what forms educational provision might take, in terms of the syllabuses and the associated activities and materials for implementing LA work that are currently available or potentially so.

2.1 Teacher resources: reaching the teachers

Any kind of educational reform must be predicated on teacher preparedness. In Britain, the Report of the Bullock Committee, *A Language for Life* (DES, 1975), while being mainly concerned with the improvement of literacy teaching, made explicit recommendations for the provision of systematic education in language for teachers, parents and pupils.

On the provision for teachers we may read:

> We believe it is essential that all teachers in training, irrespective of the age range they intend to teach, should complete satisfactorily a substantial course in language and the teaching of reading. (DES, 1975: 336)

> We consider that the basic course should occupy at least 100 hours, and preferably 150. (DES, 1975: 338)

The response to these proposals has generally been deplorably non-committal on the part of university education departments. This is through no fault of their own, but it has been the only response possible in the continuing climate of an unrelenting parsimony on the part of central government.

The Kingman Report (DES, 1988a) was yet another political response to disquiet expressed by employers and parents about the apparently falling standards in English among British school-leavers. Once again, concern was expressed about teachers' lack of knowledge about English and the recommendation was echoed from the Bullock Report that 'all teachers of English need some explicit knowledge of the forms and the uses of the English language' (DES, 1988a: 4).

Clearly, if there has to be an information explosion about language, it has to start somewhere, and that must be with the teachers. The best time for developing such knowledge is during the Postgraduate Certificate in Education (PGCE) year. The objection that this year is already too full to allow extra timetabled work on language has been slightly weakened by the recent extension of the training year by six weeks. Still there is the problem of the absence of teacher trainers in sufficient numbers and places who themselves have the necessary Language Awareness, not to mention the classroom experience of doing LA work with pupils. Some departments of education are now large enough – as a result of recent government policies of expansion of centres of excellence (and closure of smaller units!) and such 'economies of scale' – to justify engaging the services of a single LA expert. However, it seems reasonable to assume that where there is keen competition for scarce resources, LA will not be regarded as a staffing priority. Some departments happen to have the support of service teaching in what has traditionally been called 'Applied Linguistics' provided by one or two members of a linguistics department in the same university. This provision has frequently been desultory. However, we are confident that any applied linguist familiar with the LA literature and the urgency of providing LA training for teachers to be, will want to abandon the desultory attitude on reading the collection of papers in this volume.

Where pre-service provision is impossible, the next best course of action is to make LA available through In-Service Training (INSET) programmes. Some part-time MEd schemes have been doing this on a small scale. One welcome, but typically parsimonious, government reaction to the Kingman Report has been the appointment of 'expert trainers' in consortia of LEAs in English who could (although they have no brief to) liaise with local universities in order to mediate the necessary training to the teachers.

Teachers tend to be highly dependent on textbooks. If one pauses to ask why this should be so, the answer must be that, for many, the textbook is a lifeline to survival in the classroom, and an eminently good textbook can often make teaching a far more pleasurable and stimulating occupation. The textbook may function as a surrogate for training, in that you may not need to be trained to be able to use it tolerably well, and also in the sense that the textbook can itself be an instrument of training: the author of a textbook shows the teacher how. This is particularly clearly the case where a good teachers' book accompanies the working materials. So it has come about that many teachers owe their familiarity with LA to textbooks that they have used. Nowhere is this more true than in the relatively 'progressive', albeit often somewhat fashion-conscious, field of TEFL, a teaching and publishing area so lucrative that its publishers are willing to risk innovation where mainstream language teaching would fear to tread. The fashion-conscious side of TEFL may well be one (of many) sources of the variation in the use of the term LA. Teachers' interpretations of the term LA will tend to vary according to the textbooks in which they have met the term, and the activities they have used under the LA heading. For example, one TEFL methods manual (Hubbard *et al.*, 1983) includes a convincing section on LA, demonstrating (pp. 163ff) that before they plan a lesson, teachers have to be aware of the forms and functions they are going to teach. In a somewhat different vein, Gairns and Redman (1986) dedicate the entire first chapter of their teachers' book on vocabulary teaching to LA activities, in which they direct teachers' attention to problems met by English as a Foreign Language (EFL) learners when acquiring vocabulary. Ellis and Sinclair (1989) even go so far as to structure a whole coursebook around language and learner awareness activities. Then there is the 'humanistic' (and commercial) sector of TEFL, represented by Frank and Rinvolucri (1983) and Rinvolucri (1984), who make extensive use of 'awareness activities', in order to 'close the gap between all too mechanical and all too free language practice' (Frank and Rinvolucri, 1983: 8). Such activities typically take the form of personalised, meaning-focused grammar practice.

We do not wish to give the impression, however, that LA in any of its various forms is only for English teachers, either 'mainstream' or TEFL. Those are the two groups that have been addressed so far, English teachers by the Bullock, Kingman and Cox Reports, TEFL by the publishing houses.

Teachers of modern languages also will benefit from LA work. They are in fact summoned to do LA work (in nature if not in name) by the Draft Orders pertaining to modern languages teaching in the new National Curriculum; there it is stated that modern language study should:

(a) extend the pupil's linguistic knowledge, skills and understanding;
(b) lay a foundation for learning any subsequent foreign languages;
(c) widen the pupil's cultural horizons and promote international understanding.

In one respect modern languages teachers are likely already to have more LA than their colleagues teaching mainstream English. This flows from the fact that they themselves have usually learnt (in Krashen's sense of conscious learning through formal instruction) in classrooms and from textbooks the foreign language they now teach. Consequently they have experiences and memories of language learning not shared by their English, native-speaker colleagues. At least this is the case with the older teachers of languages, who studied before the audio-lingual and 'communicative' approaches were introduced: younger teachers, who learnt under the 'communicative' approach, are less likely to have such explicit knowledge of the target language. They will have been harangued on the need to teach communication in the language, rather than teach about it.

Then there are the growing ranks of bilingual support teachers in Britain's multicultural and multilingual school system. Whether Welsh or Punjabi, they are likely, on account of their bilingualism, to have great awareness of the minority language that they teach, its forms and uses. Where they are likely to fall short is in their awareness of the colloquial and non-literary norms of those languages, which they tend to devalue in favour of the prestigious standard languages, with the result that Punjabi gets ignored and Urdu is idealised. Perhaps more importantly, they will tend to have an underdeveloped awareness of the structural and semantic connections and contrasts between the community language and English. These teachers will need to be guided on how best to foster this positive spirit of disinterested curiosity about languages in contact in the same classroom, school or street.

We must be careful, however, never to lose sight of the fact that language is not the privilege or prerogative of the so-called 'language' teachers in a school. The Bullock Report devoted the whole of Chapter 12 to 'language across the curriculum', emphasising that all teachers, of what we traditionally refer to as different school 'subjects' are essentially different ways of using language, and that all teachers ought to be trained in language. Predictably, this sentiment is echoed by the Kingman Report, Chapter 6 of which (entitled 'The education and training of teachers') calls for 'all teachers of all subjects' to be given in-service and probationer instruction about language.

2.2 Reaching all the pupils

Having made it quite clear that LA is for all teachers, it must follow
that it is likewise for all pupils. It must become one of the prime goals
of the educational process for learners to gain heightened awareness
of: (a) the phenomenon 'language', whether human, animal or machine
language; (b) their MT (be it English, Welsh or Punjabi), the 'official'
language (if this is not the child's native language); and (c) other
languages of the school and/or the community. If, as we have claimed,
education consists in a large part in learning to use language (and
languages), then learners need to be able to observe and take note
of how differences in use correlate with differences in selection of
forms of language. Pupils need to be able to characterise objectively
and analytically their own choices of language forms and functions, the
language of those around them, and the potential of language to reflect
variety. They need to be able to describe and assess their own speech
and writing, as a basis for self-criticism, which in its turn becomes the
impetus for personal growth.

It must be stressed that LA is neither the privilege of the very able
nor a palliative for the less able: both claims have been made for it, as
Donmall (1985: 9) points out, and we wish to disassociate ourselves
from them. It is not a soft option for those who cannot learn to speak
and write in French – a claim some people, equally wrongly, made
against Area Studies. On the contrary, it may act as a bridge to better
FL learning, as Hawkins (1984: 4) suggests. We must avoid at all costs
the temptation of offering LA as an alternative to language learning,
as proposed by Davies (1983) for example, who seems content to
trade the traditional and still essential 'instrumental' benefits of FL
learning (i.e. gaining proficiency) for the two less substantial benefits
of heightened awareness and improved attitude. The Kingman Report
strikes the right chord here when it refers (DES, 1988a: 49) to the
'entitlement' of children to be helped to achieve the highest levels of
language competence and understanding that is within their capacity to
achieve. The question now arises as to the domains of competence and
understanding. It is to these that we now return to define and extend.
It is our opinion that there are at least five such domains of LA.

3 The domains of Language Awareness

3.1 The affective domain

We have already mentioned how some TEFL materials writers, usually
associated with the humanistic approach of Stevick (1976), have been

quick to promote LA activities. Frank and Rinvolucri offer their own definition of an LA activity: it is an activity 'to make the language activities personal' . . . 'encouraging the learner to contribute new things of personal relevance', which 'adds up to total involvement of the learner's whole person' (Frank and Rinvolucri 1983: 7–8). These are somewhat grandiose claims – perhaps reflections of the commercialism of TEFL. Nevertheless, they are in essence a definition of LA that sees the affective dimension as being the most central, a stance repeated in Rinvolucri's claim (1984: 5) that 'Meeting and interiorising the grammar of a foreign language is not simply an intelligent, cognitive act. It is a highly affective one too . . . [ ] . . . learner feelings towards specific ligaments of the target language.' There seems to be growing evidence that the possession of internal criteria is a potent factor in determining success or failure in language learning. As Sorace (1985) has shown, the feeling that one knows correlates very highly with actual knowing. The idea that grammar has its localised dark corners of terror is not so absurd either: David Crystal's *Rediscover Grammar* (1988) is founded on a very similar premiss: that learning is done with the heart as well as the head, a point stressed by Scott in this volume, where he uses the pregnant phrase 'a feeling for fact'. Nor is that definition far from the one offered in the NCLE Papers on Language Awareness, where the affective aspect of LA is specified in terms of 'forming attitudes, awakening and developing attention, sensitivity, curiosity, interest and aesthetic response' (Donmall, 1985: 7).

3.2 The social domain
In the last fifty years, most countries have experienced the effects of global migrations of peoples, with the result that the monolingual and monocultural state is now the exception rather than the rule. In Britain, the minority ancient Celtic languages have been outnumbered by the languages of immigrants from all continents. We are still trying to come to terms with the problems of ethnic diversity and inter-group relations, which often erupt into inter-ethnic friction. The solution is a long-term one, and must be based on our schools: LA, in the words of the 1985 NCLE Report, can be utilised 'to foster better relations between all ethnic groups by arousing pupils' awareness of the origins and characteristics of their own language and dialect and their place in the wider map of languages and dialects used in the world beyond' (Donmall, 1985: 8).

The Kingman Report has surprisingly little to say about LA work as an instrument for social harmonisation through the understanding of language variety, only that 'Systematic stress laid upon the regularity of usages is a step on the way to linguistic tolerance' (DES, 1988a: 36). For 'tolerance', we would prefer to see the more positively committed term 'endorsement'. In fact Kingman tends to emphasise the cognitive advantages of multilingual classrooms, overlooking two points: (i) that the advantages of such classrooms are more in the cultural than the cognitive domains and (ii) that the cognitive benefits of 'comparing different usages' (DES, 1988a: 36) are likely to be far greater for those pupils whose MT is English if the comparisons are elicited and formulated in English. In other words there is some danger either of patronising the children of some minority culture or of exploiting them to the advantage of their native language (NL) English mainstream culture peers.

3.3 The 'power' domain

This formulation of LA has been with us for a long time, at least for as long as individuals with discernment have known that language can be used as an instrument of manipulation. Its best-known formulation (which Scott reminds us of in Paper 20) is that of the Brazilian social engineer Paulo Freire (1972), who speaks of *conscientização*. Not unconnected with the idea of a school subject being a way of verbalising reality, *conscientização* involves alerting people to the hidden meanings, tacit assumptions and rhetorical traps laid by those who traditionally have most access to the media for verbal communication. These may be governments, bureaucracies, the Church, commerce, or, worst of all, unscrupulous individuals. It was Bolinger, in his book *Language, the Loaded Weapon* (1980), who argued the need for linguistic vigilance in the face of the snares of linguistic beguilement. One example he cites is the ruthless exploitation of the capacity of language to create pseudo-entities – what he calls 'reification'. Just as children create fairies by the very act of naming them, so governments can talk about 'jobs' as if they were out there (in the south of England) waiting to be 'filled'. Language deceit of the sort that commerce, particularly advertising, resorts to can be seen in the claim that a 'new' soup recently launched is 'full strength – no water need to be added'! LA work in schools can alert pupils to the mendacity of such obfuscation and develop their sensitivity to further such encounters. New impetus for such LA work is currently being provided by the University of Lancaster 'Language and Power' group (Fairclough, 1989, 1990).

3.4 The cognitive domain

If knowledge is power, then the cognitive and 'power' domains of LA must be closely linked. The NCLE definition of LA stresses the cognitive advantage to be derived from such study: '... developing awareness of pattern, contrast, system, units, categories, rules of language in use and the ability to reflect upon them' (Donmall, 1985: 7). This statement represents a rejection of what we call the 'behaviour' view of language work in school – encapsulated in the American label 'language arts' – as well as what was known in Australia as the 'new English' (Rothery, 1989), which assumes that language is something that one produces adequately well in response to social or emotional needs. The urge to communicate is viewed as sufficient – without recourse to language study – to bring about adequate language performance. In the LA definition, language in general and languages in particular are legitimate objects of study, as legitimate as other aspects of our physical or social environment that are studied in disciplines like history, chemistry, biology, etc. The effect is to reinstate 'English' and 'French' as subjects on the school curriculum, and, more importantly, to legitimise any talk about these phenomena in school lessons. On the cognitive effects of 'talk about', the philosopher Henri Bergson is unambiguous; in his words:

> Nothing is clear until we have put it into words, for words are the only means of translating impressions to the intellect. Hence the immense help expression gives to vision, in clarifying it. The growth of the power of language is not merely a technical development, it implies a growth of vision.

The Kingman Report is equally direct in its support for this analytic dimension of LA: 'If we are to help pupils function intellectually – and we take this to be a prime purpose of education – we must spend time in English classes examining words and how each contributes to the meaning of a sentence' (DES, 1988a: 8–9), since 'is is not enough to write "freely" with no thought given to the audience for the writing, or the shape and patterns of the language used' (DES, 1988a: 11).

Children should then be made aware of the forms of language. But the functions are not to be overlooked either, for LA is not in any sense a return to the arid, decontextualised grammar-grind of pre-war parsing. LA work conforms to the Kingman Report requirement that language study should be based upon a model of language in use. An Australian initiative to teaching English through use has been based on the classroom exploitation of the notion of (non-literary) GENRE: writing classes centred on helping pupils to identify the conventional patterns of organisation that we instinctively conform to when we produce instances of genres such as telling a story, applying for a job, writing a laboratory report or consulting a doctor. A genre is

'. . . the stages passed through to achieve goals in a given culture' (Rothery, 1989: 228).

But is there any evidence that the study of language (even 'in use') confers any cognitive advantage? We are assured that it can do no harm – but can it do some positive good? There is evidence that children raised in situations where there is talk about language tend to be cognitively advantaged. Hawkins (1984: 14) notes the strong correlation between socio-economic class and children's reading attainment, attributing the poorer children's lower achievement to their

> . . . deprivation of 'adult time': the opportunity for uninterrupted dialogue with an adult who can give the child individual attention at the critical age when the child is learning to match his expanding conceptual universe to the linguistic symbols of the mother tongue.

Should all this sound like a belated recourse to the now defunct 'Deficit Hypothesis' of Bernstein, the reader might just think again: as Mason (1986) has shown, in a very perceptive paper, it is an emphasis on the child's ability to handle the language-analytical demands of academic discourse that distinguishes the methods of public and private schools, and these are essentially class-related distinctions. If lower-class children are disadvantaged though their restricted access to abstract and analytical language at home, it will be in LA work where compensatory 'Headstart' education can be appropriately delivered.

Another source of evidence that LA has beneficial effects upon cognition comes from studies of bilingualism. Cummins (1978), for example, reports on the marked superiority of bilinguals over mono-linguals in evaluating contradictions, or semantic incongruities: just the kinds of skills needed, as we have seen, for spotting advertisers' sleight of hand. Ben-Zeev (1977) goes further, suggesting explanations for the observed cognitive assets accompanying bilingualism. She reminds us that the bilingual's main problem is to keep his two languages apart or 'to resolve the interferences between his languages'. Bilinguals do this by recourse to three strategies, each of which is unmistakenly 'metacognitive', i.e. it involves language analysis and LA. First, they indulge in language analysis, refining their awareness of how each of their languages 'processes a given paradigm', that is how each language organises its articles, or its relative clauses or its colour words, etc. Second, bilinguals develop 'a mechanism to emphasise the structural differences between languages and thus to keep them apart'. Third, bilinguals are 'more open to correction and guidance', i.e. to feedback cues, than monolinguals: this trait is probably enabled by the first two. It is significant that the Kingman Report should likewise observe that:

> It can only be sensible to make overt comparisons between languages which the pupils know, so that they can be led to see the general principles of language structure and use through a coherent and consistent approach. (DES, 1988a: 48)

Notable here is the ambiguity of the phrase 'languages which the pupils know': does each pupil know both languages (as is the case with bilinguals), or does each pupil know one only? If the latter interpretation is intended, most pupils will be talking about languages they do not know, with the result that the comparisons made might be at best superficial and second-hand.

3.5 The performance domain

This is the most contentious and certainly the most crucial issue in LA philosophy. The issue is whether knowing about language improves one's performance or command of the language; that is, whether analytical knowledge impinges on language behaviour. There is a large and growing body of published opinion on this issue in the FL acquisition (applied linguistics) literature, associated in particular with the work of Stephen Krashen. The LA literature itself is optimistic rather than informative on this question. Thus the National Council for Language in Education (NCLE) (Donmall, 1985: 7) says that:

> Heightened awareness may be *expected* to bring pupils to increase the language resources available to them and to foster their mastery of them . . . [our italic].

Tinkel, in the same volume, referring to an early precursor of LA (Doughty *et al.* 1971), is similarly tentative, claiming that 'a basic premise of the volume . . . is that the development of awareness in the pupil will have a positive effect on his competence' (Donmall, 1985: 38).

It is one thing for individuals to be tentative, but one expects a little more conviction from a government report. This is sadly lacking in the Kingman Report, where an appeal is made to belief [our italic]:

> And since we *believe* that knowledge about language, made explicit at the moment when the pupil is ready, can underpin and promote mastery as well . . . (DES, 1988a: 4)

and later:

> We *believe* that within English as a subject, pupils need to have their
> attention drawn to what they are doing and why they are doing it
> because this is helpful to the development of their language ability.
> (DES, 1988a: 13)

The first statement is inconsistent: if the pupil already has at his
disposal implicit knowledge (competence or ability), then the requisite
mastery is already there, so there would be no point in making it
explicit.

Nor is there any reason why we should expect LA to improve
language performance, for, to quote Tinkel again, LA work involves
'. . . exploring the students' already-possessed intuitive language ability' (Tinkel, 1985: 39). This is consonant with standard definitions of
LA. Scholars writing well before the LA movement gained momentum
defined LA as 'implicit knowledge that has become explicit' (Levelt *et
al.*, 1978: 5) and as 'focussing one's attention on something that he
knows' (Read, 1978: 70).

Clearly this issue is that which led to the strong demand for definition at the Bangor LA Seminar: while most of the participants understood LA in the sense meant by the British 'movement' (Hawkins,
1984; Donmall, 1985), some (Nicholas (Paper 6), Masny (Paper 21))
preferred the interpretation associated with Krashen and more particularly Rutherford (1987): they talk of consciousness rather than
awareness of language. But the boundaries are not clearly drawn:
the view was cogently expressed at the seminar that LA needs no
justification in terms of improvement in skill, just as biology does not
have to prove that it has led to improved crop or stock production. The
study of language is patently self-justifying. The Kingman Report, and
most writing on LA, seem not to be content to take this philosophical
stance: some kind of 'practical' side-product is piously hoped for,
even though its delivery cannot be guaranteed. What seems to be
spectacularly absent is research. Apart from the notable small-scale
exception of LA validation reported here by Heap, we know of no
significant provision of research funding to investigate this crucial
and obviously worrying question: instead, the Secretary of State for
Education in 1988 appointed individuals with certain 'beliefs' about
LA to determine educational policy into the next century! Let us now
try to summarise what little is known about the effects of awareness
on performance.

We pointed out earlier that bilinguals are particularly receptive to
feedback cues, that is, they are able to capitalise on correction they

receive: this seems to bring cognitive advantages. Taking a paper by Snow (1976) as our cue, we would like to propose something similar for monolinguals too, something which we call a *deficit view* of LA. Our suggestion is that language learners only make progress in their skills when they notice (or become aware of) the fact that their own utterances do not match those of utterances which serve as their models (Klein, 1986): to put it simply, we learn by becoming aware of what we do not know. Now, to perceive what you do not know involves a comparison of what one does with what other people do and spotting the discrepancy. Others have taken the same stand. Bertoldi *et al.* (1988) insist that LA is raised through the provision of feedback and models: 'This input allows students to compare their own performance in English with that of native speakers and writers of the language'. . . by first 'identifying their own errors' and following this realisation up '. . . via classroom discussion or small-group work' (Bertoldi *et al.*, 1988: 160). The same position is taken by Tudor (1988), in an essay on the use of translation in FL teaching. For him, translation has the virtue of creating in the learner a 'perceived resource gap' (Tudor, 1988: 364) which in turn leads the learner to adopt 'resource expansion strategies'. Thus, translation is held out as one of the keys to achieving 'enhanced acquisition' without the mediation of learning.

It follows then that definitions of LA that concentrate on the explicit-making of implicit knowledge are only half-truths: once we realise what we do know, we are able to identify what it is that we need to know. By the same token, realising what we do not know helps us to see what we do know. It is in this way that skills improve when we raise implicit knowledge to awareness. As anyone knows, honest and objective self-evaluation is the key to self-improvement. That, for example, is the secret of success in the Suzuki method of teaching the violin: learners are shown how to develop inner criteria to draw upon in self-evaluation.

The concept of 'reading readiness' has had a long and useful history in literacy theory. The deficit view of LA allows us to coin a cognate concept: we might call this learning readiness. It is commonsensical to suppose that people will learn something most eagerly when they experience a need for that particular piece of knowledge or skill. Give someone the experience of needing desperately to buy a postage stamp in a French post office, and he will be ready to learn when the opportunity next presents itself: he has learning readiness. Bravo Magaña (1986) studied his children's acquisition of English as a second language. Leticia, aged 7, could frequently be seen 'labouring with an answer . . . aware of the problem, in search of a solution and "ready" for it. Leticia learns the answer because she is ready for it and "mental readiness" can be postulated as a condition for acquisition' (Magaña, 1986: 308).

The ability to spot mismatch between present and target skill is probably enhanced by being able to talk about that mismatch. That is why it is likely that the development of a user-friendly metalanguage – that is, a language for talking about language – is a necessary condition for improvement. This is recognised by the Kingman Report, where it is conceded that if the situation arises where pupils and teachers need to talk about a class of words which grammarians label 'pronouns', then 'there is no good reason not to use that term' (DES, 1988a: 13). Similarly, the report endorses the 'process' approach to writing instruction: 'For the discussion of the first draft to be helpful, teacher and pupil need to be able to use a shared vocabulary for talking about writing' (p. 33).

Having examined the five domains of LA, we would like to stress that we do not see these as mutually exclusive, operating in isolation from one another. Proponents of 'affective' teaching presumably believe that this will lead to better learning and performance. Similarly, some models of second language acquisition are based on the social dynamics of intergroup relations (see, for example, Giles and Byrne, 1982; Garrett *et al.*, 1989); again, though, such models are still very much in need of empirical testing.

We must reiterate that much of what we have said or have quoted from the writings of other people on this issue of the effects of LA work on performance is largely conjecture. Conjecture it will remain, until such a time as research funding is made available for language educationists to address these questions empirically. Meanwhile, people with experience and goodwill can gather together and exchange their views on LA at a weekend seminar. It is in the spirit of such a 'meeting of minds' that we are privileged to present the following papers.

Section Two: Language Awareness in teacher training and education

If the classroom is where LA has to be nurtured, then the first requirement is for teachers to develop their own LA: LA begins with teacher awareness. This is why we take teachers as our starting point for this volume. We begin this section with three papers firmly grounded in the current concerns of and recommendations for the UK educational system, then shift our attention to LA in TEFL teacher training, and then to a contrasting overseas perspective.

Brumfit, in Paper 2, sets the stage by taking the current LA movement in the UK and asking the question: 'Why now?' He traces the post-war developments in British education, language teaching and linguistics, and shows how language study has repeatedly attracted interest and been endorsed by government and administration, and yet been repeatedly thwarted in its development. Gaps and mismatches between teachers and linguists, along with cuts in education resourcing, still work against LA. Yet its momentum continues. For how long though? There is no room for complacency. Brumfit draws our attention to LA's mixed parentage, and adds his voice to the calls for bridge-building. Of central concern for the survival and development of LA is the task of introducing changes into initial and in-service teacher training and education.

In Paper 3, Mitchell and Hooper show us some of the gaps to which Brumfit refers. Their focus is on the teachers in UK secondary schools. With recent proposals in mind for the teaching of English and modern languages, what are the teachers' current views and beliefs about LA, and how much agreement is there? Their study reveals some wide differences between English teachers on the one hand, and modern language teachers on the other; regarding, for example, the effects on language proficiency of explicit knowledge about language. Moreover, some central areas of LA are found to be noticeably missing from both groups. These observations raise a question: Will the present plans for training teachers in response to the Kingman Report be sufficient?

Where Mitchell and Hooper survey the topography of teacher pre-paredness for LA, Merchant (Paper 4) focuses on one of the gaps. His focus is on UK primary school teachers' knowledge about language. From various quarters, teachers have frequently been asked to respond positively to the 'linguistic diversity' of the school population. But what is this 'linguistic diversity'? As part of a European Community-funded project, teachers were asked to write a definition of the term. The survey revealed a considerable variety of understandings. From these results, Merchant suggests a number of improvements to teacher education about language, centring on a clearer definition of the term itself, and on the goals of LA work. Teachers' courses might, he suggests, emphasise features like power, politics and oppression through language.

Paper 5, by Wright, takes us beyond UK educational concerns, and the training and education of teachers for UK schools, to that of non-native teachers of English overseas. A language teacher training programme targeted at such teachers must lead them from the role of language users to language analysts and then to language teachers. Wright sees LA as the mediator here, the key element in his teacher training methodology. This is thought by Wright to work well in some ways for teachers who are non-native speakers, because of their usually high prior familiarity with the linguistic metalanguage and LA's less face-threatening qualities when there is insecurity about the language. Wright explains and exemplifies how LA can be employed in initial and in-service training, as well as advocating its use on language improvement components. Some issues, he reminds us, are yet to be resolved, however: how to introduce new information about the language (see also Little and Singleton, Paper 9) and the lack of evaluation of LA, a point explored more fully by Heap (Paper 18) and Garrett and James (Paper 22).

Nicholas (Paper 6) confronted seminar participants with an overseas perspective on LA that was quite new to many of them. He reported case studies of children under 5, seeking to explain how learners approach, acquire and use a second language. His paper is organised around several claims, one of which is that awareness of language at the lexico-grammatical level distinguishes second from first language development, but that this awareness is potentially conscious only after about the age of 7. Here, then, we see for the first time a distinction being made between awareness and consciousness. In the LA movement in the UK, LA is bound up with conscious, explicit knowledge about language, and talking about language. For Nicholas, on the other hand, learners may be aware of language, even if they are unable to articulate or consciously reflect on their awareness. Nicholas has also perhaps brought some reciprocity to the field. We often hear the claim that awareness leads to development; Nicholas maintains that development also leads to awareness. The different aspects of LA at different ages are learner factors which pedagogic programmes must take into account. Teacher training programmes at primary level will thus be different from those for the secondary level.

2 Language Awareness in teacher education

Christopher Brumfit

1 Introduction: historical background

The Language Awareness movement has taken its impetus at different times from traditions that have not previously interacted with each other. In the first part of this paper I shall try to illustrate this contention by setting the movement in a historical context.

1.1 Education

The 1960s were a period of expansion in British teacher education. An extensive debate about appropriate disciplinary bases for the training of teachers was an inevitable result of changes in the education system. With hindsight, it is possible to see the ending of National Military Service in 1959 as inevitably leading to a reassessment of the role of secondary and tertiary education. Britain had to come to terms with a diminishing international role in peacetime, with her commitments moving towards Europe and away from those of the imperial past. A major expansion of higher education was beginning, and the meritocratic system of state-funded grammar schools (probably the most effective educational innovation on its own terms in the history of British education) was increasingly subject to criticism of the principles on which it had been based. Its success had only been bought at the expense of the rest of the population.

New movements in secondary education led to new teacher training needs. Tripartite education had divided the teaching profession into separate groups (with separate trade unions that still persist): academic teachers with honours degrees plus PGCE routes through training (where training was expected at all, for it was not compulsory for recruitment to the profession) for grammar schools, and teachers' certificates in colleges for most of the rest.

But increasingly, teacher education was redefining itself as a base for both academic and practical initiation into the profession. Colleges became staffed more and more with holders of masters degrees in academic disciplines relating to education – degrees gained from university departments of education. Tibble (1966) defines educational studies as history, sociology, philosophy and psychology, and teachers were expected to have an understanding of these areas in addition to practical competence and an understanding of the curriculum and materials of their own specialised level of teaching, or their own subject discipline.

1.2 Linguistics

While expansion of teacher education led to this ferment of definition, linguistics itself was independently confronting its own role as an area of academic study. For reasons that still need clarifying, a highly technical argument about the formal systems underlying (it was claimed) all natural language, became a major intellectual force, with implications reaching far beyond what was then a fairly obscure academic discipline. True, Chomsky's precocious attack on Skinner's ideas (Chomsky, 1959) was a brilliant polemic, but his works that were most cited and, indeed, read in this period were not written to win the popular and amateur enthusiasm they received. Chomsky's classic texts of 1957 and 1965 are dense, complex and of great technical sophistication – yet they had more impact than works that were linguistically and conceptually more accessible.

In part the appeal may have been that his work was undoubtedly presented as, above all, a break with the past. The constant citation of Kuhn's *Structure of Scientific Revolutions* (Kuhn, 1962) enabled Chomsky's followers to recognise a new scientific paradigm, implicitly claiming links with Copernicus, Newton and Einstein. And other disciplines responded: reactions to Chomsky's ideas were significant in the debates of psychologists, sociologists, anthropologists and philosophers as well as educators. Language became a major topic of debate and language study became more firmly reified.

Nor should we attribute this interest exclusively to the impact of one scholar. Independently, post-Saussurean scholarship in Europe was using language as a metaphor in the exploration of social systems, and examining language itself as a major element in social structure. In Britain the post-Foucault tradition centred initially on the work of Bernstein, with his suggestion that language was a major cause of failure in state education. Over-simplification and trivialisation of his distinction between 'elaborated' and 'restricted' codes provided a base for much teacher education in the late 1960s and early 1970s, though it was not until well into that decade that such writers as Trudgill (1975) and Stubbs (1976) specifically addressed the issues from an informed linguistic perspective.

1.3 English as a foreign language

Meanwhile, there were further contributors to language awareness. American domination of the world economy reinforced the position of English as the major language of international communication, and Britain was historically better placed than the United States to exploit this demand. In addition, in The British Council, it had a highly effective means of supporting development of the English language throughout the world. This growth of demand led to an increase in serious work on language at all levels, together with enthusiasm by commercial publishers for new ideas. Textbook writers benefited, but so too did academics, commentators and theorists. An international market of students interested in understanding their own language teaching experience developed, and courses latched on to the concerns of language teachers in Europe and the United States as well as in the Third World. International associations were founded, and the study of language in education, riding on the back of second language teaching, became a major scholarly enterprise. The dates are instructive: the two major associations of teachers of English as a second or foreign language, Teachers of English to Speakers of Other Languages (TESOL) and International Association of Teachers of English as a Foreign Language (IATEFL), were founded in 1966 and 1967 respectively; in applied linguistics, the international association, Association Internationale de Linguistique Appliquée (AILA), was founded in 1964, and the national one, British Association for Applied Linguistics (BAAL), in 1967; the Centre for Information on Language Teaching and Research (CILT), was founded in 1966. What Britain lacked in funding for descriptive research it made up for in energy and, to some extent, in exciting speculation.

1.4 Post-war immigration

Within Britain, the historical consensus appropriate to wartime gave way to an awareness of different traditions in the community. At the same time, post-war immigration made awareness of cultural and linguistic variation a political issue, and the British education system responded with a range of measures, mostly uncoordinated and unplanned, to address multilingualism in the classroom. Without the political distance that enabled researchers in EFL to maintain something of a grand overview, English as a Second Language (ESL) discussion for Britain remained largely atheoretical until it was taken over by the clients, who linked language work to broader issues of racism and the structure of British society. At the moment, there is little sign of a common linguistic cause between minority users of traditionally recognised languages such as Welsh and Gaelic, and those who have only very recently achieved some measure of educational recognition, speakers of Punjabi, Urdu and other heritage languages, let alone those who remain outside the DES's lists – Polish and the others. Nonetheless, this is a further educational tradition that has placed language firmly in a central position for debate.

1.5 Modern languages

Yet these traditions can be marginalised: EFL teachers are interested in overseas work; racism ensures that bilingual work is seen as peripheral to mainstream activity – a concern for the inner cities, perhaps. The Language Awareness movement represented by Hawkins (1984) or Donmall (1985) seems to have emerged from more mainstream studies, though a sociology of those who have been active in the movement would reveal interesting links with the other traditions I have mentioned. Yet it is conventional modern language teachers who have made much of the running, and their links with conventional English mother tongue teachers that have built up much of the most interesting work in schools.

1.6 Teacher education

This may be partly because the impact of the European Community, and of work under the auspices of the Council of Europe, has forced modern language teachers to take more notice of multilingualism as a phenomenon. Similarly, it has been difficult for English teachers to have remained totally unaware of the pressures of multilingual classes on teachers. But what is interesting is how little this has grafted on to the strongest educational tradition of language study in teacher education. Bodies like NATE, BALT (British Association for Language Teaching) and JCLA (Joint Conference of Language Associates) now all relate most easily to local authorities and to departments of education in colleges, polytechnics and universities where English and modern language teachers are trained. Yet in the 1960s and early 1970s, it was largely outside departments of education that successful high-level education in language study for education had developed. Applied linguistics, developed in linguistics departments at Edinburgh and Reading, was associated with English at Birmingham and Lancaster, and with modern languages at Essex. It was these and a few other centres that developed the most sophisticated work on language in education, fed mainly, but not exclusively, by research and masters' level students with overseas interests. Very few British education departments produced courses of similar value until much more recently, and those who did often failed to exploit the resources available to them because of internal political rivalries (for example, in 1975 departments within Britain's biggest institute of education, at London University, failed to unite to form a language centre because of internal politics).

In formal teacher education, BEd courses with educational linguistics components developed in colleges of education in the early 1970s, but many of the best fell victim to cuts, on the 'last in first out' basis, as colleges diversified or reduced in size later in the decade. While they developed, though, a number of publishers such as Edward Arnold and Penguin Books produced the first large-scale series of popular books on educational linguistics. The same period saw the publication of the results of the Nuffield Programme in Linguistics and English Teaching, directed by Michael Halliday from 1964, and these included *Language in Use* (Doughty, *et al.*, 1971) with a wealth of practical linguistic activity that has reportedly been less successful in schools than in FE.

All in all, by the mid-1970s the movement towards language sensitivity for teachers looked strong. The publication of the Bullock Report appeared to offer the official push that was needed. It stated (DES, 1975: 337–8); 'Among the modules that go to make up the professional training element there should be a compulsory one on language in education.' Yet after this high point, language study in British teacher education declined as the system retrenched in the face of cuts.

The calls for language study continued. The Secretary of State for Education may not have been specifically concerned with Language Awareness when he set up the Kingman Inquiry which reported in 1988 (DES, 1988a), but the report clearly saw a major extension of knowledge about language for teachers as a necessary requirement. A year earlier, the HMI survey on the initial training of teachers in the public sector (DES, 1987:66) comments:

> The majority of courses provided students with insufficient help to understand clearly the place of English, or language, within the whole primary curriculum, that is to say how language ability should be developed in the context of the various elements of the curriculum and how in turn these can be more effectively learned by appropriate language activities. There was little evidence anywhere of the study of the structure of language.

It is in this context that we should see our current discussion of Language Awareness in teacher education.

2 The position today

The previous section has drawn attention to the diverse traditions on which the idea of language awareness has drawn. Part of the problem for teacher education is to weave elements of these differing traditions into a coherent pattern. To mention the strongest features of the different traditions (drawing upon some of the data discussed in Mitchell and Hooper (Paper 3) on teachers' attitudes to language knowledge), the conviction of modern language teachers that consciousness about language contributes to skilled acquisition of second languages, the commitment to variation and sensitivity to audience of English mother tongue teachers, and the research commitment of the EFL tradition all have much to offer.

Yet there are also negative sides to this mixed parentage. The successes in developing advanced courses in language teacher education by applied linguistics departments have been almost always ignored in recent discussion of the need to train coordinators to develop Language Awareness in schools, following the Kingman Report. This is all the more striking when we consider that few English teachers have received much linguistically sophisticated discussion of language as part of their first degree. Indeed, many English teachers may move to literature out of a humane concern for aesthetic and value-laden study in opposition to what is perceived to be an arid abstraction of language from its human origins by linguistics. Certainly much discussion by English teachers of the draft NCLE Report on language in teacher education (published in revised form as Brumfit, 1988) concentrated on the phrase 'dry, arid parsing' as an apparently adequate specification of all that language awareness could be seen to offer! To give the full feel of the findings of the survey, I reproduce pages 38–42, in which the main recommendations are discussed. It should be noted that these arise from the questionnaire on practice in British teacher education which was sent to every teacher training establishment in the United Kingdom.

Language in teacher education: recommendations

1. *Lack of cooperation*

NCLE has argued for some time that schools should have coordinated policies on language as a medium for learning and languages as subjects. There is certainly no clear evidence from our survey that teacher education reflects such ambitions. 'Language awareness' courses, where they exist, are taught either in isolation, or in association with foreign language methods courses. 'Language across the Curriculum' sometimes appears as a general title, but there is no evidence that any languages other than English contribute strongly to a serious policy for other subjects in school. (A simple example of a missed chance would be a recent lesson in which the pupils were asked to write to Paris to buy a painting for a local authority: there was no consultation with the French Department, and no opportunity to write in French at all!)

In our responses there was no evidence that the notion of a school language policy was seriously addressed at either initial or (more surprisingly) at in-service level. Nor was there direct evidence of cooperation between language departments to any great extent, though close links between English, Foreign Language, Classics and Community Language Methods tutors at secondary level training should not be hard to develop.

All in all, this is an area where some schools are thinking ahead of teacher education (see, e.g., Marland 1986). A mismatch between the most imaginative practice and the best teacher education can never be good for the latter. Perhaps a first realistic step is to encourage greater cooperation between English, Foreign and Community Language Methods tutors at secondary level, and between all these and 'Language' tutors at primary level in training institutions.

> RECOMMENDATION (1):
> Teacher education should explicitly address, through its content and organisational practice, the need for schools to bring languages together in a coordinated policy.

2. *Language across the curriculum*

But the need for close liaison goes further. There is, it is heartening to note, quite widespread acceptance that language is significant in all subject areas. Evidence of clear timetabled discussion of this in non-language subjects is rarer. What is not explicitly introduced, though, is the notion of language as a worthwhile area of content in – for example – physics and zoology within science programmes, social studies, history, or geography. If we consider understanding of language to be essential for a well-grounded education, such developments should be encouraged, especially when schools do no explicit teaching of basic ideas about language.

Yet this could happen in addition to, rather than instead of, explicit language awareness activity in schools. Understanding language development for all prospective parents, second language learning for all prospective language learners, language structure and the history of languages for some students at least, have been encouraged in some schools (Donmall, 1985). Such initiatives need to be built on and extended. Further, the role of *Language in Use* (Doughty *et al.*, 1971) should be considered seriously, as the NATE submission to the Kingman Inquiry (NATE, 1987) does. And if we want language teachers to be able to teach creatively and relevantly about language, they will need special training in this in addition to their normal language methods work.

RECOMMENDATION (2):
Teacher education methods tutors in all subjects should explicitly address the issue of language as a medium of learning.

RECOMMENDATION (3):
All language teachers should be encouraged to teach about the nature of language, and should be explicitly trained in methods of doing this and cooperating with other teachers in so doing.

3. *Bilingualism and multilingualism*

A depressing feature of the questionnaire results was the lack of general appreciation of the needs identified by the Swann Report (DES, 1985: 561–2 and 611) for satisfactory teacher education for a multilingual society. Among the few topics consistently under-represented was bilingualism and multilingualism, and no evidence suggested that the languages and varieties of language of all ethnic groups were being built upon. Mainstream work did not refer at all to the potential role of minority languages in the curriculum, nor to the major debates that have taken place in this area. This is partly, no doubt, because teacher education in language is mostly tied to the teaching of particular languages, or to other disciplines like psychology or sociology where language is not the central focus.

RECOMMENDATION (4):
That the social dimensions of language in Britain, and particularly of the languages and dialects of minority communities, should be specifically studied as part of the training of all teachers, and be seen as an essential major element for any teacher of languages.

RECOMMENDATION (5):
That primary teacher education should include components on the role of community languages, means of maintaining and developing pupils' mother tongues, and the possibilities of bilingual education.

4. *Language for work*

Nor was there evidence of language for work or life after school being taken very seriously as an issue, except insofar as it fitted in to conventional English and EFL work. On the other hand, foreign languages were clearly expected to be taught for communication in the first place.

RECOMMENDATION (6):
That there should be more research on the language needs of employment and that the relationship between such needs and the teaching of English, community and foreign languages should be explored in teacher education.

5. *Methods work*

It was striking that the historical, social and policy implications of language teaching were the areas most neglected in methods work. This perhaps links with the lack of awareness of Britain as a multilingual society referred to above – on the whole, teaching methods seems to be conceived of as primarily technical, with little regard for the links between techniques and methods used and more general educational and social questions. It is clearly undesirable to ask methods tutors to be less practical, but there is a case for asking for practicality to be embedded in social awareness. Students are being prepared to join a profession with its own history and its own view of its role in society.

RECOMMENDATION (7):
Methods work in all language teaching should be sensitive to the historical, social and policy implications of joining the language teaching profession, as well as similar implications for the teaching profession in general.

6. *Self-awareness by teachers*

There was evidence that some BEd courses introduced students to classroom research and self-awareness activities. Depressingly, there was no evidence that this happened much in language work at university level, even in in-service and BEd work (though this could be accounted for by the pressure of time on PGCEs, and the tendency to teach general research methods at Masters and Diploma levels). There seemed little if any concern for research into the description of linguistic interaction in the classroom – a particularly sad observation, as this is an area where teachers are well-equipped to find a base for research, and need to be able to monitor their own and others' performance effectively. Whatever the pressure on pre-service training, some willingness to address these issues at in-service level had been expected, and was not apparent. In this, Britain is in marked contrast to practice in the United States and Canada (see, for example, Alatis *et al.*, 1983).

RECOMMENDATION (8):
That all teachers, particularly those working at secondary level, require work to make them aware of the nature of language, in addition to work on language in particular subject areas. Current work on language for primary teachers should be supported and strengthened.

RECOMMENDATION (9):
That teacher education should recognise the need for all teachers to be familiar with research on classroom interaction and language use in educational settings. Trainee teachers should have the option of being prepared for research activity in this area. A particular priority is research on classroom interaction in multiethnic and multilingual classrooms.

7. *Structural problems*

It is possible that a substantial increase in demand for teacher education on language could develop in the next few years. Movements such as the development of Oracy testing in GCSE, the concerns of the Kingman Inquiry into the teaching of English language, the need for sophisticated Graded Objectives work in modern languages, and the pressures for multilingual education, all point in this direction. However, such a development would need nurturing, and there are few people with adequate expertise to nurture it.

The nature of language is more complex than amateurs think, and there is a long tradition of scholarship and study to draw upon. A graduate or post-graduate level understanding of applied linguistic and educational issues is essential for those who lead teacher education in this area, as well as close contact with and experience of teaching in British schools. Because of the development of applied linguistics and its close connection with EFL teaching particularly [discussed at the beginning of this chapter], such a combination of expertise is rare. Unless means can be found for experienced teachers to have at least the equivalent of a whole year studying for a Master's level retraining, the partially sighted will be leading the blind. There is a very substantial and relevant literature of research, practical discussion and theory to be mastered before language work can be developed with the sophistication that English graduates are able to bring to the work in literature. Further, the amount of time available in practice for part-time Masters level courses make it unlikely that occasional work will give awareness of language as strong a base as was provided for first degree work in other areas. Yet language is too important to be left either to amateurs who know British education but know only a little about language, or to professionals who know much about language but have little close contact with British education.

RECOMMENDATION (10):
There must be support for full-time courses in the area of Language in Education at Masters level, for advisers, teacher educators and school-based in-service and curriculum coordinators.

However patchy the information received from practice in 1984–5, there is little reason to suppose that the changes in teacher education that have taken place since then will have made substantial difference to the observations: language does not feature in the criteria imposed by the Council for the Accreditation of Teacher Education (CATE), for example. This changed in November 1989 and language does now feature in the criteria imposed by the Council.

3 Towards effective practice

Any attempt to produce good practice has to accept the constraints of current teacher education. The academic centre of British teacher education is under severe financial threat from current government policies. Funding for full-time postgraduate degrees has been effectively removed by the establishment of new in-service funding arrangements, and part-time degrees with local authority support are unlikely to survive local financial management of schools except as credit accumulation from a succession of short courses. Initial teacher education may survive the threat from the licensed teacher proposals, but it is still unclear whether there is a strong will to allow students to expect a rigorous academic/practical training for any level of classroom work. The signs are that teacher shortages in major academic areas, including modern languages, will be addressed by bypassing initial training. All-in-all, there is no sign that higher education can expect much support for degree-level courses remotely comparable to the full-time study that first degrees provide. Those courses that survive will be dependent on the diminishing number of overseas students, and the small number of privileged British students who can finance themselves.

Nonetheless, we have a responsibility to continue providing a satisfactory alternative to bootstrap operations. If language is as important and complex as all commentators agree it is, we cannot expect understanding of it to proceed from two-week courses for LEA language coordinators. Somewhere in the system we must make it possible for those who need to master their own understanding of language to have the time and opportunity to do that, and for the results of that mastery to be percolated through the education system in courses of all types. Even with the time constraints imposed by the PGCE teacher training format, we have to act as if the system will continue, and try to ensure that eventually there are models of good practice to follow.

Yet the problems outlined above, the largely unwitting attempt by a government to destroy its own teacher education structure, are less important in the long run than the gaps in belief and ideology that divide language teachers. The different traditions examined above make it difficult for practitioners to talk to each other. What is the basis of this problem?

Stephens (1989), in a fascinating analysis of the language question in mother tongue English discussion, suggests that linguists have concentrated too much on language rather than learning in their arguments with English teachers. She surveys publications (largely those associated with the National Association for the Teaching of English) since 1980, and demonstrates clearly that there is no lack of concern with language as an object of interest in itself. However, where linguists have intervened in the debates, there has frequently been an implicit transmission model of teaching that conflicts with the most deeply held beliefs about good practice of practising teachers. There are also disagreements about the degree of idealisation necessary before language-related discussion can start, but these disagreements are found within linguistics. However, recent attempts to link linguistics to education (e.g. *Educational Linguistics* (Stubbs, 1986), which has provoked substantial discussion in the NATE journal *English in Education*) have failed to attract support, in Stephens' view, because of an insistence on language as system, and an unwillingness to explore pedagogical matters sensitively.

If linguistics cannot build bridges adequately to English teachers, there will never be a useful Language Awareness movement, for English teachers are central to language work in schools, and a movement seen simply as a means of enabling students to approach second language learning effectively will inevitably be seen as a minor and instrumental detail in the total curriculum. But linguistics must start where teachers are themselves if it is to have any impact on the movement: and not to have any impact on the movement is effectively to claim that it is not really the study of language at all, but some more esoteric glass-bead game that should be left to high priests of the cult while we get on with the real work of understanding language under some other name.

The strength of the English teachers' position is their close contact with learners, and their awareness of what learners can do with language and how it interests them. The weaknesses of their position are two-fold. First, they are largely untrained in language – most do not know what it is that Stubbs is really writing about because little in their training has prepared them to look at language objectively. Second, like all of us, there is a risk that they underestimate what learners can be interested in because learners' interests inevitably reflect teachers' interests and skills. Thus, effective work needs to address mismatches between teachers' expectations of students (for example, the differences between secondary and primary teachers' assessments of what learners can do, reported by Mitchell and Hooper, Paper 3), and mismatches between the expectations of committed language communicators, like Stubbs or Crystal, and those who address language from within an English teaching tradition, like Rosen or Britton or Torbe.

I have concentrated in this discussion on the English teaching tradition, because that is where most of the mistrust of language as language lies. This is not to suggest that there is any less need to address modern language teachers, heritage language or classics teachers. Indeed, the serious issues that have been raised by current debates must be matters for all teachers of all subjects and at all levels of teaching.

4 Some suggestions

There is no reason why the agenda for language study that the Kingman Inquiry (DES, 1988a) produced as the commissioned 'model' should not be used as a checklist for language awareness for teachers: it represents a fairly conventional list of useful topics in elementary linguistics. However, as soon as the process of teaching is addressed, issues raised by Widdowson's note of reservation (DES, 1988a: 77–8), and by the English mother tongue objectors referred to above become important. Any consideration of how to link specific items of information about the nature of language to learners' current knowledge involves establishing clearly what relationships there are between the elements in the checklist.

We then have to address a standard curriculum problem: to what extent do we expect learners to be consumers of ideas, and to what extent recreators of ideas? And while this may appear merely to reopen the discovery learning debate, it is necessary to see this as a genuine practical difficulty. When there is very little time, we take short cuts in understanding: we simplify, we use 'models', we idealise, we generalise. Matters that are not central to our concern rely on stereotyping for their position in our consciousness. Only as they become central do we need to look at the complexity that is awaiting us in any area we choose to study. Consequently, simplification and prepackaging have to be seen as inevitable pedagogic devices, used to varying degrees in any learning activity. The key question for us is how to enable such packaging to be conducted in a principled way.

Let us first consider the initial training of teachers. Here, we know that time is at a premium. Two principles may therefore be appealed to: permeation and concentration.

4.1 Permeation

Permeation (which may simultaneously be practised using similar techniques in relation to other major elements in the curriculum, such as economic awareness, multicultural education and special needs, to give only three examples) involves a systematic examination of all elements on a PGCE or BEd course to see where elements of language awareness may legitimately be developed. Such an examination then requires administrative support. Specialists need to offer back-up materials and reading lists for the use of the students of non-specialist colleagues, with some ideas of activities and classroom-based exercises that will link language matters with the concerns of other subject specialists, or of specialists in education outside professional studies.

In this model, individual members of a department will feed their specialist knowledge of resources, references and ideas to colleagues in exchange for a similar service performed for them in areas that are not their own. In this way a checklist of agreed activity can be built into the educational contexts that relate most closely to students' perceptions of themselves as particular kinds of teachers: primary or middle, science or mathematics or languages.

But such permeation can only form one side of the Language Awareness activity. It is useful to persuade colleagues and students that language, like the other permeation topics referred to, influences all our work, but the process will be ineffective unless there is also something more specific. Here, the arguments of both the linguists, as characterised above, and the practitioners, become important. The linguists are important because they are concerned with making sense of a phenomenon, and have to establish a 'story' that holds it together; the practitioners are important because their insistence on language as located, power-based, and a source of personal identity, prevents the linguists' 'story' from becoming so abstract that it is simply the mechanical system of abstract relationships that recent linguistic discussion has been criticising (e.g. Harris, 1987). Specific work for language teachers must arise out of the practical needs of language teachers, but it must also be capable of systematisation as clearly as possible; otherwise the picture will be confused and incoherent and, consequently, neither intellectually appealing (so that it will alienate the teachers we most want to attract) nor memorable (so that it will alienate everyone). This means that language understanding needs to have its exemplification not from texts that are externally provided, but as far as possible from examples that are essential for classroom activity. Language to understand reading (and learners' misreadings); language to understand the possible causes of slips in writing by learners; language to understand the range of personal relations needed in the classroom; and language to understand the code that learners are being taught in foreign language classrooms. If the features of the Kingman model are related to specifications – for English teachers, for German teachers, for Welsh teachers, and practical examples adduced on the basis of videos of classroom performance, examples of pupils' writings, and recordings of teachers, learners (and outsiders whose words may be used in class) – a core of material will be available for teacher education. But at the moment we have to pick and choose from inadequate data, with each institution approaching the task as best it can.

4.2 Concentration

Specific work, albeit brief, for all initial training students will draw upon sources in school-based material. However, all of this has to be seen as a prompt only for work within the school environment. The increased school experience that all teacher education is being pushed towards can be a major asset here. The principles that emerge from use of the Kingman checklist will make no sense if learners are not expected to produce their own examples from observed practice both in school and in their own daily lives. Where examples are needed, they should be produced by students, not by textbooks or staff (Wright (Paper 5); Rutherford, 1987). The advantage of language's omnipresence in education is that illustrations of any point are available in almost every classroom. If there is no example to hand the linguistic principle is probably unimportant for non-specialists.

But such a programme, student-centred, example-based, and with student-teachers providing the examples as far as possible, can only be devised and taught if the people running language in teacher education have been trained to a high level of sophistication. Language simultaneously locates us as ourselves, links us to each new social setting we encounter, develops through and along with us and itself causes concept development, provides us with play and precision, enables us to lie and to confuse, and ties us by freeing us – and to understand all this requires a depth of thought about spoken and written language that has only been available to a relatively small number of people who either have taken educationally orientated linguistics courses or have had so much time and talent in thinking of such matters that they are probably teaching on such courses already! For we have to pursue a consensus that unites Barnes and Crystal, Britton and Stubbs, Rosen and Sinclair and Quirk and Wilkinson and Torbe. We have to accuse all of them of partial blindness; of failing to see that in so far as there are others of this group who have spent a lifetime thinking about language in schooling or language in education or society whose position they cannot encompass, they have failed to comprehend a legitimate aspect of language use in education. There are, of course, differences of political and social intention between all of these, and these differences will inevitably colour their views of language in education – but the consensus for a phenomenon that is as pervasive as language must start from the points of view of those who have spent most time examining it.

Out of this concern must develop a basic linguistic practice for initial teacher education. But it cannot, in my view, develop out of the continuing antagonisms, many of them defensive in the extreme, that have characterised past debate. There is nothing wrong with intellectualising language, as linguists do, any more than there is anything wrong with intellectualising any important phenomenon. If we fail to do that we cannot think about it clearly enough to criticise other people's arguments. But that does not resolve problems of teaching, and much linguistic discussion has intellectualised parts of language and ignored the aspects that are too difficult to handle. Teachers are concerned with language development and have to handle anything that learners are willing to associate with. Linguists must recognise this, and must see the insights of teaching-based commentators as contributions to the same understanding from a different viewpoint – as data to be seriously examined. But no language awareness will emerge in a principled way in teacher education without a high-level attempt to examine these traditions from all sides.

So, finally, where will that examination take place? The school-based model I have described for initial teacher training has value at the stage when learners are concerned with developing their own initial practical abilities. Some later in-service work will require a similar model. But the thinking will not normally benefit from too immediate a contact with the classroom. It will require a retreat from the classroom in order to reflect and to consider research findings from Britain or overseas, to practise empirical investigation or to meditate on teaching experience recollected in relative tranquillity. As mentioned earlier, opportunities for this to happen are fewer than they were, and could disappear altogether. If they do, thinking seriously about education will become the prerogative of the very rich and the very lucky. Education is so important in the structure of society that such a change will inevitably be a step towards tyranny.

3 Teachers' views of language knowledge

Rosamond Mitchell and Janet Hooper

1 Introduction

This paper reports some preliminary findings from a research project conducted in Hampshire schools in autumn 1988, in which primary and secondary school teachers with special responsibility for language teaching were interviewed to discover their views on the place of explicit knowledge about language (KAL) in the school language curriculum, and on possible rationales and strategies for developing such knowledge.

The project took its immediate stimulus from the publication of the Kingman Report (DES, 1988a), which argued the case for such teaching at least partly on the grounds that children's language proficiency would thereby be improved. This connection between the development of children's explicit understanding of language as a system, and that of their practical language skills, is controversial, and disputed in much contemporary writing by English mother tongue specialists (e.g. Allen, 1988; Barrs, 1988) as well as among some second language acquisition researchers (e.g. Krashen, 1981). On the other hand, the Language Awareness movement in British schools has in the 1980s been promoting the development of children's explicit language knowledge on other, broader grounds, and asserts its value regardless of any direct impact on language skills (Hawkins, 1984; Donmall, 1985).

However, the knowledge and beliefs of practising classroom teachers on the issue have been explored only to a very limited extent. Brumfit and Mitchell (forthcoming), and Dennison (1989), have explored the personal knowledge about language of student teachers, using a structured questionnaire first developed by Bloor (1986) for use with language undergraduate students. Mitchell (1988) documented a continuing commitment to grammar explanations among Modern Languages (MLs) teachers in Scotland involved in communicative language teaching initiatives in the early 1980s. Chandler (1988) used a postal questionnaire among English teachers to investigate current 'grammar teaching' practices, finding that while over 80 per cent of his sample claimed to teach 'some grammar', explicit knowledge of language appeared to be declining among English teachers themselves, with younger teachers appearing to have 'little more than a fragmentary knowledge even of traditional grammar' (Chandler, 1988: 22). Despite much polemic in teachers' journals (see review by Stephens, 1989), little else is known about ordinary classroom practitioners' beliefs.

The study reported here was designed to explore teachers' knowledge and beliefs more fully, on the assumption that these are key factors which largely determine the manner and degree of implementation of any given language curriculum. The prospects for the proposed National Curriculum for English and Modern Languages (DES, 1988b), and in particular for the implementation of Kingman-style Language Awareness work, depend critically on a clear understanding of teachers' views.

The research strategy adopted was that of the semi-structured individual interview. An hour-long discussion covered teachers' overall aims in teaching language, and the place within these of the development of explicit KAL; goals and strategies for teaching particular age groups were reviewed. Teachers' rationales for KAL were explored, and in particular their perceptions of its relationship with the development of language proficiency. Further themes to emerge were teachers' own beliefs about the nature of language, and continuities/discontinuities between the beliefs and practices of primary and secondary school teachers.

The sample of teachers interviewed was randomly selected, from primary, middle and 11/12–16 schools in the Southampton/Winchester area. In primary and middle schools, language consultants were interviewed: these are class teachers who have undertaken a specialist advisory role on language for their colleagues, but continue to teach the full primary curriculum to their own class. In secondary schools, heads of English and of modern languages were interviewed: as far as practicable these were chosen in pairs from individual schools, so that the issue of liaison across the 'subject' divide could be explored in more depth.

This paper reports on the views on the KAL issue of seven secondary school heads of English and a similar number of heads of modern languages, which have so far been analysed in detail. The views of the remaining secondary school teachers, as well as of the primary teachers, will be reported in full elsewhere.

2 The English teachers

2.1 Background and overall aims

The English teachers interviewed were hardly aware of the Language Awareness movement as such. If they had heard of it, it was as 'something which has come down the modern languages side': curriculum cooperation with modern languages staff for Language Awareness work was virtually non-existent. (Indeed, despite initiatives in several schools which had linked the English and Modern Languages departments together in new 'faculty' structures, little active curriculum cooperation of any kind between language departments was reported).

The English teachers recalled little of value on language topics in their own initial professional training (with the exception of one, who vividly recalled discussions on class, accent and dialect under Harold Rosen's tutelage at the London Institute of Education). In one or two cases further qualifications had been undertaken: but overall, this group of teachers seemed to have little curiosity about language itself. While most seemed to be maintaining active personal interests as far as literature was concerned, few were doing any reading on language (one commented favourably on a recent book by David Crystal; another reported buying but not understanding some contemporary linguistics books).

These English teachers generally reported their overriding aim as being to produce pupils who were effective communicators, orally and in writing: only one individual argued at this point that children should understand language as a system. The predominant strategic means reported for achieving this aim was the study of literature, though some were working through non-literary themes and projects with at least some age groups, using, for instance, Inner London Education Authorities (ILEA)-produced materials on topics such as 'Myself' or 'The Island' (a 'castaway' simulation).

In this overall framework of aims and means, the development of knowledge about language was generally seen as a secondary, if not marginal, issue. It was noticeable that interview questions regarding the development of KAL were frequently reinterpreted and answered in terms of the development of children's practical language skills.

2.2 Conceptualisations of knowledge about language

Across all three teacher groups, there was considerable variation of views regarding the usefulness of developing pupils' explicit knowledge about language, and the extent to which this should be done. However, throughout the extended discussions that took place on this topic, certain dimensions of language were given much more prominence than others. It appeared that there were some aspects of language which individual teachers were able/willing to discuss with a reasonable degree of fluency, whether favourably or unfavourably, while others were hardly mentioned. The topics that were given prominence in this way varied significantly between the different teacher groups, though there was a considerable degree of consistency within each group. Those topics that were prominent in the English teachers' interviews could be grouped under four headings: Syntax, Language variation, The writing system, and Literary analysis.

2.2.1 Syntax

This was in fact the dominant interpretation of 'knowledge about language' overall; the English teachers, like the others, constantly tended to redefine KAL in the narrow sense of syntactic knowledge, and to express overall positive or negative attitudes accordingly. The construct of 'grammar' was, however, analysed as having a range of subcomponents. Thus, the traditional parts of speech were mentioned by all English teachers whose transcripts have been analysed. A clear majority reported that they taught all or some of these explicitly to their pupils, though a minority argued that this was not appropriate. Sentence and/or phrase structure was also mentioned by a clear majority, who all claimed to teach at least some aspects of this topic. Clause analysis was mentioned by a majority, mostly to be repudiated as a subject of study: only one teacher reported that this was taught. Otherwise, one teacher each reported the systematic teaching of English morphology (prefixes, etc.), and of vocabulary.

2.2.2 Language variation

Almost all teachers mentioned variation in styles and genres in the writing of English, and perceived a need to discuss these explicitly with their pupils; as far as teaching was concerned, this was the most fully supported KAL topic. A clear majority also mentioned the related topic of 'awareness of audience', though neutrally as between speech and writing. These points were concretised by those teachers who claimed to teach particular types of writing (e.g. diaries, letters, autobiography). Lastly, almost all teachers mentioned variation between standard/nonstandard English and their contexts of use, and most felt it right to heighten pupils' awareness of this issue, though with differing degrees of 'normative' emphasis.

2.2.3 The writing system
Almost all teachers said they explicitly discussed and taught aspects of
the punctuation system and paragraphing; a minority mentioned spelling 'rules', and claimed to teach them. One teacher explicitly discussed
the alphabet and sound–letter relationships with his pupils.

2.2.4 Literary analysis
A majority mentioned the traditional 'figures of speech', and claimed
to teach these; a minority mentioned poetic forms such as rhyme and
metre.

Other KAL topics to emerge, though each was mentioned by one or
two teachers only, and not necessarily because they felt it appropriate
to teach about them, were language and the media; language fami-
lies/the history of language; and 'non-verbal' aspects – presumably
paralinguistics.

It is arguable that these discussions about the kinds of KAL which
it was/was not appropriate for pupils to develop in school were tapping
at a deeper level the teachers' own personal models of language, and
that the dimensions outlined above constitute the English teachers'
own main ways of construing/conceptualising language itself. Certain
features of this particular 'model of language' rate special comment.
First, the 'Syntax' and 'Literary analysis' components are strikingly
traditional, and seem to have been affected very little by contemporary
developments in linguistic and literary theory. Second, it is worth
considering what is *not* included in the topics which figure prominently
in the programmatic syllabuses of the Language Awareness movement,
or indeed of the Kingman Report: there is little developed analysis of
the spoken language, or ways of talking about it; there is no reference
to the structure of text above the level of the sentence (apart from
the traditional concept of 'paragraphing'); there is nothing at all on
language acquisition/development. (This is not to assume that the
teachers know nothing about these matters, or do not think they are
important; but somehow they were defined as 'not relevant' throughout
an interview which repeatedly presented opportunities to identify and
give personal views about a range of KAL topics.) On the other hand,
English teachers have clearly taken on board the non-traditional ideas
of register and stylistic variation in written English, and of dialectal
variation in the spoken language (traceable presumably to the influence
of English educationalists such as James Britton, and of socio-linguists
such as Labov and Trudgill). In this they contrast very clearly with
their modern languages colleagues, as will be seen below.

2.3 Rationales for developing knowledge about language

In discussing possible rationales for developing children's explicit knowledge about language within the school language curriculum, the English teachers (like all the rest) were preoccupied with its supposed relationship with the development of language proficiency. Generally speaking, when for the time being interpreting KAL in the narrow sense of syntactic knowledge, teachers felt it had a limited role in promoting practical language skills: a considerable number felt that the relationship was actually negative, with grammatical analysis getting in the way of skill development. A clear majority of the teachers argued that pupils differed in the extent to which their personal language skills could benefit from metastatement and analysis: the consensus view was that academically able pupils could indeed so benefit, but not the rest. However, when thinking about the 'language variation' dimension of KAL, teachers' views of the relationship with language proficiency development were much more positive, and there was a widely held (though not unanimous) belief that explicit discussion of stylistic variation had a direct payoff in improving children's writing skill.

When asked about other possible rationales for KAL (of kinds advanced within the Language Awareness movement, for example), the English teachers mostly had little to add: two explicitly said there was no other, while the rest advanced a variety of suggestions, on the whole tentatively (that it could help MLs learning or literary appreciation, provided intellectual discipline, was in itself pleasurable). Just one teacher presented a strong and well-developed argument for the study of language as an abstract system, as (a) accessible to 90 per cent of pupils, and (b) empowering/liberating for the individual language user.

3 The modern languages teachers

3.1 Awareness of Language Awareness

It was clear from the sample of transcripts analysed so far that the modern languages teachers possessed a degree of familiarity with the Language Awareness concept, particularly arising in connection with the name of Eric Hawkins and his initiatives in this field (Hawkins, 1984). In addition, the concept had been familiarised through the Hampshire Modern Languages Skills Development Programme (HMLSDP, 1988). Under this scheme a range of French, German and Spanish materials are being piloted in Hampshire secondary schools, including an introductory half-term unit entitled

'Language Matters', which falls under the umbrella of Language Awareness (and is taught through the medium of English). Typically then, questioned as to their familiarity with the concept, the MLs teachers interviewed cited topics characteristic of the Hampshire scheme, such as similarities and points of comparison between languages, language families, looking at pronunciation and at different alphabets and scripts, recognition of patterns in language, and so on – or they cited Hawkins and, sometimes, the Cambridge University Press series of booklets *Awareness of Language*. There was also some familiarity with the Language Awareness concept through new course materials such as 'Arc-en-Ciel', which introduces discussion of points of language such as pronunciation, gender, appropriacy and so forth.

Significantly however, this group of teachers all tended to see such Language Awareness teaching as a luxury, rather than part and parcel of their everyday teaching. It was generally regarded as an adjunct, usually a preliminary one, to the real business of teaching the language, and in the schools where it was practised, was viewed as a four-week or half-term introduction in the first year, rather than a continuing dimension to foreign language learning. Thus topics dealt with systematically at this stage only rarely cropped up later in the school, and then only on a very *ad hoc* basis. It was generally felt that, though interesting and valid in their own right, such consciousness-raising activities would have to cede precedence to the all-important business of learning to communicate in the target language.

3.2 Conceptualisations of language

On the whole it would be fair comment that for the MLs heads of department, even more than for their English colleagues, knowledge about language tended to be equated with morpho-syntactic knowledge. In spite of their admitted familiarity with a broader spectrum of topics as discussed under the Language Awareness umbrella, and in spite of the interviewer's attempts to broaden the scope of the term, when questioned about the place of explicit talk about language in their classrooms, the teachers constantly returned to discussion of grammar. (Most commonly, this was in terms of parts of speech, sentence structure, verb tenses and gender.)

The MLs teachers were, however, somewhat on the defensive regarding their own state of knowledge about language; a question about teachers' own use of reference sources in this area was generally perceived as threatening, with one teacher commenting 'a degree in linguistics wouldn't help me very much'. Clearly, such knowledge as they did have owed little to their original degree and teacher training courses, where the component of language knowledge was generally deemed very slight (if not non-existent). The general background was a literature-based university degree in a modern language, followed by a PGCE where the main emphasis was on teaching methodology. On the whole the state of the MLs teachers' knowledge about language was perceived to owe more to their later, personal professional development: to a limited extent through reading, and more significantly through discussion with colleagues, the advisory service, in-service training and encounters with new materials and methodology. (There were regretful comments from teachers on the relative lack of intellectual challenge and stimulation to be found in 11/12–16 schools: 'Teaching 12–16 stultifies one's urge to know – it has stifled my natural curiosity', said one; 'You don't get too far, you don't get too high,' said another.) The fact that questions probing the extent of teachers' own knowledge about language aroused a degree of suspicion and distrust perhaps itself suggests more regret than was overtly expressed, and some perceived need of further knowledge.

3.3 MLs rationales for developing explicit KAL

Unlike their more sceptical English mother tongue colleagues, the MLs teachers generally believed that a clear positive relationship existed between explicit knowledge about language and the development of practical language proficiency, as the following quotations make clear:

> I have not thought it through, I just assumed intuitively that if you are aware of how something works that must help you actually do it, and it does for lots of things.

> Yes, knowledge about language gives the confidence to be able to manipulate it.

> If they have knowledge, it will improve the range of their language and their ability to adapt language. People NOT aware of how language works may memorise a sentence and re-use it, but people WITH knowledge of how language works could take the sentence, adapt it and use it in another context.

The view is clearly expressed in the last of these quotations, that explicit knowledge about language is required to move beyond phrasebook learning to the creative use of the target language (or in other words, for the internalisation of a generative FL system). This view was generally advanced, despite running counter to much current second language acquisition theory: it closely paralleled the views of the sample of Scottish MLs teachers interviewed previously by Mitchell (1988).

In advancing this view, however, the MLs teachers tended consistently to close down their interpretation of KAL to embrace only (morpho)syntactic knowledge. This was clear from the exemplification consistently given for the kind of ongoing 'talk about language' which it was felt appropriate to undertake with pupils in the 11–16 age bracket, after broader preliminaries had been completed. It emerged from the teachers' accounts of their day-to-day class teaching that such talk was typically limited to aspects of sentence structure, with verbs and tenses being much mentioned, together with topics such as gender and adjectival agreement. Indeed, KAL was frequently translated into classroom teaching in the form of an inductive approach to grammatical patterns.

As with the English teachers, there emerged a general feeling among the MLs teachers that the importance of developing explicit KAL varied substantially, according to the perceived ability of the pupil:

> For some children, the less able, I don't think that explicit knowledge is something that will support them too much. But I think, for the brighter ones, it is again an additional tool. If you want really to grow and to go on to further work, then I think you must have a knowledge of it. I know there are some children for whom this is not appropriate.

Almost universally, then, it was felt that for the 'less able' pupil, talking about language is mystifying and off-putting, and is therefore neither appropriate nor helpful. For such pupils the best approach was seen to involve practising with and learning unanalysed chunks or patterns of language, and the analysis of language structure was viewed as best ignored, since such pupils were thought not to be capable of applying the knowledge to help them manipulate the language. Conversely, the more able the pupil, the more helpful, indeed necessary, talking about language was perceived to be.

Implicit in these views, of course, are worrying assumptions about the ultimate level of achievement in a foreign language which is seen as possible for the 'less able'. If explicit knowledge of syntax is essential for developing a generative target language competence, and yet some pupils are not capable of acquiring such knowledge, the expectation is created that the most such pupils can achieve (at least in school contexts) is an accumulation of global phrases. In this way, the MLs teachers' commitment to a particular view of KAL can be seen as actually limiting rather than enhancing pupils' ultimate target language proficiency.

As with the English teachers, the MLs teachers' rationales for developing pupils' knowledge about language other than the perceived positive relationship with FL achievement were fragmentary and undeveloped. Suggestions made by individuals included: '... reduction of insularity', 'enrichment of them as people ... and academic interest', 'being more aware of other people, perhaps in their difficulties in expressing themselves in language'. But such ideas were clearly marginal, by comparison with the perceived link with language proficiency.

4 Conclusion

These two key groups of language curriculum specialists had entered teaching with little or no specialist training in language. The models of language they controlled could thus be explained primarily as a combination of that transmitted in their own time as school pupils, plus newer ideas internalised during their active professional life via new curricula and materials, in-service activity, and informal contacts of all kinds.

These processes evidently continue to operate somewhat differently in the English and MLs traditions. Both groups of teachers shared a strong tendency to equate KAL with morpho-syntactic knowledge of a traditional kind, centred on the written language system. However, attitudes towards the place of such knowledge in the curriculum differed significantly between the two groups. Generally speaking, the English teachers were sceptical of its value to many pupils, as far as developing practical language skills was concerned, and saw little other point in it. The MLs group, however, retained a surprisingly strong consensus that KAL in this narrow sense did contribute vitally to language learning, at least for some pupils.

On the other hand, the English teachers' view of language had other fairly well-developed, non-traditional aspects, notably their concern with, and ability to analyse, language variation. This socio-linguistic dimension was largely absent from the MLs discussion, rather surprisingly, given the promotion of the concept of 'communicative competence' in relevant theoretical literature over the last decade at least (see, e.g. Canale and Swain, 1980).

Missing from the discussion of both groups, however, were some key topics in contemporary 'expert' models of language (the Kingman model, for example): notably, the structure of discourse beyond the level of the individual sentence, the spoken language in all its aspects, and first/second language acquisition and development. Of course, this does not mean that these topics were not felt to be important by each group. It was clear, from the rich accounts of everyday practice provided by all teachers, that much classroom time is spent in practical activity devoted to elaborating pupils' ability to produce and evaluate long texts, and also that increasing importance is given in both English and modern languages to developing spoken language skills. Both involve continuing discussion with pupils about their work, which must include metalinguistic feedback of rich and varied kinds; but somehow neither emerged as salient themes when teachers were asked to discuss in more general terms their own views on language, and the kinds of explicit knowledge it is desirable for pupils to develop. Similarly, teachers' accounts of classroom practice gave insights into the implicit language learning theories to which they adhere; it seems impossible that, in day-to-day classroom work, teachers are not regularly giving explicit advice to pupils on what, in their view, constitutes good language learning strategies. But again, this area was not tapped in interview despite repeated opportunities. On the evidence, it would seem that language teachers have not yet fully theorised these key aspects of their work or, at least, that they lack a technical language through which they can easily analyse and discuss them with their pupils (and with visiting researchers).

On the basis of the evidence presented here, it would seem that ordinary language teachers have a much more limited conscious commitment to the systematic development of their pupil's KAL than is envisaged in their different ways by either the Language Awareness movement or the Kingman Report. Nonetheless, it is clear that consciousness-raising about aspects of language has some place in most language classrooms, though perhaps in differing degrees for different pupils. Just how this talk about language works out in practice, and how it impinges on the developing models of language held by pupils, cannot be known until documented through further studies involving the longitudinal observation of classroom interaction. But it seems likely that it will take more than the limited cascade training programme presently envisaged by the DES in support of Kingman to 'normalise' on the Kingman model the variation in current teacher knowledge, beliefs and practice.

4 Linguistic diversity and Language Awareness: the views of primary school teachers

Guy Merchant

1 Introduction

The view that teachers should respond positively to the linguistic diversity of the school population is now widely supported in the educational literature of policy documents and research reports as well as HMI investigations, DES statements and committees of inquiry. As a result, linguistic diversity has become a familiar term in professional debate and staffroom discussion. Conflicting versions of what such a positive response entails in terms of classroom practice are representative of the variety of ways in which practitioners interpret the concept of linguistic diversity in the light of their own theories of teaching and learning.

Through the work of a three-year development project funded by the European Commission, we now have a much clearer picture of professional thinking and practice in this field. The Linguistic Diversity in the Primary School Project (LDIP) has involved groups of primary school teachers in a number of LEAs around the country. Their work has explored a range of themes from developing the use of minority languages in school to raising the status of non-standard varieties of English as well as activities that fall under the general category of Language Awareness.

In 1985 the Swann Report recommended that the British education system should cater for 'the linguistic needs of ethnic minority pupils' and also 'take advantage of the opportunities offered for the education of all pupils by the linguistic diversity of our society today' (Swann, 1985). Underlying this statement was the Swann Committee's notion of a two-pronged educational response to cultural pluralism that distinguished between the specific needs of ethnic minority groups and the more general needs of all children (Craft, 1982).

Although educational provision for ethnic minority children remains an important and sometimes contentious issue, the emphasis on multicultural education as an aspect of every child's school experience has tended to take precedence as the school's role in maintaining social cohesion and providing a more uniform curriculum has been reaffirmed.

The distinction the Swann Report makes between the specific needs of some children and the general needs of all children has influenced thinking on language education in primary schools. One consequence of this is that the move to provide bilingual teaching support for pupils from linguistic minorities, which gained considerable support in the late 1970s and early 1980s (Khan, 1980; Tansley, 1986), has tended to lose momentum as attention shifts to a consideration of how all children can benefit from linguistic diversity. The most recent testimony to this change of emphasis is to be found in the report of the National Curriculum English Working Party (NCC, 1988), which is quite clear about the enriching effect of linguistic diversity: 'Pupils whose first language is not English can help other members of their class to extend their understanding of language' (1.20) and 'their knowledge and experience can be put to good use in the classroom to the benefit of all pupils to provide examples of the structure and syntax of different languages . . .' (12.9).

The enriching effect of linguistic diversity is clearly seen in terms of the benefits for monolingual children in learning about language rather than the potential for developing the language skills of bilingual children. In this way the minority languages of Britain are seen as an important resource in developing the kinds of Language Awareness described by Hawkins (1984) and Donmall (1985).

2 Developments in linguistic diversity

Recognising and valuing children's languages became an important aspect of multicultural education in the early 1980s. Houlton and Willey's 'Why support children's bilingualism?' (1983) was influential in helping schools and LEAs to reconsider their responses to the changing linguistic profile of the school population. 'Linguistic diversity' or 'language diversity' work came to be seen as a way of enriching classroom life. At first this was done in rather a superficial way. 'Welcome' posters in many languages were displayed on classroom doors; notices and labels were translated into Urdu and Gujerati; dual textbooks were ordered from the libraries; dominoes, matching games and teaching clocks began to feature Arabic and Punjabi numerals. The intention was, of course, to create a multilingual environment – an environment in which children's curiosity about language was aroused and one in which all languages were valued as being equally important.

Unfortunately much of this early work on linguistic diversity failed to engage children in meaningful interactions or any sort of systematic learning. Pioneering work was often done in isolation by committed classroom teachers without the benefit of support from colleagues or official policy guidelines. This initial enthusiasm was criticised by some for being superficial and tokenistic. The work in primary classrooms often depended upon visual impact – classrooms displayed a variety of scripts – mysterious shapes in a variety of calligraphic styles, running in different directions, left to right, right to left, horizontal and vertical: essentially decorative and often meaningless to many. Luckily not all of this work was confined to labelling and other kinds of window dressing. Committed teachers were beginning to explore ways of encouraging the use of a variety of languages in a more purposeful way in the classroom and were keen to make Language Awareness an integral part of topic planning (Houlton, 1985).

Innovatory developments in the classroom were spurred on by curriculum development projects such as the Schools Council Mother Tongue Project (1981–5) and research studies like the DES-funded Linguistic Minorities Project (1980–3). The major achievement of this work was its contribution to a changing awareness of the languages of Britain. Other languages, once seen as a handicap, are now more likely to be seen as an asset. The idea of 'responding positively' to linguistic diversity is now widely accepted. Exactly how to 'respond positively' is still open to interpretation.

Following the Swann Report's distinction between the specific needs of ethnic minority pupils and the general needs of all pupils (DES, 1985), primary school responses to linguistic diversity can be seen as falling into two distinct categories. The first is derived from a change of attitudes towards the education of minority group children and emphasises the importance of valuing home languages and providing some sort of continuity in their language learning experience. To this end an increasing number of local authorities are providing bilingual support for ethnic minority pupils (Bourne, 1989). This provision focuses on the specific educational and linguistic development of bilingual pupils.

The second kind of response to linguistic diversity calls for Language Awareness programmes for all children. Work in this field is still in its infancy. This is a more general response in which schools are encouraged to recognise the multicultural and multilingual nature of British society. It is the line taken in the Cox Report where it is argued that 'difficult issues of language in an increasingly multicultural society require informed citizens' (DES, 1989b: 3.9). The report goes on to suggest that schools have a vital role to play in changing attitudes and encouraging 'a tolerance of linguistic diversity through the recognition that all languages are rule-governed and systematic'. To put this into practice we need teachers who are informed citizens with a particular kind of knowledge about language.

3 Investigating teachers' definitions of linguistic diversity

Teachers' knowledge about linguistic diversity varies considerably according to their own experiences and professional development and their individual theories of teaching and learning. As part of the preparatory work for a programme of in-service courses initiated by the EC-funded Linguistic Diversity in the Primary School Project, teachers were asked to complete a pre-course questionnaire consisting of three open questions. These were:

1. What motivated you to come on this course?
2. What do you expect to gain from this course?
3. What do you understand by the term linguistic diversity?

For the purpose of this paper we concentrate on responses to the third question only: definitions of linguistic diversity.

The teachers involved were all employed in primary schools and worked in seven different local authorities. Courses were based in LEAs in London, the Midlands and Yorkshire – authorities with quite different policies on multicultural education and varying degrees of commitment to training in this area. Responses from 138 teachers were analysed. Table 1 shows the biographic information collected to describe these teachers, the schools they worked in and the courses they had previously attended.

The problem of coding responses to open-ended questions is frequently discussed in the research literature (e.g. Cohen and Manion, 1986) and strategies for ensuring the reliability and validity of such data need to be developed. In accordance with established practice, a coding frame was devised on the completion of the questionnaires by selecting categories that were typical of the responses found in the sample. Following the approach used by Atkins (1984) the initial coding frame was checked for reliability with an independent judge. After reaching agreement on categories to be used for the coding frame, the data were analysed first by the author and then by the independent judge. A high level of intercoder agreement (93 per cent) suggests that this content analysis is reasonably valid. The coding frame for responses to the third question (defining linguistic diversity)

TABLE 1   The sample

	Course 1	Course 2	Course 3	Course 4	Course 5	Course 6	Course 7	Total	% of total
Language background of teachers									
1. English/monolingual	5	15	5	12	4	8	20	69	50
2. English + other langs.	9	5	10	6	5	7	6	50	36
3. Bilingual	4	0	1	3	4	5	2	19	14
Ethnic composition of schools									
1. All white	3	0	0	0	0	0	2	5	3
2. 50% or less ethnic minorities	13	6	6	9	5	11	18	76	55
3. 50% or more ethnic minorities	2	6	10	12	6	9	10	57	42
Previous courses attended									
1. None	5	1	1	3	3	4	3	20	14
2. Language development	2	1	2	2	1	1	0	9	6
3. Bilingualism	0	0	1	2	1	0	0	4	2
4. Multicultural 6	10	8	8	1	7	17	50	36	20
5. Previous l.d. course	6	7	5	7	5	0	4	28	20
6. Racism awareness	5	3	2	3	4	5	6	28	20
7. Section XI training	6	10	0	2	0	10	3	29	21
No. of course members	18	20	16	21	13	20	30	138	

is set out on Table 2. Quotations from the questionnaires are used to illustrate the categories agreed upon.

Question 3: *What do you understand by the term linguistic diversity?*

Category 1. Community language/language variation: '. . . speaking of different community languages, ranges and varieties of languages in society.'

Category 2. Accent and dialect: 'different languages, different dialects, different accents present in Britain.'

Category 3. Use in the classroom: '"using" different languages in all aspects of the curriculum.'

Category 4. Valuing community languages: 'to have respect for the many languages in the community.'

Category 5. Language deficit: 'the ability to appreciate and understand the difficulties of bilingual people in the community.'

Category 1 responses use the term to describe the linguistic profile of the school population. Descriptions include reference to minority community languages and varieties of English. There is no indication of what the educational implications of linguistic diversity might be; the term is used as a straightforward statement of fact. Teachers' definitions classified in Category 1 appear to be accurate but rather simplistic or incomplete.

Category 2 responses make specific reference to regional and class variation in the language of mother tongue English speakers. As in the case of Category 1 responses, the term is used descriptively. These responses are, for the most part, fairly accurate, but again avoid any evaluative comment.

Category 3 responses emphasise the language rights of children. Here definitions focus on the use of languages other than Standard English in classroom contexts. The underlying importance of the language of the home in subsequent language development is central to these responses. Valuing and using the languages of children (and particularly those from ethnic minorities) is also a dominant theme. Linguistic diversity is defined in educational terms with reference to the needs of specific groups of children. Underlying these responses is the view that the school system has played a major role in linguistic oppression and should change fundamentally in order to legitimise the variety of languages spoken in the community.

Category 4 responses refer explicitly to the importance of giving recognition to minority community languages in school settings. Working from the belief that community languages have a low status in society and that linguistic prejudice is a significant problem. These definitions stress the need for raising the awareness of all pupils and suggest that teachers could respond to linguistic diversity by providing Language Awareness programmes for all children.

Category 5 responses see diversity as a problem particularly related to the educational achievement of ethnic minority pupils and their white working-class peers. Definitions of this type embody popular interpretations of Bernstein's theories of language disadvantage as well as a belief in the idea of widespread semilingualism. The educational implications of these definitions are that there is a need for remedial or compensatory programmes and, in the case of bilingual pupils, an expansion of ESL provision.

4 Results

Analysis of these data provided by the course members gives a general impression of current professional needs in responding to linguistic diversity. Their responses proved invaluable in the planning of subsequent course provision and offer insight into current professional thinking in this area.

The independent judge's coding of the participants' responses to Question 3 is shown in Table 2.

Where responses fall into more than one category they have been double-coded or multiple-coded.

Definitions of the term linguistic diversity proved to be the most difficult of the responses to categorise and code. Nevertheless, the analysis shows that the majority of teachers on our courses came with the view that linguistic diversity is a broad descriptive concept which embraces the newer community languages as well as the varieties of contemporary English. A typical definition in this category relates the term to: 'Variation of languages spoken including a wide variety of ways of using the same language, e.g. English.'

References to linguistic minorities tended to use examples drawn from the languages of the Indian sub-continent – no mention was made of Celtic languages and very few examples were drawn from European language groups.

A third of the teachers responding saw linguistic diversity as an important aspect of classroom life. Rather than taking a broad view of language in society, these definitions tended to be prescriptive in flavour – arguing that schools OUGHT to use different languages in the classroom. By contrast, a smaller proportion (14 per cent) focused exclusively on the need to raise the status of community languages

TABLE 2 Definitions of linguistic diversity

	Course 1	Course 2	Course 3	Course 4	Course 5	Course 6	Course 7	Total	%
1. Community languages/language variation	12	19	9	9	8	12	29	99	72
2. Accent and dialect	8	10	5	4	0	8	14	50	40
3. Use in the classroom	3	0	11	12	2	7	6	41	30
4. Valuing community languages	5	2	3	5	4	1	0	20	14
5. Language deficit	4	0	5	2	1	4	0	16	12
Total number of course members	18	20	16	21	13	20	30	138	

– again examples tended to be drawn from Asian languages such as Punjabi and Gujerati.

Finally, a smaller number of teachers in each group wrote definitions which seemed to embody a 'deficit' view of other languages. References to children's 'problems of communication', 'difficulties with English' and 'low self-esteem' were typical of these responses.

Teachers' perceptions of linguistic diversity vary quite considerably. Fortunately we are now in a position to see from an independent evaluation study commissioned by the LDIP project that courses have helped to raise teachers' awareness (Dhingra, 1989). Changes in perception were observed in each of the LEA courses. Some of the interviews conducted by the course evaluator illustrate this:

> Before the course I had too narrow a view – being in a mainly Gujerati/Punjabi-speaking school, I tended to think of language only in terms of the school community.

> I had not before seriously considered feminist, Irish or West Indian dimensions of diversity.

> I now have much more awareness of the importance of linguistic diversity in relation to self-esteem and also to the position of individuals and groups in society in terms of power and status.

However, the pre-course data are probably more typical of current professional thinking than the thoughts of those who have attended courses designed to raise their awareness. These data suggest that many teachers have fairly limited knowledge of the languages around them. There is a tendency, for instance, to adopt an over-simplified view in which linguistic diversity is equated with South Asian languages. One teacher's definition illustrates this trend: 'It is the many different languages from the sub-continent of India.' While another is ambiguous, confused, or both: 'a variety of languages and cultures – a spaghetti junction.'

Category 1 and 2 definitions (Table 2) do not, however, express any particular views about how schools should respond to linguistic diversity. Categories 3, 4 and 5, on the other hand, give us an impression of the sort of classroom activity associated with the concept. Teachers involved in the LDIP project, the majority of whom were employed in multilingual schools, emphasised the need to use the language skills of pupils in the classroom. Thirty per cent of the sample were concerned with 'the linguistic needs of minority pupils' (DES, 1985). A smaller percentage of responses were coded in Category 4 and this illustrates the need for more development in the area of Language Awareness.

Although over-simplified definitions were quite commonplace, the number of references to regional variation in English was surprising – 40 per cent of the sample included specific references to accent and dialect. However, there were few references to the influence of class and gender on language use.

Finally, as a result of the project's experience in contributing to a wide range of in-service courses we were surprised to see a comparatively small number of responses coded in the 'language deficit' category. If this is an accurate picture of changes in professional attitudes, the information is encouraging to say the least. However, it must be recognised that our rather crude research tool was not designed to measure specific language attitudes but merely to gain an impression of teachers' thoughts about linguistic diversity.

5 Conclusions

The results of this small-scale survey suggest a number of ways in which teacher education about language might be improved. A broader and clearer definition of linguistic diversity and its implications for classroom practice needs to be developed within the teaching profession. This will be particularly important in developing training programmes to support the recommendations of the Cox Committee (NCC, 1988) and the Kingman Report (DES, 1988). The DES-sponsored Language in the National Curriculum (LINC) project may well provide useful materials for in-service work in this field. More attention should also be given to the topic of linguistic diversity in initial teacher training.

We should be moving away from the notion that diversity is only a matter of importance for multicultural schools. When the Swann Report suggested that: 'all schools should seek to foster among their pupils an awareness of the linguistic diversity of our society and a real understanding of the role and function of language in all its forms' (DES, 1985: Ch. 7, 5.1), this was, in fact, a plea for more Language Awareness work. As our research has illustrated, there is a continuing need to develop this sort of approach. However, we also have to recognise that this awareness work has to be accompanied by the kinds of educational provision that support the development of bilingual and bidialectal children.

Other questions also need to be asked. If Language Awareness is to be part of our response to linguistic diversity we need to be quite clear about its goals. This is likely to depend upon our analysis of the role of language in society. We may, for instance, suggest that children's knowledge about language should at least be informed and up-to-date and argue that there is a need for schools to reflect the languages of society at large. All children should *know* about the languages and varieties around them in order to become informed citizens – this is the main thrust of the English Working Group's recommendations (NCC, 1988).

Alternatively, we may feel that linguistic prejudice is a widespread phenomenon and harmful to the development of good intergroup relations. This, too, has implications for Language Awareness work and suggests that the problem lies with the *negative attitudes* of individuals towards particular language groups. A Language Awareness programme following this analysis would need to complement work on knowledge about languages with an exploration of attitudes to language. But, if we are honest, the difficulty with this analysis of language in society is that it implies that individuals are directly responsible for the status of languages, and this is clearly not the case. Language status tends to reflect and determine the pattern of intergroup domination and subordination. A more radical view of language in society would suggest that Language Awareness programmes need to include an understanding of power, politics and linguistic oppression and the ways in which groups and institutions can alter circumstances. This, after all, is the real challenge of linguistic diversity.

5 Language Awareness in teacher education programmes for non-native speakers

Tony Wright

In designing and implementing a language teacher education programme for non-native speakers, either initial training (ITT) or in-service (INSET), one naturally becomes aware of the complex network of issues that such a venture generates. These issues range from the nature of the curricular perspective being mediated, through questions of 'appropriate methodology', to issues derived from an examination of specific classroom activities. Concerns such as these are thrown into sharp relief when the programme is conducted not in the teacher's country of origin – as is the norm worldwide – but abroad. Recent experience at Christ Church College on a number of programmes with participants from environments as varied as Madagascar, Cyprus, Sweden and Malaysia, has provided us with ample opportunity to explore these and other issues.

Our experience has also brought us into contact with one of the key elements in language teacher education and training programme design: the relationship between the study of languages and the study of teaching methods. This relationship – between content and method – appears to be central to a discussion of the design and implementation of any teacher education programme; the special issues raised by working with non-native speakers in English Language Teaching (ELT) give the debate a further dimension. In our work we have been especially concerned with the question of appropriate content knowledge for language teachers and how this knowledge is acquired on courses. Further, we are interested in how this knowledge might form a basis for effective classroom language teaching. While I shall discuss our response to these questions from an ELT perspective, I believe that many of the problems we face are not unique and may have relevance for foreign language teacher education in Britain and even for mother tongue English education.

1 General principles

In our work in language teacher education we have tried to respond to the new agenda in language teaching (see Breen, 1987, for a review of the perceived paradigm shift from content to process in language teaching) and in particular the move towards raising awareness about the nature of the language being learnt or taught. We have opted for language awareness as a key element in our methodology for reasons that are simple yet at the same time complex because of the multitude of issues raised by the choice.

It has not been easy to reconcile what appear to be differing perspectives offered to us by applied linguists. On the one hand, for example, there is renewed interest in 'grammar' and, on the other, a strong pull in the direction of classroom practices designed to be as 'communicative', and therefore unselfconscious with regard to the nature of the linguistic system, as possible – and our own experience as language teachers and tutors on training programmes, concerned with the day-to-day practicalities of teaching and learning as well as attempting to satisfy the needs and demands of sponsors and participants. Furthermore, particularly in the early stages of our work, there was precious little in texts or journals to guide us methodologically, apart from the extremely valuable *Discover English* by Bolitho and Tomlinson (1980), various materials designed for learners rather than teachers (see some of the material in Rinvolucri (1984) for example, and some of the ideas advanced by Hawkins (1984) in L1 learning and teaching).

In many ways, the approach we have developed parallels that reported by Edge (1988). Edge sees the development process for the trainee as moving from user to analyst to teacher of language. We see this route as one of a range of possibilities, but, with the needs of the initial trainee in mind, we are broadly in sympathy. In INSET, we believe that we could enter the framework at any point and work in any direction – INSET demands a more flexible approach and one that recognises that the user/analyst/teacher route has, to all intents and purposes, already been followed. Language Awareness, as we conceive it, is in a pivotal position in the user/analyst/teacher framework, mediating between user competence and teacher competence. The approach is summarised in Figure 1.

The primary focus of our approach is ultimately on the relationship between the content and method of language teaching – the analyst/teacher axis. As minimal requirements, we believe that language teachers need expertise in the language they are teaching and skills to handle the management of the learning process. However, we do not see the former, for instance, as a licence to lecture learners about obscure grammatical points. Knowledge about language is first and foremost an enabling knowledge that provides the teacher with the

64

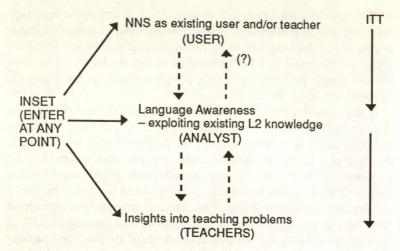

FIGURE 1   The user/analyst/teacher approach

tools to carry out such basic tasks as interpreting a syllabus document and translating it into a scheme of work, explaining code errors to learners, providing accessible information about the language to learners, making decisions on behalf of learners regarding the content of instruction and ensuring that there is a linguistic focus – either on language skills or language items or both – in any particular lesson.

Language teachers have to make informed decisions on the content of teaching. However, we do not see these decisions being taken in a vacuum. There seems to be little point, for instance, in preparing materials for learning a grammatical point without a methodological framework in which to place the material. Thus skills and expertise are not seen as separate – in many ways they are mutually supporting. This is the essence of the analyst/teacher axis.

Knowledge about language also makes a powerful psychological contribution to the teacher's work – confidence. This confidence may be seen as vital for any teacher, but even more so for the non-native speaker who may be held up as a model user and source of information about the language. Very often, demands similar to those placed on native speakers of English are placed upon non-native-speaker teachers. They are expected to know their language, both as user in the everyday sense and as technician in the pedagogic sense. Here, user and analyst combine.

The central issue on both of these axes – the user/analyst and the analyst/teacher – is *how* the teacher comes by linguistic knowledge. There would, I feel, be fairly broad agreement about the types of linguistic knowledge that a language teacher requires, whether native or non-native speaker. How the teacher acquires that knowledge is probably an area of some controversy. For the non-native speaker, there are additional factors to consider.

Non-native speakers approach the language with very different perspectives from those of native speakers. Owing to their previous experience of learning English, non-native speakers often have a very well-developed metalanguage born out of a structural/grammatical approach. Of course, this could be seen as a problem, especially if the view acquired is regarded as 'traditional' or 'out-of-date'. We see it as highly advantageous in encouraging Language Awareness. The non-native's view of language may also be impermeable through a basic insecurity regarding proficiency in the language or even inferiority about the variety spoken. We have encountered both these problems and have opted for an awareness-raising approach precisely because of them. We sense that it is far less face-threatening than an approach which persists in giving trainees the notion that the rules of language are somehow 'outside' them, as a language improvement course or a series of lectures on linguistics or phonology might well do. The affective element in Language Awareness is very powerful. It is our experience that non-native speakers are capable of interesting and valid insights into the nature and system of language once opportunities have been provided. Often we have found ourselves discussing with trainees an observation they have made about an aspect of language that we, as native speakers, have been 'blocked' from. Opportunities such as these do not seem to be afforded by a top-down theoretically grounded approach. Our approach aims to give trainees the confidence to reflect upon their L2 knowledge and to see it as internalised and, therefore, their property. I would not claim that this confidence is easily won; it runs counter to many prior assumptions, both of trainee and tutor, regarding the nature of linguistic knowledge.

2 Language Awareness in initial training

The first priority in initial training, as previously intimated, is to begin the transition from user to analyst – to begin the often painful process of standing outside language, dissecting it, reflecting upon it, hypothesising about its nature from existing knowledge; in short, challenging assumptions and views. This process has to be tempered by the knowledge that, eventually, these insights are to become part of teacher competence and must thus be well based in practice. For initial trainees, with no previous experience of teaching other than as consumers, this requires a willing suspension of disbelief on their part in the early stages of their course. At this juncture, I shall report on how we attempted to overcome these difficulties with an initial training group and how we developed the programme of specialist training to effect the transition from user to teacher.

In 1985, our first intake of Malaysian students began a specially written BEd (TESL) course. (An outline of the course can be seen in Figure 2.) The students were proficient users of English – they had followed a two-year matriculation programme, the major goal of which

Methods	*Language study*	
Year 1	Learning languages	Attitudes to language
	Teaching methods – 4 skills	Language Awareness – lexis – grammar
	Teaching materials – construction and evaluation	– phonology – text
	Teaching practice (3 weeks)	
Year 2	Teaching methods – skills and systems – learner language – teaching syllabuses	Language Awareness – grammar topics – phonology – text and discourse
Year 3	Preparation for teaching practice – analysis of syllabus for skills and systems – preparation of schemes of work and materials	Language in context – introduction to pragmatics
	Teaching practice (12 weeks)	
Year 4	Curriculum study testing/assessment/ evaluation ESP CALL	Socio-linguistic issues – variety study – language planning/policy – inter-ethnic communication – SLA models

FIGURE 2   BEd (TESL) – Language study and methods programme

was to raise proficiency levels – and had lived in Britain for two years. They had, in addition, followed a structure-based English programme at secondary school in Malaysia, completed just two years previously. Thus, we could safely assume a fairly comprehensive metalinguistic knowledge. But we knew they had many misgivings about teaching – based principally on their own learning experiences at school. Our initial decisions as to the content and conduct of the Year 1 programme were based on these facts. On the one hand, we believed it necessary to begin the move from user to analyst of language and to assemble some of the tools they would need as teachers of language. We also had to dispel their fears about language teaching and to demonstrate that it was a richer and more challenging activity than they assumed. We had to challenge two sets of assumptions – about teaching and about language. There was a further, hidden, set of assumptions about the nature of learning. These surfaced as the course progressed.

We had, in addition, two major long-term landmarks to guide us: a short teaching practice in Malaysia at the end of Year 1 and an extended practice in Year 3. We therefore aimed to complete specialist training by the end of the long practice. The final year would be used to broaden students' perspectives on language teaching through curriculum studies and an examination of contexts of language use.

We could have chosen to use language study modules in years 1 to 3 to provide knowledge about language through a study of linguistics, to lecture and prescribe reading, but we felt that this approach would not have provided the students with an adequate pedagogic base as content and method would have been irreconcilably separated. Instead, we made the decision to work on parallel tracks in methods and language study in years 1 and 2, seeking points of crossover at every opportunity. For example, if we were looking at grammar on the language study course, the methods course would endeavour to incorporate this when studying a teaching principle and associated techniques.

In language study, the first year was devoted to a survey of language topics under the umbrella title of Language Awareness. This title also reflected the approach we adopted in contact sessions. The key principle was to work on language data and information about language, with differing focal points – on lexis, grammar, phonology and text, with text as the primary unit. The aim, in linguistic terms, was to develop an appreciation of the influence of linguistic context on language use. In the methods module in year 1, our aim was to examine the factors involved in learning languages and to acquire a basic repertoire of techniques for teaching the four skills, sufficient to teach basic lessons on the short practice at the end of that year.

While the Language Awareness course began with questions related to attitudes to language, the methods course began with the students being exposed to a range of possibilities for teaching and learning languages; they were taught a foreign language – French – in four very different ways in four separate sessions with a follow-up focus in each instance on the method used and the view of learning implicit in the method, the management skills required by the teacher and the view of language implicit in each method. By the end of the first month of the programme the two parallel directions of language study and methods had been mapped out. In year 3, the two were brought together in the intensive work leading to the preparation for teaching practice – analysing the syllabus, devising schemes of work, preparing teaching materials. Language and methods work was deliberately, as it is in reality, integrated. In order to see how language awareness developed towards this goal, let us examine three tasks, one from the year 1 and the others from the year 2 language study programmes.

The year 1 task (see Appendix 1) was designed to provide opportunities for students to comment on the effect of context on the meaning of utterances. This task followed work on different approaches to grammar during which we examined samples from different sources (reference grammars and course books) which gave information about particular grammar points: present continuous and simple present. It also laid part of the foundation for an approach to teaching grammar that took pains to place grammar in context, and also for more complex issues raised by 'functions' and pragmatics later in the course.

During the short practice at the end of year 1, students were asked to collect samples of students' written work for use in year 2. The aim of the tasks (see Appendix 2) was to establish the difference between formal and conceptual views of the verb in English. Previous work on the course had examined formal aspects of the English verb such as morphemic changes, negation, question formation and auxiliary usage. This series of tasks was designed to effect a link between a study of time, tense and aspect and this previous work as well as to provide direct input to the methods course which was to examine learner language, error and correction. At this stage, early in the year 2 course, we were beginning to establish direct links between the analyst/teacher positions.

A further example of the type of task used on the year 2 course (see Appendix 3) examines article usage. Here, the link with pedagogic concerns is even more overt, raising the key issue of the role of grammatical explanations in the classroom. One great danger of acquiring specialist knowledge about language is the possible desire to show learners that you have this knowledge. Combined with an examination of grammar reference works and, again, learner error (from the samples), this proved to be an invaluable way to study a difficult point of English grammar. In 1989 we included as a follow-up, an exercise from Ur (1988), where newspaper headlines have to be written out as complete sentences. It provoked a very interesting discussion of the links between grammar and background knowledge and helped put the 'rules' of article usage into perspective. It also enabled a discussion of the use of Language Awareness exercises with learners – a surprise from our point of view, as our agenda had not previously included a discussion of this issue.

Before moving on to a brief discussion of the role of Language Awareness on INSET programmes, it is worth noting a problem that we faced in the early stages of the BEd language study work. Although the students were metalinguistically well equipped at the outset – i.e. they knew basic grammatical terminology – there were considerable barriers to their using the metalanguage without embarrassment. They associated terms like 'verb tense' and so on with their very recent learning experience. They declared their misgivings on numerous occasions: refining and using the vocabulary of the experts was a very arduous process for them. Informally, from our perspective, progress could be ascertained by the students' increasing willingness and confidence in using the terminology and talking about language. Significantly, the merging of language study and methods courses in year 3 accelerated the process: conscious exploration had become unconscious and 'natural'.

3 Language Awareness in INSET

If INSET is broadly regarded as a medium of change and innovation, where does Language Awareness fit in? Each INSET group has different needs and goals. However, one of our main goals must be to present new viewpoints on language and language learning, not with the aim of forcing change, but rather providing the wherewithal for teachers faced with change (often imposed) to understand and confront these changes in a spirit of inquiry. Language Awareness does have a part to play in this process, but with a different emphasis from the approach taken in ITT.

As pointed out previously, the framework of user/analyst/teacher can be entered at any point by an INSET group. I have reported elsewhere (Wright, 1990) on attempts to integrate language work with broader curricular and methodological issues in INSET. Here I shall examine two Language Awareness exercises devised for INSET groups.

The first is an adaptation and extension of the year 1 BEd exercise (see Appendix 1 – alternative rubrics). The content is identical, but the orientation different. This time, the exercise is done in response to the question 'What are the disadvantages of a focus solely on form in language exercises?' The first task draws explicitly on teachers' prior analyst/teacher knowledge. The second challenges that perception explicitly in preparation for further work on communicative grammar tasks in the classroom.

The second set of activities is based on a text (see Appendix 4). The exercises can be attempted in any order and for different purposes. For example, Exercise A can be used to develop a discussion and a subsequent consideration of discussion exercises as a classroom technique. The text would be the focal point of the discussion, leading to a consideration of the elements of a text which activate background knowledge and how the language and organisation of the text contribute to its overall effect on the reader. On its own that would not be sufficient, however. Exercises B and C could be used with a group of teachers from a structural teaching tradition in order to provide support and guidance during and following Exercise A. Alternatively, Exercise D could be the entry point – overtly a teacher entry point – with B and C used as support exercises. A further, exciting, alternative is to invite the INSET group to devise their own route through the exercises. This could be used to generate further discussion of their own views of language and also to consider the value of Language Awareness as a methodological tool in language teaching.

Many non-native-speaker teachers on INSET courses ask for 'language improvement'. A possible response to this would be to provide what basically amounts to a language course. This, I believe, is an easy solution and one which may also reinforce feelings of perceived inferiority *vis-à-vis* native speakers. The types of exercise outlined above are, I believe, a more satisfactory response to this need, for they do not separate language from teaching method and they exploit and necessarily challenge participants' views of both of these. We believe that Language Awareness is a valid alternative to language improvement on short courses. In this way we acknowledge all aspects of the participants' knowledge and experience. As a final point, we also wish to avoid the 'tips for teachers' approach to methodology through our approach. Again, language and method are seen as different aspects of the same venture – language teaching.

4 Further issues

While this report has, of necessity, been brief, there are two points that remain to be made, not in conclusion, but as a prospective.

1. Language Awareness naturally seems to entail an inductive methodology in practice. We have also sought ways of enabling students and teachers on our courses to acquire information about language. Our exercises and tasks often involve the use of reference works – grammars, etc. – in order to provide information. This has been invaluable with ITT students in learning how to make use of a reference grammar, dictionary, thesaurus and textbook (see Figure 3 for schematic outlines of LA tasks). We need to give more thought to ways in which we can incorporate information on language into

Type A

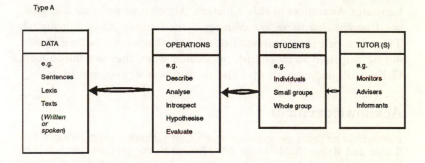

Type B

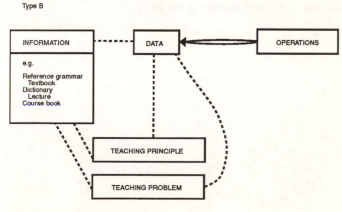

FIGURE 3   Sample task types

Language Awareness exercises for non-active speakers in addition
to introspecting on existing L2 knowledge. There is also a danger
in inductive exercises being 'found out'. We need to be aware that
students are quite entitled to ask the question 'Why didn't you tell us
this before we did the exercise? You must have known, otherwise you
wouldn't have set the exercise in the way you did.' A balance between
exploration and information needs to be maintained – not an easy task
by any means, but one with much potential for future development.
(See Bowers *et al.*, 1987, for a possible pattern.)

2. Not all tutors, let alone ITT students and INSET teachers, are
convinced of the value of Language Awareness. There is an evident
need for research into attitudes towards this type of awareness and
its efficacy as a teaching method. Although we at Christ Church
are in broad agreement about the need to integrate language and
methods studies, there is still a great deal of debate about the role of
Language Awareness in this equation. My own view is that it is vital,
but I accept that there are colleagues who remain to be convinced.
These are rich issues for staff development sessions, but we should
not be surprised to meet with opposition when they are introduced.
Debate will undoubtedly give rise to new perspectives and ideas.

Acknowledgement

I would like to thank my colleagues at Christ Church College, notably Roy
Taylor and Roger Budd, whose contribution to our programmes has been
immense. Many of the ideas I have reported here are the product of intense
debate and collaboration over the past four years. I would also like to express
my gratitude to all students and teachers who have participated in our
programmes both for their patience while we have experimented and for
their contribution to the development of the ideas.

Appendix 1: Formal and functional approaches to grammar

TASK 1

(a) *Describe the structure of the following sentences, using terms such as verb, tense, noun, pronoun, noun group, etc.*
(b) *Account for the meaning of each sentence in terms of time reference.*
(c) *Compare the meanings of the different sentences. Is there a relationship between forms and meanings?*

1. I'm hungry.
2. I declare the meeting closed.
3. He works in London.
4. They live in a rented house.
5. They are living in a rented house.
6. He's walking to work while his car is being repaired.

TASK 2

Look at the following A/B exchanges. Each one contains a sentence from Task 1. What is the meaning of each of these utterances? Are there different types of meaning expressed?

1. A: Would you like a drink?
   B: I'm hungry.
2. A: Hurry up and pass the meat.
   B: I'm hungry.
3. A: I think you ought to work harder.
   B: I'm hungry.
4. A: I declare the meeting closed.
   B: You can't do that.
5. A: What about item 11 on the agenda?
   B: I declare the meeting closed.
6. A: He's always home late.
   B: He works in London.
7. A: I think he's a bit of a country bumpkin.
   B: He works in London.
8. A: I saw him in a Porsche.
   B: He works in London.
9. A: What a dreadful couple they are.
   B: They live in a rented house.
10. A: Mrs Jones is expecting again.
    B: They live in a rented house.
11. A: They've just come back from Thailand.
    B: They live in a rented house.
12. A: Who made those muddy footprints?
    B: He's walking to work while his car is being repaired.
13. A: What a complete idiot that one is.
    B: He's walking to work while his car is being repaired.

Comment on the relationship between the forms and meanings in the set of sentences in Task 1 on the basis of the exchanges in Task 2.

Alternative rubrics for INSET groups

Aim: To examine the relationship between forms and meanings with a view to evaluating exercises which focus on formal aspects of English.

TASK 1

(a)   Describe the structure of the following sentences, using terms such as *verb, tense, noun, pronoun, noun group, etc.*
(b)   Account for the meaning of each sentence in terms of time reference.
(c)   Compare the meanings of the different sentences. Is there a relationship between forms and meanings?

(Following Task 2)

What conclusions do you draw from Task 2 with reference to the relationships between forms and meanings?

What are the general implications of Task 2 for teaching grammatical items?

Do any of these implications conflict with your current practice?

Appendix 2: Present tense and time – forms and meanings

TASK 1

Examine the sentences which follow. They all contain errors of the sort frequently made by learners of English as a second or foreign language. Decide what the error is in each case, describe it and say whether it is an error of FORM or of MEANING or both. Suggest possible reasons for the errors.

- He looking for his dog.
- John is resembling his father.
- This watch is belonging to me.
- I am thinking that you are wrong.
- I am swim very well.
- At the moment, they build a new computer block.
- He see your point of view.
- A: What do you do?
  B: I am writing an essay.
- I am hearing that you are in trouble.
- We are living here since 1965.
- He is usually walking to work.
- Do you eating fried rice?
- Are you sleep well these days?
- He not liking tea with milk.

TASK 2

Examine a sample of the work you collected while you were in schools in Malaysia. Identify and note 5 examples of FORMAL errors and 5 examples of errors of MEANING from your sample. Describe the error in each case, suggest a correction and a possible cause of the error. Write your examples on an OHT to show to the other group members.

Appendix 3: Specific and non-specific reference

TASK 1

Examine the sentences which follow. Each one contains a possible error (or errors) in article usage. What should the correct form be, and what is the rule or principle that the learner could be getting wrong in each case? (Use your reference grammar to help you formulate statements about the errors.) Are there any examples which cause problems? If so, be prepared to say why.

1. Tiger is almost extinct.
2. He went up North on bus.
3. There were many expeditions to South Pole at turn of century.
4. I phoned up man I interviewed yesterday.
5. Mary bought new dress and shoes.
6. The language is a complex phenomenon.
7. I went to the bed at 10 o'clock.
8. He lives on the Headcorn Drive.
9. The eighteenth century London was violent place.
10. One of best stories I have read is the 'Pride and Prejudice'.
11. You reach market through the narrow alley.
12. He stayed for the breakfast.
13. It was the face to face confrontation.
14. He spent large proportion of his life at the sea as a cook.
15. The thieves approached at the nightfall.
16. One of the most problematical aspects of the English is definite article.

TASK 2

English language teachers have long wished that there was a rule of thumb for article usage in English. Look at some of the ones teachers have formulated and see if they work. Work out your own examples to show the effectiveness (or non-effectiveness) of the 'rules'.

1. 'When you come across a noun, ask the question "what particular one?" or "which one?". If there's an answer put "the" before the noun.'
2. 'We always put the definite article if we know what it is we are talking about.'
3. 'The indefinite article "a(n)" is used when the reference is vague.'
4. 'Abstract nouns are not normally preceded by the definite article.'
5. 'Mass nouns do not normally take the definite article. They behave rather like abstract nouns in this respect.'
6. 'Names of countries do not take an article unless they precede a noun phrase like "the Soviet Union", but for areas of water and land with accepted limits, the definite article is always used.'

Appendix 4 Text function and realisation

Exercise A

Read the text 'The Happy Mean'. How do the views on fitness expressed here compare with views commonly found in your country?

THE HAPPY MEAN

Keeping fit and healthy does not have to be a painful experience. It isn't essential to deliberately reduce your food intake to starvation levels or to run in marathons. You may well find later that, as you become fitter, you want to enter a marathon because it doesn't frighten you any more and you feel fit enough to face the challenge. But it's not necessary at the start of your campaign for fitness; the essential point is one of balance between doing too much or not enough.

Of course, you've got to do more than the person who just potters through a normal daily routine and makes no real effort to keep the body fit.

This person might claim that he has all the fitness he needs and that there is nothing physically wrong with his body. That's partly true but not the whole story, for although their condition may appear to remain stable for years, the body is slowly deteriorating and it will continue to do so unless some regular physical activity is undertaken.

On the other hand, there is no need to sweat for hours every day lifting heavy weights to build prize-winning muscles, or to pound the pavements for dozens of miles a week. A 'muscle builder' has the correct intention but the wrong approach: if you only develop muscular strength you may not have the endurance or flexibility necessary for all-round fitness.

This is what you need to do to achieve that all-round fitness:
Stimulate the heart and the circulation of the blood. Exercise joints and muscles throughout the body.

Running is one of the best ways to do it, but research has shown that, if what you want is a good level of fitness for enjoyable, healthy everyday life, then exercising two or three times a week is usually quite sufficient.

So don't worry; to be fit and healthy you haven't got to steel yourself to hours of agonising pavement-pounding in the rain every day – you can enjoy getting fit.

Physical fitness is a relative rather than an absolute state. Anybody, from an elderly person to an Olympic athlete can become fitter. For somebody who has not taken any exercise for some time, an improvement in their state of fitness can be made by doing gentle and simple exercise. But an athlete already in training would have to work very hard just to achieve a small improvement.

Whoever you are, you have to accept the body that you've been born with; but with careful handling it can be developed to optimum fitness. Your optimum fitness will be different from the marathon fanatic next door: so don't compare your efforts with his and don't give up because you can't run as far and as fast as somebody else.

Exercise B

1. If you were asked 'What does *have to* mean?', what would you reply? And if you were asked the meaning of *don't have to*, what would your answer be?

2. Similarly, can you give a definition of *may* and *can*?
3. Now read the first paragraph of the accompanying text 'The Happy Mean'.
4. What is the writer's purpose? In other words, what are the functions of this paragraph?
5. Can you pinpoint certain words in this paragraph which realise these functions?
6. What happens to the meaning of the paragraph if we substitute *is not* for *does not have to be*?

Exercise C

1. Read the whole of the text. What purpose/function does each of the paragraphs have?
2. Look again at paragraph 7. What function(s) does it have? Can we say which word is essential for this function to be realised?
3. What happens if we substitute another modal for *can*?
4. Now look at the other instances where *can* and *may* are used.
   What functions do they realise, and therefore contribute to the overall meaning of the text?

Exercise D

1. What do you consider to be the problems in teaching modal auxiliaries?
2. Give some examples of how you would teach *can* and *may*.
3. Look at the way *can* and *may* are used in the text. Try to devise some teaching tasks that take account of these different uses.

6 Language Awareness and second language development

Howard Nicholas

'Language Awareness' is defined in a number of different ways. In Britain, Language Awareness is particularly associated with an educational movement, the purpose of which is to make students in schools more *conscious* of 'the nature of language and its role in human life' (cf. Brumfit, this volume; Donmall, this volume). As a macro-educational issue, this movement takes as its common theme the view that increasing students' conscious reflection on the language(s) they use will enhance the development of their human potential by making them more aware of the influence that language has on them and that they in turn can exercise through language. This view argues that increased conscious reflection on language by students and teachers leads to improved language use and better overall education. The direction of this relationship is from awareness to development, with development being understood in macro-human terms.

In contrast, this paper examines a differently oriented relationship and its central claim is that aspects of macro-human development influence the 'awareness' that learners have of language, *independently of conscious reflection on language*. It is argued that learners can be 'aware' of aspects of language without being able to explicitly articulate that awareness. This awareness is evidenced through the language use of the speakers. Further, it is argued, the 'awareness' so viewed has consequences for the manner in which second language development can be constructed. As such, this view of Language Awareness has educational consequences in that it suggests that there are constraints on language teaching brought about by the language awareness of the students. This view of Language Awareness has, however, little to say about the macro-educational issues of whether or how Language Awareness programmes should be mounted, except to suggest that different kinds of Language Awareness programmes would be needed with different age groups – hardly a novel point.

Although these two views of Language Awareness contain opposing directions of relationship, it is important to see them as complementary rather than as in opposition to each other. Both make reference to the same elements: awareness and development. Both argue that the relationship between the elements is of significance for humans. Both have implications for educational policy and programming. The central point of contrast is the place of *conscious* reflection. This is the feature which distinguishes the two views: one as an educational theory, in which conscious reflection is an essential part of the educational process, and one as an account of aspects of language development in which consciousness plays a *variable* role. An adequate implementation of the educational theory requires an understanding of the issues of the developmental account. The developmental account does not, however, have to answer to the educational theory since it does not propose to answer the question of whether Language Awareness ought to be part of the school curriculum.

The developmental account seeks to explain how learners approach, acquire and use language. As such the account can delimit which aspects of language are accessible to learners in any manner, and which are susceptible to conscious reflection. This paper describes the process of second language development through case studies of three children under age 5. It seeks to describe which aspects of language awareness influence their second language development and which aspects of second language use are susceptible to conscious manipulation. It seeks, further, to demonstrate how these aspects, conscious and unconscious language awareness, interact with the language use of the learners' interlocutors. The paper will be organized around five claims. These claims are:

1. Second language development can be distinguished from first language development by the presence in second language learners of awareness of the lexico-grammatical level of language organisation.
2. Awareness of the lexico-grammatical level of language organisation is unconscious in children under age 7 and potentially conscious in older children, adolescents and adults.
3. In both younger and older second language learners, awareness of the need for and constraints imposed by interaction is accessible to reflection and can be made conscious. As a consequence, interaction is deliberately manipulated by all second language learners (with varying degrees of success).
4. 'Adult' second language development can be distinguished from 'child' second language development by the emergence in 'adults' of conscious pragma-linguistic awareness. This leads to the manipulation of discourse as a means of conveying information otherwise encoded through morpho-syntax.

5. The emergence of pragma-linguistic awareness enables instruction about morpho-syntax to profitably complement communicative instruction.

1 The role of lexico-grammatical awareness

This section requires a definition of 'second' language development in contrast to 'first' language development.

It should be noted that 'second' language development cannot be defined by claiming that it occurs *after* first language development is completed. Karmiloff-Smith (1979) demonstrates very clearly that significant aspects of the grammar of determiners and reference are still being acquired up till age 11. Equally clearly, second language development cannot be defined according to the *number* of languages presented to the learner since this would fail to distinguish between second language development and simultaneous bilingual development. Neither can 'second' language development be distinguished by its *degree of dominance* in a speaker's repertoire since this dominance can and does change according to time and circumstance. It is also not possible to use speakers' *attitudes* as a permanent basis for distinguishing between first and second language development since these attitudes are also transitory. More positively, any definition of second language development must accommodate both child and adult learners and, therefore, cannot be based on arbitrary nominations of *age*. As a consequence of these constraints, any definition of second language development must attempt to define the *additional insight* into language which is available to second but not first language learners.

Halliday (1975) has pointed out that (some) children pass through a proto-language phase before they begin to make use of elements of the target language. In this proto-language phase children have a two-level language system in which sounds have meaning, but only through specific one-form-to-one-function relationships. The forms consist of intonation contours; the functions are defined within Halliday's systemic-functional framework. Of critical importance for our purposes here are (i) that the functional meanings are not uniquely encoded in the language of the surrounding community and (ii) that the forms selected are not related to the meaning contrasts made by the child in the speech of members of the surrounding community. Thus, the child is seen to be forming its 'own' language until it becomes aware that 'words' and 'grammar' are the major means through which sound and meaning are related. In essence, the critical insight which children need is that there is a lexico-grammatical level of organisation within the speech of the surrounding community. Until this insight develops, the child either babbles or makes use of proto-language. After gaining this insight the child can be said to have begun speaking the particular language.

In contrast, in the course of second language development, whether by children or adults, neither babbling nor proto-language is exhibited. The absence of these two features is the result of the awareness shared by all inter-language users that language has lexico-grammatical organisation (cf. Nicholas, 1987). As a consequence of this awareness, all second language development begins with variably correct or complete target-language units of one of the following three types:

(a) words or phrases;
(b) sentences;
(c) formulae.

Depending on a range of socio-psychological factors (cf. Meisel *et al.*, 1981; Meisel, 1983) these units may be more or less accented and more or less grammatically complete. They are, however, clearly derived from the 'target' language.

2 Consciousness and lexico-grammar

In very young children, some under 3 years of age (cf. Nemoianu, 1980; Zobl, 1983), this lexico-grammatical awareness is only demonstrated through their second language behaviour. At such a young age, indeed sometimes also up to and including 6 year olds, children have an unclear understanding of the term 'word'. It is sometimes taken to mean 'word' and is sometimes equated with 'sentence'.

Thus, children's explicit comments about this aspect of language vary, but their behaviour in relation to 'lexico-grammar' is remarkably consistent. The younger children can be seen to demonstrate their awareness of the lexico-grammatical level of language by the way in which they begin producing second language utterances. Their lack of babble or proto-language demonstrates this awareness. It is only when second language development occurs in older learners that this awareness can be explicitly verbalised.

3 Interactional awareness

In young children (those under approximately 7 years of age), success-ful rapid second language development is characterised by the use of one of the three above beginning units as a means of *controlling the conversation* without supplying much conversational content. As will become clear below, the viability of this strategy depends on the interactional context in which the children find themselves and to some extent on the child's personality.

An example of successful, rapid second language development is 'Cindy' (cf. Nicholas, 1987). Cindy was a 3 years and 4 months old monolingual English speaker when she was first exposed to German. Although her father was a native speaker of German, he and his family had lived in an English-speaking environment for nineteen years prior to their return to West Germany. Upon arrival in West Germany his language of communication with Cindy was English. Immediately after her arrival in a small town in south-east West Germany Cindy was enrolled in a monolingual German kindergarten and in addition was visited twice weekly by me for recordings of informal play sessions. Initially, Cindy was not aware that I understood or spoke English. She was, thus, constrained to attempt to interact through German. Figure 1 provides the proportions of synoptic and dynamic utterances in Cindy's initiations (for definitions see below). Responses were excluded because they were too heavily conditioned by interlocutor contributions.

Figure 1 shows that in the initial recordings Cindy produced dynamic initiations more frequently than synoptic initiations. Dynamic initiations consist of (i) topic nominations (ii) turn disposals (iii) confir-mations and (iv) confirmation requests. Synoptic initiations consist of nine other functions such as statement, question, command, offer, etc. As this list demonstrates, the difference between dynamic and synoptic functions is that the former manipulate the shape and direction of the conversation whereas the latter supply the content or meaning of the conversation.

The effect of Cindy's initially dominant use of dynamic functions was that she was able to engage in sustained interaction and through this gain wide exposure to the second language while remaining in control of the meanings being negotiated. As a result, Cindy acquired a range of morpho-syntactic features of German over eight months, which many adults did not acquire over much longer periods (cf. Clahsen *et al.*, 1983).

It needs to be noted, however, that the success of this *interaction* strategy depends on the cooperation of the interlocutor. The following

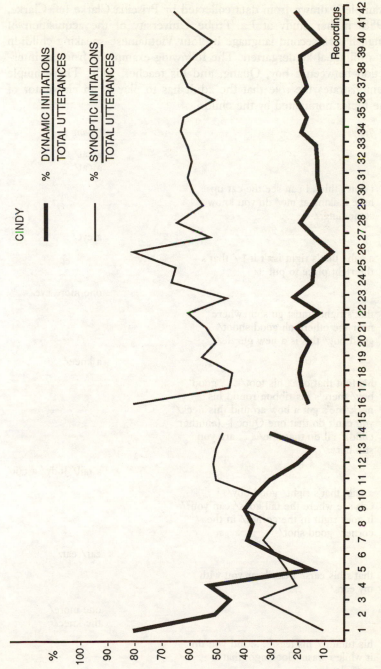

FIGURE 1 Relative frequency of dynamic and synoptic initiations: CINDY

example is drawn from data collected by Priscilla Clarke (cf. Clarke, 1988) in her study at La Trobe University of the acquisition of English as a second language by four Vietnamese-speaking children in a bilingual kindergarten. The following example is from an interaction between a boy, Quang, and his teacher, Judy. The example demonstrates the role that the adult has to play as an elaborator of the topics nominated by the child.

Judy	*Quang*
	a cat/
	a cat/
i don't think i can see the cat up here looking at me/ do you know something?/	
	a eye/
a aah/ that's right isn't it ↑ / that's the right place to put it/	
	one more eye/
that's right/ must go somewhere near the other/ oh good shoot/ good boy/ this is a new puzzle/	
	a knee/
his foot that one/ his foot/ . . . good boy/ there's his ribbon round his neck/ he's got a bow around this neck/ you can't do that one Quoc ↑ (another child)/ i'll do that one/ . . . are you still here?/	
	a tail/ Judy/ a tail/
a tail/ that's right/ good boy/. i can see where the tail goes/ can you?/ it goes right in the corner/ in the corner/ good shot/	
	ear/ ear/
that's his ears/ i can hear you with my ears/	
	one more/
	the knee/
his tummy/ his legs/ . . . did you do it while i wasn't looking?/ that is very clever/ . . .	

This example clearly demonstrates that the success of the child's interactive strategy depends on the cooperation of the interlocutor, who must elaborate the child's topics in such a way that the elaboration is meaningful to the child. In this extract Judy provides information about the items nominated by Quang. Judy's comments are restricted to information about the items nominated by Quang. She keeps her references to items both can see or manipulate and allows Quang to set the pace of progression from one topic to the next. Note also that the 'topics' occur within the same discourse context, i.e. discourse roles are preserved. Thus Judy's utterances serve to elaborate Quang's topics rather than to introduce new ones. As a consequence Quang is better able to comprehend and also analyse the linguistic content of Judy's utterances.

The question is whether the children are aware of the role of interaction and take any steps to influence the type of interaction in which they engage. This sort of evidence is only available when interaction breaks down. The following examples come from a study being undertaken at La Trobe University by Liu Guo Qang of a Chinese-speaking boy, Bob, in the course of his acquisition of English (cf. Liu Guo Qang, 1988). Bob was aged 4 years and 11 months when he was first exposed to English in a child care centre in Australia. Liu Guo Qang reports that Bob attended the child care centre with expectations that he would learn English. In the first two recording sessions he was observed to be trying to speak English, but the manner in which his attempts were taken up by adult and child interlocutors led to Bob gradually withdrawing from English interactions before beginning various attempts to engage others in interaction. The course of events demonstrates (i) Bob's awareness of the importance of interaction and (ii) Bob's reflections about alternative means of initiating interaction.

The first example demonstrates how the interlocutor's take up of Bob's conversational initiative led away from Bob's intended meaning. Bob began the interaction by showing the centre supervisor that he was able to tie the 'Superman' cape he was wearing.

Supervisor	Bob
	look look/
do you know how to tie your shoelaces?/	
	what?/
do you know how to tie your shoelaces?/	
	yeah/ (without comprehension)

who taught you how to tie your
shoelaces?/ your daddy ↑ /

yeah/

he must be clever/

(Bob does not respond. He
walks away; unties the cape
and ties it up again and
says:)

can you tie this?/

Although the supervisor's comments were superficially related to Bob's
initiation via the use of the word 'tie' in response to Bob's implied 'tie',
in fact the interaction moves so rapidly away from Bob's intended
meaning that he loses any sense of control and thus any sense of
meaning. Notice, however, that he retains his sense of the importance
of sustaining the interaction. His two 'yeah' utterances do not demonstrate comprehension; they are 'empty' responses to questions. Bob is
aware that it is incumbent upon him to fulfil his interactional role, i.e.
sustain the discourse – even if the discourse is 'meaningless'.

This example brings out an important difference between sources
of evidence for language awareness. Awareness of lexico-grammatical
organisation can be demonstrated through almost any successful or
unsuccessful second language utterance. Awareness of the role of
interaction is, in contrast, much more readily demonstrated through
interaction which goes wrong. When interaction is working smoothly,
it is very difficult to determine precisely whether the learner is aware
of the significance of various of its aspects. The only means of knowing
precisely is the use of introspective research methods (cf. Faerch and
Kasper, 1987). Using these data we can gain access to conscious
knowledge. However, when interaction breaks down we can gain
access to the steps that the learner takes to repair or continue the
discourse. This kind of evidence reflects what the learner is aware of
without any necessary claim that the awareness can be verbalised. If
we see a learner alternating between various interaction strategies it
is possible to claim that the learner is, at some level, reflecting on the
various strategies and their respective effectiveness. Bob's behaviour
thus clearly demonstrates awareness of the strategies.

Liu Guo Qang (1988) reported that Bob, having experienced limited
success in his initial attempts to obtain English interaction, resorted to
a series of alternating strategies in an effort to engage English speakers
in conversation.

Initially, Bob left the conversational initiative to others and merely repeated what they said to him. The following example is from the second recording.

Supervisor	*Bob*
the car must be clean now/ are they clean?/	
	are they clean/
are they clean?/	
	are they clean/
they are washed/	
	they are washed/
do you know what this is for?/ do you know what this is for?/ (Supervisor points) horse/	
	horse/

However, this approach does not provide a basis for successful, sustained discourse in English. Bob also tried other strategies. One of his most frequently used strategies was talking in Chinese. In the same session he tried, using Chinese, to instruct another child in the use of a typewriter. Translated, he said:

and there is a zero/ first hit this/ this is mine/ press this/ that's right that's right/ this is my name/

The girl's reaction was an angry 'Bob!'. Clearly, therefore, this strategy was not creating sustained interaction. However, Bob continued to talk *to himself* in Chinese. Liu Guo Qang (1988: 12) notes that this strategy seems designed to inform others 'of his very existence in the group' and further notes that this strategy was only used 'when he was with other people, for example, playing at the same table or in the same group with some other children . . .'.

Bob also had other strategies which he used in an effort to generate interaction. Liu Guo Qang (1988: 15) records how Bob would make increasingly loud noises to accompany his play while looking up at approaching adults. The following example comes from the third recording.

Supervisor	*Bob*
	(Bob sees the supervisor approaching him while he is at a table playing with a toy bus)
	da gong gong/ (big bus)
	wu . . . (bus noise)
(The supervisor looks at Bob and seats herself at his table)	
	da gong gong. you you yi ge/ (big bus. another one)
Bob. what's this?/	
	what's this/ (no comprehension)
(The supervisor leaves the table)	
	wu . . . wu . . . (bus noise)
(The supervisor looks but continues to depart)	

Bob also tried initiating in English. In the second session he approached a girl and said 'hello'. She replied 'hello', but the conversation went no further (Liu Guo Qang, 1988: 17–18).

What we see in the above examples is a clear demonstration of the young child's awareness of the importance of interaction and his awareness that there were various means by which it might be initiated. However, we see equally clearly that he did not have sufficient means at his disposal to sustain the discourse. Bob was left in a very vulnerable situation because his interlocutors did not know how to sustain the discourse either. Thus, despite Bob's attempts to manipulate interaction, his exposure to the second language and thus also the degree to which he could gain input was limited. Despite the lack of success these strategies met with, the fact that various interaction strategies were initiated demonstrates that Bob was aware of the role of interaction as a means of obtaining input. The only conscious reflection on the strategies produced by Bob came in the first recording session (Liu Guo Qang, 1988: 13) when he commented in Chinese that a supervisor had not heard him after she failed to respond to a question which Bob had addressed to her in Chinese. This is the only evidence we have that these strategies are accessible to reflection at a conscious level.

4 Pragma-linguistic awareness

A number of different forms of evidence point towards approximately age 7 being a significant point of change in learner approaches to second languages. Indeed I would like to go so far as to suggest that after approximately age 7 second language development follows 'adult-like' paths.

Long (1988) and Stock (1977) both report evidence of emerging phonological transfer in learners who begin second language acquisition after age 6. Fletcher and Garman (1988: 102ff) pointed out that by age 7 first language acquiring children were using adverbials in different sentence positions and with different functions (*NB* for more frequent temporal reference) than 5 year olds. They point out (1988: 105) that these features, together with differences between the 5 and the 7 year olds in the explicitness with which temporal reference is marked in contextually underdetermined utterances, constitute an aspect of the children's developing pragmatic ability. They further note (1988: 106) that language impaired children are 'much less certain of the appropriate conditions for overt RT (reference time) provision than either of the two normal groups'. Meisel (1987) reports that older children use adverbials to mark past reference whereas younger children acquiring their first language use verbal inflections. Nicholas (1987) pointed out that children under age 4 who were acquiring a second language also used verbal inflections instead of adverbials for this function. Nicholas (1987) also pointed out that the use of equational structures to nominate topics of conversation no longer appeared to be used as an interactive strategy in children beginning second language acquisition after age 7. This range of features, together with the observation that psychologists as diverse as Piaget and Vygotsky both nominate age 7 to 8 as a key point in cognitive development, suggests that this age is a crucial point of change in language development.

I would like to exemplify the change by examining the kind of discourse which is produced by those second language learners in the older group. The particular feature I would like to describe is the relationship between time adverbials, temporal reference and extended turns. I suggest that the changes in discourse relations which emerge at about 7 years of age mark the emergence of pragma-linguistic awareness, which is the emergence of an understanding of how morpho-syntactic features of language relate to markers of social identity.

Discourse organisation is the device through which morpho-syntax and social identity can interact. When extended turns are produced, it becomes possible to make use of general devices such as adverbials for temporal reference to substitute for more specific morpho-syntactic features. Thus, in the following example, the date enables both the preceding and the following references to be interpreted as 'past' despite their lack of appropriate morphological features.

> i'm coming with Australia with my family in 1976/ in the West Australia/ first time be very hard because no understand language/ stay in the West Australia five months/

In *this* context, it becomes clear that 'am coming' means 'came'; 'be' means 'was'; 'no understand' means 'didn't understand'; and 'stay' means 'stayed'. Thus, this example indicates how particular non-morphological devices ('in 1976'; 'first time', etc) can serve to disambiguate quite different form–meaning relationships. Given that the speaker intended to convey past reference, this example demonstrates how general contextual references can serve to replace or reinterpret specific morpho-syntactic forms: 'in 1976' changes 'i'm coming' from a present progressive meaning to a simple past meaning; 'first time' gives the non-finite, non-tensed 'be' a simple past meaning. While it is unlikely that these conversions were deliberately planned, it is reasonably clear from this and many similar examples in adult second language development that the ability of general features such as adverbial marking to compensate for information conveyed by specific morpho-syntactic forms in the standard language is extensively exploited. I suggest that this reflects a generalised awareness in adults of the interaction between morpho-syntactic form on the one hand and features of the discourse, interactional and social situation on the other hand.

The emergence of this awareness at least correlates with changes in the kind of discourse in which the different age groups engage. The principal feature of relevance here is the presence and organisation of long turns such as in the previous example. In young children acquiring a second language this kind of turn is infrequent and as a consequence there is comparatively little call for contextual disambiguation via non-morpho-syntactic means.

To return to data from Cindy (Nicholas, 1987), five points distinguish her temporal referencing from older learners (at least initially):

1. no adverbials are used to highlight temporal reference during the first phase of her second language development;
2. initially, aspectual relations are marked via either 'so', which

approximates the meaning of 'there' on the completion of an action or event or a formulaic verbal form 'hast(u) gemacht' (have done);

3. later temporal reference via adverbials is via '(und) dann' (and then) to mark immediate sequence or 'jetz(t)' (now) to mark an existing state;

4. only in the third phase of her inter-language development (from the eighteenth recording on) and simultaneous with the emergence of a variety of syntactic forms do deictic adverbials such as 'morgen' (tomorrow); 'nachher' (later/afterwards); and calendaric adverbials such as 'montag' (Monday); 'in juli' (in July) begin to emerge. However, these references hold for single utterances only and exist in contexts in which turns rarely consist of more than a single utterance;

5. even when more complex and non-immediate temporal references are attempted they usually occur through sequences of short turns in which both interlocutors take a role in specifying temporal reference.

The following example illustrates how *both* interlocutors act to establish the temporal reference rather than having it clearly established by the L2 user as in the previous, English example. The context is the discussion of a pet cat (Cheetah) which had been run over in Africa and the possibility that Cindy's current family pet (a dog, Tutzi) could also die if she jumped from the balcony on which we were playing.

Howard	*Cindy*	*Approx. translation*
	wenn jemand hier aufgeht kann kann er hier runterfallen/	if someone climbs up here he can fall down/
=mhm/=	a ↑ /=dann wär ma tot/ a ↑ /	then he would be dead/
ja/ dann wäre er tot allerdings wenn er vom balkon hier so runterstürzt/		yes/ he would be dead if he fell from the balcony/
	wenn–wenn–wenn Cheetah hier rüberspringt dann wird er tot/ a ↑ /	if Cheetah jumps he'll be dead/

aha/	yes/
dann haben wir kein hund mehr/	then we don't have a dog anymore/
nee/ wenn–wenn der–wenn die Tutzi das machen würde dann würde sie sterben/	if Tutzi did that she would die/
ja/ wei–weil mai katze auch mal–wenn eine katze das macht dann wird es auch sterben/ a ↑ /	if a cat did that it would also die/
genau/ hast du eine katze?/	exactly/ have you got a cat?/
nein/ sie ist tot/	no/ she is dead/
ist sie über die straße gelaufen?/	did she run across the road?/
a+a ↑ / sie hat bloß hier aufgemacht/ die Cheetah hat mit ihm gespielt und	no/ she simply opened here/ Cheetah played with him and then he
dann war er tot/	was dead/
sie hat mit einem hund gespielt ↑ /	did she play with a dog?/
=ach so/=	ich muß–ich–ich will= i want back there/
=was ist hinten?/=	den–dahinten jetz is= what is back there?/ dahinter/ die kann it can see my cat/ meine katze sehen/ it has run back there/ meinst?/ dahinten is gelaufen/
aha/ . . . ganz hinten/ hm/	all the way back/
ganz hinten/	all the way back/
wo ist dann die katze gestorben? hier oder in Afrika?/	where did the cat die?/ here or in Africa?/
ö.a/ Afrika!/	Africa/
in Malawi ↑ /	in Malawi?/
a!/ in Malawi/ das	in Malawi/ that isn't

	Ghana ga: nich/	Ghana/
die katze ist hier		did the cat die
gestorben ↑ /		here?/
	ö!/ die katze is hier	the cat died here/
	gesto: ben!/	
wo ist dann die		where did the cat die,
katze. gestorben?/		then?/
	oa!/ oa!/ in das licht/	in the light/

From the excerpt it can be seen that, though known to both participants, the precise location of the pet cat's death, and thus the time
of its demise, were not clearly indicated. Indeed the first reference
which moves temporal reference from unreal future to real past is, in
fact, the present 'she is dead' without explicit mention of when her
death occurred. Thus, the remaining turns are devoted to attempts
to establish more or less precise temporal reference; as it transpires,
unsuccessfully. The contrast between this and the explicit temporal
referencing of the adult extract is obvious. Of equal significance is the
far greater accuracy of temporality marking on the verbs in Cindy's
utterances. Where there are errors they are principally in the marking
of real/unreal distinctions or in lexis (*dead* 'tot' vs *die* 'sterben').
Consequently, it cannot be said of Cindy's discourse that she is using
general contextual or discourse features to compensate for inaccurate
morpho-syntax. Her morpho-syntax is, if anything, more informative
than her discourse organisation. It is the older learner who has the
awareness of, and the need as a result of the discourse organisation
for pragma-linguistic aspects of language.

5 Pragma-linguistics and grammatical instruction

There is increasing evidence that communicative instruction alone is
not sufficient to ensure mastery of the second language grammatical
system (cf. Harley, 1986; Clyne, 1986). There is also evidence (cf.
Harley *et al.*, 1987) that phonological development in French in children in Canadian immersion programmes changes at about age 7, i.e.
native-like French accents begin to sound more 'English'. These two,
superficially different observations serve to indicate that attention to
linguistic form is a necessary part of second language development *and*
that learners of a certain age begin to perceive a relationship between
linguistic form and the projection of social identity. That accent is
not only an articulatory, but also an interpersonal phenomenon has

long been recognised (cf. Schumann, 1975; Hatch, 1983; Giles, 1977; Labov, 1966). Usually, however, the point at which the connection is established is puberty (cf. Schumann, 1975). However, the evidence for a much earlier connection would now seem to be clear (cf. Long, 1988; Nicholas, 1987). Thus, it seems possible to suggest that *during* the course of primary education, learners become aware of how social identity can be projected through the forms of the language used by the speaker. As a consequence of this realisation, the students in the French immersion programmes, who have little if any contact with francophone peers, begin to orient more to the linguistic forms (both phonological and morpho-syntactic) of their anglophone peers than of their teachers. Inasmuch as there is also evidence that as of a similar age (7 to 8 years) children in other circumstances begin to develop grammatically non-standard forms of the second language as a result of the recognition of power and group relations (cf. Brent-Palmer, 1979), the claim that linguistic form takes on social meaning can be extended to morpho-syntactic aspects of language. In other words, from approximately age 7, children are in a position to appreciate the meaning of grammatical forms.

Thus, from this age on, it becomes possible to integrate grammatical instruction with communicative instruction in such a way that grammatical choices can exemplify the exploitation of meaning potential. Grammar can, from this time on, be presented as a means of exemplifying social and individual identity with divergent grammatical forms representing significant choices about the identity the learner seeks to project. This becomes possible as a result of the learner becoming aware of the pragma-linguistic dimension of language and thereby being provided with a means of making grammar meaningful.

6 Conclusion

I hope that this paper has demonstrated how different aspects of Language Awareness can account for different dimensions of second language development and how Language Awareness can be used to differentiate between second language development in different age groups.

All second language development is united by the awareness of the lexico-grammatical level of language organisation. However, younger and older (adult?) second language development are distinguished by the additional presence in older learners of pragma-linguistic awareness, the awareness of (i) how language form is related to the projection of social identity and (ii) how discourse and contextual factors can relate to morpho-syntactic features.

I hope also that this paper has demonstrated how pedagogic initiatives need to take account of learner factors, even though their inspiration does not need to come from studies of language development.

Section Three: Language Awareness in schools

In this section, we move into the schools and classrooms. We begin in the UK again, looking first at an English-focused LA programme, then at LA in the area of modern languages in Britain and Ireland, and then at LA work with a cross-curricular focus. The final two papers are directed at language learners' awareness of their needs in the learning process and the learning strategies they use.

We begin with Tinkel's paper (Paper 7). His LA has addressed itself to the grammatical analysis of English. He outlines the development and structure of his LA course, methodology and LA examination, and reports on their successful 'export' to another UK secondary school of a quite different character. Tinkel's is a private school, while the adopting school is a large comprehensive in the public sector. Tinkel lists the perceived benefits of LA and suggests LA as a possible complement to English teaching.

With Donmall (Paper 8), we move away from LA with its primary focus on explicit knowledge about English to LA aimed at UK foreign languages classrooms. Her starting point is the disappointing record of foreign language achievement in the UK, and she goes on to outline the main problems teachers encounter when trying to teach foreign languages for communication in secondary schools. These range from problems of how best to present new language to whether or not to use the mother tongue in the classroom. She defines and delineates LA, then matches these features of LA work with the problems she has identified in foreign language teaching, and suggests that solutions to many of these problems lie in the provision of LA work.

Little and Singleton (Paper 9) see LA as a solution to the problem of ensuring that learners get the most out of authentic texts in foreign languages. They describe a chain of classroom activities based on lexical problem-solving, during which learners spontaneously turn to discussion and consciousness-raising of the formal features of the target language. The success of the inductive approach in their activities leads them to call for a reorganisation of pedagogical grammars. They describe their own LA manual which is intended to support the learner working with authentic texts, and has won acceptance from many teachers and pupils in British and Irish secondary schools.

Anderson's LA work (Paper 10) is conducted in a London secondary school. He reports on the dismantling of barriers between teachers and the establishment of a 'broad context' for language work. He cites several urgent reasons for this, not least to allow a greater contribution to course planning from the teachers supporting bilingual pupils, and to achieve more consistency when confronting issues such as racism. For Anderson, LA work provides a useful focus for dialogue, a context for deepening understanding that extends across subject boundaries. In his school, staff from different language faculties collaborated to implement an LA scheme, based on agreed topics, timing and methodology. Such teamwork reduces the risk of the initial LA impetus petering out, and helps avoid isolation. Soon other staff came seeking involvement. Anderson looks for subsequent development both 'horizontally' to more subject areas (see James and Garrett, Paper 1), and 'vertically' through the school years, and he urges a parallel removal of barriers in teacher training.

A somewhat different area of LA concerns the language learners' awareness of how they can best master a second language. Here LA is not concerned with explicit knowledge about language or about languages, but with learners' perceptions about the process of language learning and their awareness of themselves in that process. The final two papers in this section, one by Toncheva and the other by Chryshochoos, are both concerned with this aspect of LA in the classroom.

Toncheva (Paper 11) notices how learners sometimes 'switch off' in language lessons. At times, this may be facilitative to language learning, stemming from learners' awareness of their needs. Toncheva suggests a number of factors that may lead to the employment of this strategy – for example, a mismatch between learning style and teaching methodology. Teachers have much to gain from being sensitive to and tolerant of such classroom behaviour.

Chryshochoos (Paper 12) fetches data from the language learners themselves, from a secondary school in the UK, and a high school in Greece, asking them what difficulties they experience in language learning and use, how they think effective learning occurs and how their learning situation could be improved. Among other things, his findings suggest that learners would prefer more involvement in the learning programme. We have seen a great deal of work elsewhere on needs analysis for specialised foreign language learners. It has often been said that needs analysis cannot be undertaken for the schoolchild learning the foreign language 'for no particular purpose'. Chryshochoos is questioning that assumption, and is attempting to identify the needs of groups of general learners of foreign languages in order ultimately to carry through their implications for general syllabus design.

7 Language Awareness and the teaching of English language in the upper secondary school

Tony Tinkel

1 The course background

Between 1981 and 1988 a course in Language Awareness was organised in the first year of the sixth form at The Oratory School, Reading. The one-year course ended with an AO level examination certificated by the Oxford and Cambridge Schools Examination Board.

The starting point for the course was a conviction that, given the appropriate presentation, 16–17-year-old students could study how language works with both profit and enjoyment. The experience of the seven years' evolvement of this course has confirmed that conviction.

The original inspiration for the course content came from the linguistic sciences, but since the language of exemplification was English, the course was also, inevitably, an introduction to the English language in particular. The emphasis came to be placed increasingly on the examination of English as the scheme evolved. For example, the topics of first language acquisition and animal communication were dropped; explicit theoretical formalisms were omitted. However, the systematic analysis of the structure of English was not affected by this shift of focus. If anything it was enhanced in the students' eyes by the more specific attention being placed upon it.

The final group at The Oratory School in 1987–8 consisted of twenty-two students, forming just over a third of the total year group. They had joined overwhelmingly because of interest in knowing more about their language and because of reports they had heard of the course. They were not drafted in. Their main sixth form studies covered the whole range of A level courses, not just English literature and foreign languages. For the last four years, the one-year course and AO level examination were adopted by Hinchingbrooke School, Huntingdon. The fact that it was as successful in this co-educational comprehensive day school as in the single-sex private boarding school of The Oratory, shows that the essentials are 'exportable' and not dependent on particular circumstances.

One reason for the successful adaptation of the course to another context may be that it was designed as a framework, within which different elements could be given greater or less prominence according to the needs of the group. This framework consisted of three different parts, each part addressing itself to one of three questions: How should we go about defining what constitutes 'language'? How does one particular language system work (in this case English)? How is that particular language used?

The first two parts of the course are preparatory to the third and it is significant how interest increases as that third stage is approached. It is also significant that, in retrospect, students accept the importance of the first two parts. They realise then that without the systematic examination of overall definitions and of the structure of English – however trivial or irrelevant it may have seemed at the time – they would not be fully equipped to analyse how language is used. They would not be properly aware of language.

In more detail, the first part gets the student to think of the difference between human communication in general and language in particular, and to consider the distinction between language and the measurable means by which it is conveyed. This latter distinction leads, through the systematic examination of speech sounds, intonation and stress, into the second part. This part examines English word structure, lexically based word classes (noun, verb, adjective and adverb), simple, compound and complex sentence structure and discourse structure. The final part, examining language use, begins with lexical meaning, moves on to meaning conveyed by structure, deictic reference, connotation, speech acts, differing levels of formality, regional dialect and register and is rounded off by emphasising the changing nature of language. A more precise idea of the content of the course can be obtained from *Explorations in Language* (Tinkel, 1988), which is a selection of teaching materials developed during the course. It also gives a more detailed explanation of the topics presented to the students, the manner of their presentation and the sequence.

2   The examination

The AO level examination that terminated the course was under the control of the then O Level English Language Committee of the Oxford and Cambridge Board, who chose the title 'Principles of Language' for it. It consisted of an extended essay of 2500 words on a topic of the students' choosing (one-third of the total mark) and a three-hour written paper. The questions in the written paper were designed to present the students with extracts of actual language usage for them to 'handle' in an open-minded and original way, rather than with topics requiring essay-style answers which would place undue emphasis on the reproduction of other people's views about language. The marking would then reflect the quality of their insight into how language was being used, rather than how well they could discuss topics to do with language.

It is significant that during the seven years of the scheme it was felt necessary to stiffen the requirements in both components of the examination several times. We had underestimated the potential of the candidates to show their own insights about language in a systematic manner. Some idea of what can be achieved by language awareness students at this level can be gathered from the 1988 list of extended essay topics chosen by The Oratory School's candidates (Appendix 1). The twenty-two candidates gained six A grades, three B grades, ten C grades and three D grades between them.

3   Presentation

The manner of presentation has been as crucial a part of the course as the content. The *point de départ* for the presentation is that the students possess the language already. The aim of the course is therefore to offer them an ordered, clear and systematic tour of exploration of it. It is a guided tour of something of whose functioning they are, to a greater or lesser degree, unaware, but which they nevertheless intuitively know and act upon. This fact is central to the thinking behind the course and the shaping of the materials and the examination. The students are seen, not as passive recipients of information new to them, but as fellow native speakers who, once they are made aware, are just as capable as the teacher of producing insights into how their shared language functions. The teacher's task is to organise the topics, to present each one with the maximum of clarity and the minimum of fuss and to set up relevant material as the starting point for the students to explore their own knowledge for themselves. In my experience one can then not only leave them to their native-speaker knowledge, but they begin to probe with pertinent questions.

When the teacher comes to present a topic to the students, it is an indispensable help to have examples from everyday use which will unambiguously illuminate the topic ahead. For example, the slogan of a waste disposal company 'We will not refuse your refuse' will illustrate the use of stress in English words better than a general statement about how the feature is used. Once they have grasped what the teaching point is, then they are best left to explore for themselves the materials which the teacher will have prepared to guide them.

Getting the students to explore their own language knowledge for themselves also affects the use of terminology. If the students explore effectively for themselves, it is an easy step for a technical term to be added to the object of their exploration. Terminology is therefore not seen as being based on definitions made beforehand, but on experiencing examples to which a term can then be affixed. This approach also helps to ensure that the terminology used is terminology that is needed.

If the students are taken into a partnership in the examination of language, this is a guarantee that the presentation will be non-prescriptive. It is the facts of language that have to be presented, not any theoretical or social interpretation of those facts. The students' knowledge of their native language will soon make them critical of any other approach. That same knowledge will also enable them to appreciate that language is not something immutable, but that it is a set of constantly evolving norms; that those norms can be adapted for our own individually creative use of language; that we vary our language use according to who we are with, where we come from and what we are doing; and that, therefore, what is felt to be appropriate should be the guide to usage, not absolute notions of what is right or wrong, pure or corrupted. If this is felt to be too confusing for 16 to 17 year olds, it must be remembered that they have their native-speaker knowledge to give them the necessary perspective and reassurance. Since they put language into practice in their daily lives, why should they not be able to appreciate its complexities, when they are properly guided towards that appreciation?

4 Experience and beliefs

Over the seven years of the Principles of Language Course at The Oratory School, the experience of those involved has lent increasing credence to the following beliefs:

(i) As the students explore, they become more aware; as they become more aware, they also expand and perhaps even improve their grasp of their language.

(ii) As the students become more aware of how language works, they become more sensitive to how they use it and, equally vital in these days of bombardments with words, how it is used upon them.

(iii) Possessing a technical understanding of language effects underpins appreciation of their use and satisfies a hunger among young
people to know about how language works as well as about how
it is used.

The part of the course that aims to get the students to analyse
the structure of English through guided exploration of their own
native-speaker knowledge of how it works, provides an interesting
complement to the approach to English teaching that seeks to use
language as a vehicle for the students to express and explore themselves. In the fact that both aims centre on the students' possession
of language may lie the germ of a consensus to respond constructively
to what *The Independent*, in a leading article on 28 March 1989, called
one of 'the main educational issues of the day', namely the 'role of
grammar and spelling in English teaching'.

Certainly the experience at both The Oratory School and Hinchingbrooke School is that the course has raised the level of consciousness
about language among pupils and staff. This has happened even
though the course was aimed at a small proportion of the overall pupil
total and addressed itself directly to grammatical analysis. For example,
at Hinchingbrooke it inspired a successful Language Awareness course
for second-year pupils struggling with a foreign language. At The
Oratory, third-year language groups, having heard about it, have been
pressing to know more.

The experience of the course at the two schools has also been fed
into the new AS Level English Language examination of the COSSEC
(Cambridge Local, Oxford and Cambridge and Southern Universities)
alliance of boards, which had its first sitting in the summer of 1989.
Much of the course work component of this examination and of the
format of the final question papers is inspired directly by what was
learned during the seven years of the Principles of Language AO
examination. In addition the administration of the new AS examination
was able to draw upon the accumulated knowledge in the two schools,
as to what an examiner could justifiably expect sixth form students to
know and to do under the heading of Language Awareness.

With the assimilation of the pioneer work into the mainstream
examination system it is an appropriate moment to take stock. It
seems a long way now from those early doubts and discouragements
that inevitably beset the introduction of any new perspective into
the curriculum. It is at that stage that encouragement to persist is
crucial; such encouragement in this instance came above all from
Dr John Trim, former Director of CILT, who gave indispensable

academic stiffening, from Adrian Snow, then Headmaster of The Oratory School, who found space on the timetable for the course to be taught, and from Howard King, Secretary of the Oxford and Cambridge Board, and George Wiley, a member of its O Level English Language Committee, who guided the trial examination to fruition. In the context of the examination board's backing for such a new initiative, it is worth asking the question whether such backing of an untried curriculum proposal would be encouraged, or even at all possible, in the world of GCSE and AS examinations. If not, why not? Once the course and examination were under way, the students themselves ensured its survival and success. It was their positive response to the opportunity to learn how language works that made certain that the project took root and thrived.

So what of the future? If the COSSEC AS English Language examination consolidates its encouraging beginning and becomes fully established, then it could be expanded into a full-scale A level. Its success could also encourage the AS and A Level English Language examinations of other boards, such as those offered by the University of London board, to embrace more fully the rigorous and systematic analysis of how the English language system is constructed, as well as how it is used. The Principles of Language experiment has shown that sixth form students can absorb the notions of a pre-theoretical introduction to linguistic study, that English language courses at this level do not need to be restricted to a socio-linguistic inspiration. This in turn has implications for the secondary school English curriculum as a whole, particularly in the light of the statements in the National Curriculum document 'English for Ages 5 to 16' (DES, 1989b, para. 6.8) in support of the explicit teaching about language. There is to my mind now an opening and a timeliness for some experimental research to establish the validity of claims that students' greater awareness of language leads to a greater sensitivity to the way they use language and to the way it is used upon them.

Appendix 1: Oxford and Cambridge Schools Examination Board – The Oratory School

AO Principles of Language – 1988 – Extended Essay Component

List of Candidates' Titles

An introduction to Articulatory Phonetics.

An analysis of recorded examples of UK English, with reference to own recordings.

Change in English, based on a comparison between modern English usage and the language of Chaucer's 'The Franklin's Tale'

Examples of how language is affected by the area of activity in which it is used.

A comparison between the sounds of RP English and those of Standard High German pronunciation.

Varieties of English accents in the United Kingdom: an analysis of sounds in recorded examples of speakers.

Techniques of persuasion used in advertising.

A comparison of the vowel sounds of standard British English and those of Caribbean, particularly Trinidadian, English.

Change in Spanish between the language of the Golden Age (17th century) and that of the present day, with reference to particular examples.

The use of pictures for communication in the media.

Cultural differences in the use of gesture between France and England.

The use of gesture alongside and independently of speech.

Language use in advertising.

Ideographic scripts, with special reference to Chinese characters.

An examination of the use of irony by English writers.

An examination of varieties in the design of company logos.

An introduction to articulatory (or possibly acoustic) phonetics.

An analysis of the presentation of events by English national newspapers.

Human communication outside language.

Language use in Uganda.

An examination of problems involved in fitting linguistic stress patterns to musical phrasing.

An examination of changes in the meaning of words.

Rhyming slang.

8 Old problems and new solutions: LA work in GCSE foreign language classrooms

Gillian Donmall

1 Introduction

Despite the new aims and objectives laid down for foreign language teaching and learning programmes in recent years with emphasis on the spoken word, despite the positive psychological approach which underpins the Graded Test movement and its emphasis on achievement (Page and Hewitt, 1987), and despite the impetus given to learning by new technical aids, the situation remains less than satisfactory. The DES document *Modern Languages in the School Curriculum* (1988b), confirms this view. It states that 'the general picture is of under-achievement with many pupils being capable of accomplishing more' (p. 11).

The numerous independent initiatives which developed in the years following publication of the Bullock Report (DES, 1975), supplemented by the publications of individual scholars, found impetus and support for their work as two successive working parties of the National Congress on Languages in Education (NCLE), acting on the basis of experience of teachers in schools and together with them, took developments a significant stage further. Among other initiatives, with the help of local education authorities, they undertook two surveys of Language Awareness activities throughout the United Kingdom (Donmall, 1985: 257–66). These showed that, although some teachers of English as Mother Tongue (EMT) were active in the field (and indeed some would suggest that EMT is the proper main 'home' for Language Awareness), the majority were teachers of foreign languages. What, then, might be a suitable relationship of Language Awareness to foreign languages; what might it contribute to the learning of foreign languages? Why is it of significance for the report of the DES (1988b: 14) to state: 'work on language awareness . . . is an essential part of the foreign language curriculum . . .'?

2 The definition of the term and its use

2.1 The definition
The definition of the term 'Language Awareness' is that agreed by the

NCLE working party, viz.: *Language Awareness is a person's sensitivity to and conscious perception of the nature of language and its role in human life.*

The working party added that the teaching of Language Awareness in schools 'involves both making explicit and conscious the knowledge and skills pupils have themselves built up in the course of their experience of language, and developing powers of observation and purposeful analysis of language in their immediate environment and more widely in the world'. The focus of attention is language in use.

The above definition will be understood for the purposes of the paper and reference will be made to the teaching associated with it.

Methodology associated with the teaching is that of pupil exploration, with his or her own competence in language as the springboard, the focus and the goal.

2.2   Use of the term
Why has it been experienced as necessary to coin and use the term 'Language Awareness'?

There are scholars who have carried out work which accords with that of the Language Awareness movement. Some of that work preceded the movement and contributed to it, and some supplements and supports it, but without being associated with the term. Their work may perhaps have been associated with different terms, e.g. language education. It should be added, however, that the NCLE Language Awareness movement did not set out to be exclusive. It is important that the work of all scholars beneficial to these initiatives should be incorporated.

Benefits from use of the term may be as follows:

1. Newness arouses interest and may lend impetus.
2. A term requires definition. When agreed and widely understood, practice is informed by it and may retain coherence thereby. Misunderstandings leading to 'poor practice' may be avoided.
3. Developments have occurred on the basis of the above definition and its applications which have definite intentions and would exclude others. This should give clarity and purpose to the work carried out.

2.3   The place of Language Awareness
Language Awareness is the point of commonality between languages, be they mother tongue, second or foreign languages. Study of languages may be carried out in such a way as to enhance a person's 'awareness of language'. Language Awareness work can also usefully

influence other language areas. A person who is sensitive to the way in which language functions will have a valuable basis for the learning of individual languages. It is important to note that teachers of EMT, of foreign languages and teachers in primary schools undertake Language Awareness work.

3 Misconceptions

Fears have been expressed by teachers, advisers, Her Majesty's Inspectorate – and with some justification – that Language Awareness work may be interpreted to mean or may inadvertently bring about a reversion to former practices which are now considered unhelpful. For foreign language students, 'talking about language' could be interpreted to mean that they are given the 'rules' for 'construction' of a language together with vocabulary lists either with the sole intention that they memorise these and show that they have done so by recitation of them, or in the hope that they can, with these tools, construct statements for their own use in the foreign language. Lack of competence in the latter and change of intention from the former indicate that these undertakings are not beneficial to foreign language learning. The agreed definition of Language Awareness and associated practices should dispel these fears. (Similar fears are expressed for EMT and parsing of sentences.) The Cox Report indicates a difference in approach to use of terminology for talking about language, however: 'Terms are necessary but should be taught in context for a purpose' (DES, 1989b: 26, para. 5.55) and 'The reasons for the terminology come before the terminology itself. Terms are used as a way of encouraging active thinking about language and its uses' (DES, 1989b: 21). These views reflect those of the Language Awareness movement.

Other practices sometimes associated with Language Awareness may not in themselves lack value but are not the intention. An example might be the study of the geographical 'distribution' of languages in the world, although this may provide a useful springboard for Language Awareness work or the learning of foreign languages.

Emphasis placed by the initiators of Language Awareness work in schools on general educational benefits in the affective sphere alone may lead to aims for language-related activities which do not accord with improving pupils' sensitivity to language in use. It is possible that learning little bits of the different languages spoken by pupils in one class may lead not only to tolerance but to an appreciation of the richness of linguistic diversity represented. This is an admirable goal but may not lead to any significant increase of pupils' conscious awareness of language unless it is associated with the cognitive aspects. It is important that prime intentions are not lost from sight through undue emphasis on the affective sphere. Alternatively, a different term may be applied to such activities.

The cognitive sphere is an essential focus for Language Awareness. One would like to think it difficult to dissociate it from affective aims, but care should be taken to avoid such separation.

The method of treatment of certain language-related initiatives may lead to different outcomes. 'Taster Courses' in foreign languages are a case in point. Some pupils, for example, in their first year in secondary school, learn French for one term, Spanish for another, German for the third. If this is carried out entirely by the inductive method it is unlikely that any conscious reflection on the languages will have taken place. Perhaps the purpose of such courses is to allow pupils to make a choice of which foreign language they wish to continue to learn; Language Awareness is not a feature.

Alternatively, this could be the start of a course designed to help pupils develop skills related to learning foreign languages in general rather than one language in particular; Language Awareness is unlikely to feature. However, it is quite possible to carry out such undertakings for the purpose of developing pupils' sensitivity to language differences: to develop an explicit understanding of the skills of learning any foreign language and the skills which are specific to each separate language, to gain insight into the ways in which different languages are structured; and to realise that there is no word-for-word equivalence between languages.

At the point of planning work in schools, clarity of purpose, method, conclusion or outcome, and careful matching of all three should serve to ensure the efficacy and validity of the undertaking – and also whether it is one which promotes Language Awareness and can therefore be labelled as such.

4   The teaching and learning of foreign languages: aims and objectives

It will be some time before attainment targets and proposals for study are produced; the committee set up to make proposals for foreign languages in the National Curriculum did not report until February 1990. The document *A Statement of Policy. Modern Languages in the School Curriculum*, published by the Department of Education and

Science (1988b) is undoubtedly serving as a basis for its deliberations. One of the report's five main messages is that emphasis should be placed on improving standards of communication in foreign languages among pupils of all abilities, with emphasis on practical skills. There are implications for methods of teaching:

- the foreign language should be the medium of instruction;
- there should be adequate time for practice;
- a sense of achievement should be fostered;
- a disciplined and active approach to learning should be promoted.

At this stage of developments relating to languages in the school curriculum, the foreign language specialist might well wonder what his or her role is to be. Until very recently that role was to be a teacher of a specific foreign language. It has been appreciated, however, that the country does not have need of numbers of speakers of any one modern foreign language (MFL) more than others and individual preferences would show a range of interest. In particular, it may be expected that learners will wish or need to learn one or more MFLs later in life. Recognition is given to this in the DES *Statement of Policy. Modern Languages in the School Curriculum* (DES, 1988b: 3 para. 5) and is reaffirmed in the Statutory Orders for the National Curriculum (1989: 3 para. 8): 'the first modern language should (b) lay a foundation for learning any subsequent foreign languages'. It is clear that the teacher's role must be adapted and extended to that of the mediator of skills of foreign language learning which can be applied to any language in later life, as need arises.

5 Classroom practice: teachers' difficulties

This section presents some aspects of practice based on observations made by Her Majesty's Inspectorate, those contained in *Language Teachers at Work* (Peck, 1988), the findings of the York Project on observing foreign language teachers, my own and my students' observation of practising teachers, observation of students and recounted experiences of teachers on INSET courses.

Over the years a number of different approaches have been applied to the teaching of foreign languages. In order to achieve the goal of 'communicative competence' which is widely accepted at present, some aspects of practice appear to have been embraced within the profession as the optimum means of achieving this end. The starting point is the foreign language in use in authentic – or as closely as possible akin to authentic – situations. The starting point is also the goal. Learners are to reach the point of being able to use this language themselves and for their own purposes in the foreign country. Teaching and learning using only the target language is widely favoured and arguments for so doing are persuasive.

Use of the mother tongue in any circumstances reduces opportunities for use of the target language. It can invite learners to believe in the notion that there is wide-ranging word-for-word association between languages. In the country where the language is spoken, it impairs development of skills of language learning which require concentration on the target language for gist and later for a more precise understanding in combination with non-verbal behaviour which helps to convey meaning.

The monolingual classroom also allows day-to-day transactional behaviour between teachers and learners to take place in the target language. This includes instruction, praise, encouragement, admonition, asking questions, seeking information, comment of various kinds. In this way the learners appreciate early that the language is something which is intended for practical use. It is as 'real' to them as possible in the classroom. It exists for their own purposes, not merely for the simulated reality of the tape or the textbook. The language of classroom interaction, which I call 'extrinsic' language, is quite different from the 'test-tube' language of the course. The former is unstructured, cannot always be anticipated, may need to be complex at an early stage, will in some cases only be taught for comprehension, and is not part of a sequential learning programme. The latter is structured, can be prepared in detail, and will develop from the simple to the complex in the full teaching/learning programme.

No matter how convincing the arguments, however, monolingual teaching can create problems for teacher and learner. The following areas of difficulty, the majority of which arise from the requirement to use the target language only, are not all experienced by all teachers but the frequency of their recurrence merits our consideration.

5.1 Presentation
The presentation of a new language (i.e. the teacher makes clear to learners the meaning of the language that has been heard (or read), and the function of each word independently and in relation to others) only in the target language can be extremely difficult. Many techniques are available to the teacher. Many possibilities for misunderstanding or partial understanding are available for the learner. Questions put to pupils at the end of lessons (in their mother tongue for research

purposes) in which presentation has featured can show up a host of interesting variables in comprehension on the pupils' part.

5.2   Checking
Checking comprehension by all pupils can be difficult and it can easily be the case that when some have shown comprehension the teacher moves on, leaving the others confused and uncertain.

5.3   Understanding of pattern
It is often said that the more able pupils are anxious to discuss the insights of language which they have achieved by means of the inductive approach, but that they are rarely given the opportunity to do so since it may involve a complexity of language use which they cannot handle in the target language.

5.4   Diagnosing difficulties
This can be a very difficult area in the monolingual classroom. Sometimes when a pupil makes an error or finds difficulty in producing an appropriate response, the teacher will ask another pupil to produce the required language and the first pupil to repeat it. Unless the problem was recollection, it has not been resolved. There is, however, a wide range of possibilities. Without finding the relevant one and putting it right, further learning related to this point may cease (e.g. if the concept of the future associated with a given verb form is not understood, any teaching of the past based on contrast with the future will be unsuccessful). In addition, the pupil is left in a state of uncertainty and insecurity.

5.5   Feedback
To enable teachers to progress successfully with their pupils it is essential that they get feedback about their pupils' success or failure at each stage of the learning programme and respond to it. This puts them in a position whereby they can begin to penetrate problems, if necessary. *Explicit* feedback from pupils about their problems is naturally largely absent from the monolingual classroom.

5.6   Transfer
At this stage the teacher presents opportunities for pupils to produce language for which the stimulus comes from within, when newly learnt items may be adapted for personal use. The able linguist, the teacher, is adept at conveying messages in the target language. To do so very well demands a high degree of accuracy, and a large part of the teaching

programme places emphasis on this area. The transfer state may be impaired for learners by interruption for purposes of correction of or comment on accuracy. Fluency may thereby be impaired on future occasions and willingness to attempt to convey the ideas conceived by the pupil in his or her own mind may be lost. Personal manipulation of the language for the individual's use, the goal, may not even be attempted. Development of the person through his/her language use does not happen. In fact it is only too easy to miss out the transfer stage altogether.

5.7   The message
Emphasis on accuracy may lead teachers to lose sight of the fact that when pupils speak, they want the listener to be interested in what they have to say. The teacher's response to 'J'ai une soeur et quatorze lapins' or 'Ich habe heute einen grünen und einen roten Sock an' may be of the ilk of 'très bien' or 'das war sehr gut' (= 'all genders and endings right') not in terms of the interest the pupils hoped it would stimulate.

5.8   Learning from listening
In a number of subject areas pupils are led to believe that the only valuable work they do is writing; the main focus of attention is the book. It is essential for purposes of efficient foreign language learning, both in the classroom and in the real linguistic environment, that pupils are weaned away from this view.

5.9   Association of spoken with written form
Teaching to the point of transfer in the oral mode is a complex process requiring a high level of competence in a range of skills. The process of reading and writing which follow are susceptible to the view that they are relatively easy and the essential interim stage of associating written with spoken form may be lost, thereby impairing a learning activity otherwise based on success.

5.10   The mother tongue
Some teachers do use the mother tongue while teaching the 'test-tube' language. Sometimes it is used in presentation to avoid misunderstanding. Sometimes it is used to check comprehension. Sometimes it is used for the purposes of problem-solving. Reasons are readily understandable and can reflect a teacher's concern that these important areas are not overlooked to the detriment of the pupils. Disadvantages which it may bring have already been indicated.

5.11 'Extrinsic language'

Some teachers do not use the target language for interaction with pupils in class. The difficulties in doing it, pointed out earlier, render that particularly understandable but the loss can be crucial. (It should be said that some teachers do use the target language in this area but without *teaching* it. Pupil confusion and uncertainty follow. Others teach just so much – e.g. ten instructions and no more – encouraging the view that language is always used in the same sequence and is not susceptible to development for real use.)

5.12 Work on texts

Work on texts of various kinds in the target language may be carried out for a variety of purposes. They may be used only for reading, to understand the message conveyed. They may be used so that the pupil can understand and use the writing conventions related to a given text for his or her own purposes. They may be used in order to stimulate reaction and comment by the pupil; this requires an appreciation of language used to convey, e.g. attitude, argument, emotion, and the ways in which this is done. Learning programmes are not always suited to the given intention.

5.13 Learning

Pupils are often required to carry out 'learning' for homework. They may be given a specific purpose for doing so over and above consolidation of class-work, e.g. in order to be able to answer given questions in the following lesson without support from text or friends. They may be required to perform a dialogue from memory. It can be that they are not given helpful guidance as to how to carry that learning out; no attempt may be made to do it, through ignorance of possible methods.

6 Language Awareness courses: aims and objectives

During the existence of the NCLE working parties on Language Awareness (1981–6), surveys carried out with the help of local education authorities showed that many Language Awareness courses existent in schools fell into the category 'a course for 11–13 year olds; to create awareness of and interest in language as a preparation for foreign language learning'. Can it help to overcome any of the difficulties described in learning foreign languages?

I think it is important at this stage to emphasise that the Language Awareness 'movement' has always been a 'grass roots' one, i.e. it is the teachers of English and foreign languages in schools who have (a) understood what it is, (b) understood its potential value in response to perceived benefits, needs or deficiencies, (c) initiated and developed work and (d) persisted in doing so. These teachers would not merely agree with Kingman that there is no merit in ignorance (DES, 1988a) but would go further and agree with Tinkel (1988) that 'language is so crucial in our lives . . . that it is a natural object of study in its own right'. Tinkel also, as do many teachers, sees valuable spin-offs: 'By becoming more aware of English sounds, grammar and usage, you will become more sensitive to how you handle the language and how others do as well, and as you explore your understanding of the language you cannot fail to expand it at the same time' (Tinkel, 1988: 2). A number of teachers gave detailed information about their Language Awareness work to the NCLE working parties and a number have done so since.

The following gives a rough indication of the sort of aims which they associated with their work.

– To make explicit and conscious the pupils' intuitive knowledge of their mother tongue.
– To strengthen study skills for the learning of EMT, FLs, and other subjects.
– To bring about perception and understanding of the nature and functions of language, both for its own sake and also to increase effectiveness of performance in languages.
– To give insight into the language learning process.
– To increase the language resources available to the teacher.
– To foster mastery of languages.
– To develop the sensitivity and level of consciousness they bring to their experience of language.
– To improve their effectiveness in language in and outside school.

Terms which recur in aims/objectives which they listed, are: developing, heightening, enriching:

– perceptions about language
– appreciation of language
– insight into language
– understanding of language
– sensitivity to language
– awareness of language
– performance in language

With the latter we note that some teachers are hoping for benefits over and beyond the intrinsic value of study of language *per se*. Certainly not a few look to strengthen study skills and to develop skills of language acquisition. 'Language acquisition' and 'how to learn languages' are recurring syllabus items and thus topics for pupil exploration. One area which is still overlooked and has not featured widely with regard to aims for Language Awareness work is recognition of the fact that the individual expresses himself or herself in language (not exclusively, of course) and may develop as an individual through language. The relationship between use of the language by the individual and the effect on the individual of sensitivity to and awareness of language as well as of its use, is a crucial one which must strengthen claims to the value of this work.

Aims and objectives laid down by teachers also include affective ones, e.g. forming attitudes (one frequently mentioned is tolerance for improved relations between ethnic groups), arousing curiosity, receptivity and interest leading to increased motivation in particular for the learning of foreign languages.

During the course of work with pupils in the main group mentioned above it is essential for the pupils to reflect, observe, analyse, interpret, make judgements and convey meaning themselves. Performance in these skill areas should be heightened as a natural concomitant of the process of study as it is carried out according to the pupil exploration method.

7 Benefits of Language Awareness work for the learning of foreign languages

Can the time some foreign language teachers take from curricular time to carry out activities of a Language Awareness kind be justified? We shall respond to this firstly by looking at areas of difficulty experienced in foreign language classrooms and Language Awareness modules which might help to overcome them.

PROBLEM AREA   LANGUAGE AWARENESS MODULE.

Presentation and checking 'How we learn/acquire language/s.' Pupil participation in achieving insight into the process heightens interest, establishes greater clarity, fosters active search for clarity if it is still lacking.

Pattern 'Comparative/contrastive view of structure of languages (incorporating insights into lack of word-for-word equivalence).' Pupils involved as part of an LA undertaking actively seek and draw conclusions about patterns themselves. This is a good example of how an essential feature of LA *per se* may interact with FL learning goals to mutual benefit.

Problem-solving and explicit feedback 'The role of error in language learning.' The generality of the expressions shows up the range of possibilities (lexical item; insight into functioning of, manipulation of pattern; memory). Discussion may lead to usefully amended teacher and/or pupil behaviour, as well as to increased confidence.

Transfer. The message 'Differences in nature and use of language at different stages of the language learning process. Communication.' Pupils gain insight into the relationship between accuracy and fluency in relation to 'the message'.

Listening 'How we learn/acquire language/s.' Pupils acquire understanding of the nature of and need for the process.

Spoken/written language 'Conventions of the spoken and written word. Similarities and differences between speech and writing.' A specific syllabus item should ensure that this topic is tackled!

Texts 'Intentions, structures, styles and use of language in writing.'

'Extrinsic'/'test-tube' language 'How we learn and apply learning of FLs.' Pupils will become aware of problems associated with learning a language outside its natural linguistic and cultural context and within classroom constraints. Focus on the goal and the means for achieving it (pupils' own use of the language) should ensure greater participation by pupils in the 'extrinsic' field.

Learning 'How we learn language/s.' The pupil-based process towards achieving insights, helps them to gain insights into their own learning – idiosyncratic ways as well as those common to all. Explicit insights into language for learning as well as language as the goal has value for teacher and pupil alike.

Use of English Almost all of the above problems are related to the necessity for teaching exclusively in the target language. The value in doing so has already been ascertained. LA may serve to alleviate problems which make it difficult for a number of teachers to do that. It is evident from the above that LA and FL learning may interact to mutual benefit.

Personalizing language 'Language and Me.' Most of us would feel obliged to agree, that we are especially interested in ourselves. We find our own views on any topic of great interest and we have a strong desire to convey our views to others, for them to want to hear them – especially when we're young. The pupil-based explorational method in LA work invites constantly development of the individual's own insights. An LA module on how we have used, do use, might use language to reflect and to develop the person we think we are is the starting point and the goal. It has evident relevance for LA *per se*, the learning of FLs and for developing oneself in social contexts. The pupil is still only too frequently the 'recipient' of the FL at present.

A small number of foreign language teachers who have been carrying out Language Awareness work for some years now were consulted in Spring 1989 as to whether the work was difficult to dissociate from old 'grammar grind' teaching and whether they found problems in keeping Language Awareness work separate from specific foreign language learning lessons in order to allow quite different methodologies to pertain, whether they found it difficult to teach foreign languages monolingually. This was a small number of teachers, but they said they had not experienced such difficulty.

A problem which is a feature of the foreign language classroom-based learning process is the question of 'recall'. In order to be able to speak or write the language, having once learnt it, pupils must have continuous access to it and this is most readily ensured through its constant use. However, the problem areas referred to above necessitate much retroactive teaching in response to inadequate performance. Removal of them should foster continuous recall and therefore successful usage by the learners.

On the subject of language learning/acquisition, as we know, much remains open. Teachers perform in class according to the knowledge they bring and insights gained from experience. Much still can be learnt, however, and not least from and together with the pupils. Focus on the learning process as experienced by the individual pupil, within a Language Awareness programme, may serve to improve performance.

We have shown with the above that Language Awareness is relevant to the learning of foreign languages. This grouping of problems together with responses from Language Awareness work can readily be associated with the aims and objectives laid down by teachers of foreign languages. It can also be associated with the recommendations contained in the Kingman Report and also with aspects of language study referred to by Cox. While both of these documents had as their remit the EMT field, both referred to the benefit of association with the learning of other languages in a comprehensive programme based on language (DES, 1988a: 48, para. 51; DES, 1989b: 25, para. 5.53).

Hitherto positive benefits of Language Awareness for foreign languages have been sought in relation to areas of difficulty. However,

Language Awareness work should enhance all aspects of a foreign language course as well as lending the learner additional personal benefits. The following are quite simply one or two insights which might usefully be gained. There are many more.

- Languages have rules.
- Rules can be broken intentionally for purposes.
- Rules can be broken and communication is not lost.
- Even native speakers do not perform perfectly.
- Written language is different from spoken language.
- Most written language will never be spoken in its original form.
- Languages are different in many ways, e.g.
  - there is no word-for-word equivalence
  - like-sounding words may not mean the same
  - some languages have several words for only one word in another
  - some languages do not have a word that others have
  - languages may have different word orders
  - some languages are inflected where English is not
  - we can use the language in ways which make it our own.

An examination of the examples given will serve to show that while a foundation in Language Awareness prior to learning the foreign language is valuable, the process should not terminate there. As learning proceeds, so the potential for teaching or taking insights a stage further proceeds with it. It may be valuable at any stage of learning to precede a new foreign language item by establishing existing awareness and associating it with a learning programme, then carrying out the learning monolingually and subsequently reflecting on outcomes in the light of it.

The role of the teacher of foreign languages in this country is increasingly that of mediator of general skills of foreign language learning. A course in language *per se* in combination with a contrastive analysis of how different languages function and an understanding of the process of learning foreign languages will serve as a useful foundation for this.

The role of the teacher in Language Awareness work is that of enabler or facilitator. It is the pupil who is the setting-off point, who carries out the investigations, who gains the insights, and who reaches the conclusions. There are procedures essential to reaching the goals. For example, the pupil must reflect, interpret, analyse, evaluate, make judgements and will describe, report, summarise, explain, request, argue in working with other pupils and the teacher. These skills are developed as a fundamental part of and development from the process. Explicit insight into language and language learning informs the teacher and encourages the pupil to foster optimum interaction for foreign language learning.

Clearly, there is still something of a mismatch between aims and objectives, methods and outcomes in foreign language learning. There is widespread agreement that more could be achieved but the level of success is not yet generally high. What has been offered here are suggestions, based on teachers' activities, as to how goals might be reached within a harmonious framework of sensitisation to language.

8   Some conclusions

It has been necessary for the development of Language Awareness work to bring together knowledge and expertise gained in the fields of linguistics, psychology, sociology, education, English, foreign and second languages. Much progress has been made but there is some way to go if the proper enriching of the individual in relation to his or her unique feature, the ability to express himself or herself in language, is to be ensured. The recommendations of the Kingman committee encourage this and the response made by the DES in setting up the Central Training Package on the Kingman Model of English to begin to break the vicious cycle of ignorance is a further positive step. Statements made about the importance of knowledge about language in the Cox Report and the importance of Language Awareness for foreign languages in the DES document lend weight to the view that this should be pursued.

Given the way in which the syllabus is drawn up in the Cox proposals – viz. under the four skills of speaking, listening, reading, writing – there is however a danger that Language Awareness will be distributed in 'droplets', which does not augur well for substance or coherence. In addition, 'awareness' and 'sensitivity' are hardly susceptible to assessment but the increase in assessment requirements made by the Government will inevitably place teaching emphasis on those issues which are to be assessed. General educational issues, including Language Awareness, should not be lost from view. The work of the committee on assessment criteria for foreign languages should take account of teachers' (and pupils') appreciation of the value of Language Awareness. Assessment (and teaching) targets for EMT are being established in advance. This should make feasible a coherent programme of Language Awareness embracing all languages, since subsequent committees can take account of what has already been established. (English as a second language, or community languages, should of course feature in an over-arching Language Awareness framework.)

A word should be said about initial teacher training courses. Time allocated to train teachers in the most apposite methods and techniques for helping pupils to learn foreign languages in schools even now is hardly adequate. A comparison of the number of hours available to train students for Teaching Practice (TP) on Initial Teacher Training (ITT) courses with those, for example, on EFL courses at International House shows this up. If a job is worth doing it is worth doing well! In the case of teaching/learning foreign languages there is no real alternative to doing it well. It either happens or it doesn't. Placing students with teachers in schools is not the whole answer since, although there are a number of successful teachers, a number still struggle, and understandably so, given the problem areas set out in this paper. They rightly look to training departments for new ideas and welcome students as purveyors of them. It will be necessary to have still more time to train teachers effectively in this associated field. 'Give us the *time* and we will finish the job' might be the appeal. Implications for in-service training are also clear.

Research and teaching should go hand-in-hand. The project carried out recently by Mitchell and Hooper at Southampton University with teachers of foreign languages and EMT in Hampshire into their knowledge and perceptions of Language Awareness is to be welcomed. More needs to be done, not least into how learners learn foreign languages and involvement of the learner in observation and monitoring the process. Useful contributions exist already. Perhaps it is time to work more closely with learners in matching their experiences with insights already gained. I hope that this paper has shown that further research into the possibilities for beneficial association of Language Awareness with foreign language learning would be valuable and should be carried out soon. Despite all the problems, the movement is still with us. A significant number of teachers do seem to agree with Trim when he says: 'the growth of language skills should go hand-in-hand with an awareness of the workings of language within us and in our environment' (Trim, 1988: vii).

9 Authentic texts, pedagogical grammar and Language Awareness in foreign language learning

David Little and David Singleton

1 Introduction

This paper has two sources: our long-standing interest in the role and possible modalities of grammar teaching in second and foreign language courses, and the specific desire to provide fixed support for learners using the *Authentik* newspapers and audio cassettes as their principal source of foreign language input.

For those not already familiar with *Authentik*, a brief explanation is in order. Authentik Language Learning Resources Ltd is a campus company of Trinity College, Dublin.[1] Five times in the course of the academic year it publishes newspapers and cassettes in four languages – French, German, Spanish and English. The newspapers comprise (i) 24 pages of paste-ups from authentic target language sources, organised according to broad themes like 'world news', 'fashion', 'sport', 'holidays and travel', and (ii) a pedagogical section of 16 pages made up of exercises and activities based on the corresponding cassette as well as the newspaper, a complete transcript of the cassette, and competitions. The cassettes comprise recordings of radio news bulletins and other broadcasts, slow readings of some of these items, and interviews with native speakers; as far as possible their thematic content coincides with items in the corresponding newspaper. The exercises and activities in the pedagogical section of the newspaper seek to address learners directly, involving them in various kinds of reflection about the target language and helping them to come to terms with some of the central problems of language learning.

In the first part of our paper we describe a chain of activities that Authentik has developed to help learners cope with authentic texts; in the second part we consider why the strong lexical orientation of our pedagogical procedures should be so successful in stimulating learners to ask questions about the target language system; in the third part we consider some implications for the development of pedagogical grammars; and in the fourth part we briefly outline the practical approach that we are developing to Language Awareness in general and grammar in particular.

2   Some pedagogical procedures for coping with authentic texts

Authentik was originally launched in response to the perceived need to provide learners of French with a steady flow of texts derived from French-language newspapers and magazines. The texts have always been reproduced in newspaper format, but to begin with teachers and learners were provided with no pedagogical assistance: authentic texts were the order of the day, and it was assumed that teachers would know what to do with them. Perhaps not surprisingly, this turned out not to be the case. Accordingly, *Authentik* has gradually developed a pedagogical section for each of its newspapers and now provides users with a fair amount of prepared learning activity.

The classic arguments in favour of using authentic texts in foreign language teaching are (i) that they are more interesting, and thus more motivating, than invented texts, and (ii) that they provide a rich source of target language input. However, much of the feedback we have received from teachers using *Authentik* suggests that in the language classrooms of Irish and British secondary schools authentic texts have often been used simply as comprehension practice for learners nearing the end of their school careers. In other words, many schools were probably not getting full value from *Authentik*, partly because it was being exploited in a very narrow way, and partly because it was usually being given only to senior learners. Accordingly our colleague Seán Devitt set out to devise a chain of activities that would demonstrate to teachers attending Authentik's in-service training days that even pupils in the early stages of learning could cope with authentic texts provided they were given the right kind of preparation.

The original intention was that the chain of activities would be undertaken entirely in the target language; but experience has shown that it is most productive if learners are encouraged to use their mother tongue whenever they need to express thoughts or ask questions that are beyond their target language competence. In its original version the activity chain is organised as follows. Learners work in groups of three or four. They are given a jumble of perhaps three dozen words and phrases derived from an authentic text, and any items they do not know are explained to them. Their first task is to write each word or phrase on a separate Post-it and then sort the Post-its into overlapping categories of TIME, EVENT, PEOPLE and PLACE on a Venn diagram (see Figure 1). This is intended to activate processes of reflection that enable the learners to perform the second task, which is to construct a story outline, usually by arranging their Post-its in an appropriate linear order and adding whatever additional elements are needed. When they have completed their story outline, they are given a jumble of sentences derived from an abbreviated and simplified version

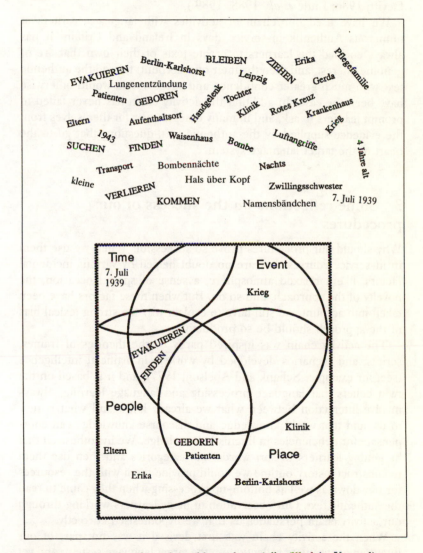

FIGURE 1 Example of word jumble and partially filled-in Venn diagram. (Reproduced with permission from *Authentik: the Learner's Manual*, a supplement to the September 1989 issues of the *Authentik* newspapers)

of the authentic text: their third task is to arrange the sentences in a plausible order (there is often more than one possible solution). The learners can then use the reconstituted text as a reference source to flesh out and correct their own story. After this they are given the authentic text to read. (For a fuller account of these activities, see Devitt, 1986; Little *et al.*, 1988, 1989.)

We have used our chain of activities with language learners at numerous Authentik in-service days in Ireland and Britain. It has always enabled the learners to create texts of their own that are of genuine interest, and then (by their own account) to read the authentic text with much greater confidence and success than would otherwise have been the case. In addition the activity chain has never failed to prompt learners to ask, and in many cases answer for themselves from the evidence supplied by the authentic text, questions that go to the heart of the target language system.

3   Some reflections on the success of our procedures

Why should our procedures prove so successful? When we use them in in-service courses they are no doubt helped by various incidental factors, like a relaxed atmosphere, a sense of special occasion, the novelty of the approach, and so on. But when these factors have been taken into account, we still have to explain why the strong lexical bias of the approach should be so productive.

The activity chain was inspired partly by the theories of frames, scripts, and scenarios developed by workers in artificial intelligence (see, for example, Schank and Abelson, 1977); and it is based on the twin beliefs that language processing and language learning always involve interaction between what we already know and what is new to us, and that world knowledge and discourse knowledge can compensate for deficiencies in linguistic knowledge. We hypothesised that by getting learners to sort words into categories and then use them to construct a story outline we could provide them with the resources for top-down as well as bottom-up processing when they came to read the authentic text. Our observation of many learners working through our activity chain persuades us that we hypothesised correctly.

When the activity chain was first devised it was not part of our intention to stimulate reflection on the target language system; and yet the things that learners say about the target language system, though always incidental to their main purpose in completing the activity chain, are usually among the things that teachers find most striking about our in-service days. Two issues discussed with considerable penetration by learners at a recent in-service day were the use of definite and indefinite reference in French and tense sequence in German.

There seem to us to be two likely reasons why our activity chain stimulates learners to critical reflection on the target language system. They have to do with learners' perceptions of language and – surely not unrelated to these perceptions – basic facts of naturalistic language acquisition.

The lay person tends to think of language as consisting of 'words', as is indicated by expressions like 'I want a word with you', 'How shall we word it?', 'She has a wonderful way with words', and so on. This perception is carried over to language learning: learners typically see their difficulties and learning tasks in terms of how particular words and word-types behave in relation to each other rather than in terms of general rules and processes. Even if we wish to take account of general rules and processes, it is surely sensible to adopt the same point of departure as the learner, especially if this point of departure coincides with the order of things in naturalistic language acquisition.

Traditional approaches to pedagogical grammar have sought to describe the structures into which words fit, thus maintaining a clear distinction between form and meaning. However, first and naturalistic second language learning begins not with abstract rules but with words, which the learner gradually comes to use in increasingly complex structural relations. In other words, discourse precedes morphology. Much the same can be said of our activity chain. The first two tasks encourage learners to deploy words so as to create general semantic relationships; and it is later in the chain, when they draw on the resources provided by simplified and authentic texts to correct and elaborate their own texts, that they tend to focus sharply on grammatical issues – morpho-syntax, word order, tense and aspect, and so on. Without wishing to press the comparison too far, there seems to us to be a general affinity between the successive stages of our approach (admittedly passed through in an hour or so!) and the way in which naturalistic first and second language acquirers gradually attach morphological and syntactic features to the words with which they build their utterances.

Reflecting on the fact that learners apparently find it easier to deal with issues of structure *after* they have used words to create skeletal discourse, we note that there is some evidence to suggest that lexical consciousness develops very much earlier than syntactic consciousness in first language acquisition. Referring to research on the ways in which children modify their speech to younger children and to less proficient speakers of their language (non-natives, retardates, etc.), Brédart and Rondal (1982: 27) note that the degree to which children are *conscious* of such modifications varies according to the nature of the modifications:

> La prise de conscience des modifications syntaxiques du discours n'est pas assurée, même à douze ans, selon le rapport de Brami-Mouling. Ces données s'accordent avec celles de Brédart (1980) indiquant que jusqu'à douze ans la majorité des enfants ne peuvent invoquer la complexité syntaxique du discours pour expliquer l'incompréhension d'un jeune enfant dans une situation d'échec de communication *alors que les difficultés liées à la complexité lexicale ne leur échappent pas.* (our italics)

It seems possible that words are the best way of feeding the natural mechanisms which underpin not only the internalisation of the target language system but also the developing awareness of the system on which the capacity to plan, monitor and edit discourse depends.

4   Some implications for pedagogical grammars

The priority of lexis, both in language acquisition generally and in the naturalistic development of Language Awareness in particular, seems to us to carry the same general implication as the success of our activity chain: pedagogical grammars should have a much stronger lexical orientation than has traditionally been the case.

In recent years there has been much talk of the need for a 'return to grammar' in language teaching, but no great effort has been devoted to establishing an appropriate theoretical orientation for such an enterprise. Indeed, applied linguists too often show a worrying disdain for matters of linguistic theory. Yet it is surely incumbent on designers of pedagogical grammars to ensure that their work is informed by general linguistic research (cf. Cook, 1989), especially when that research is intent on elaborating a grammar that possesses not just observational or descriptive but explanatory adequacy – a grammar, in other words, that is not content with showing how the sentences of a language are generated or how it is that speakers can match words to sounds, but seeks to explain how the language can be learnt in the first place.

Two important strands in current linguistic theory are (i) a preoccupation with broad grammatical parameters posited as part of an innate linguistic faculty (see, e.g., Cook's 1988 introduction to current Chomskyan theory) and (ii) an increasing concentration on the lexicon as the generator of morpho-syntactic as well as semantic and collocational detail. Even those who are enthusiastic about a parameter-setting perspective readily admit that there is a lot more to learning a language than getting broad parameter settings right (Cook, personal communication), and that the principal task of the language learner is situated at the lexical level. This is reflected in the increasing weight being carried by the lexicon in Chomskyan grammar. More generally, lexis is occupying an increasingly important place in theoretical models emanating from a number of schools – cf., for example, 'lexical functional grammar' (Bresnan, 1982) and 'word grammar' (Hudson, 1984). In lexical functional grammar the reason given for this is the desire to achieve 'a computationally precise and *psychologically realistic* model of human language' (Sells, 1985: 135; our italics), which coincides neatly with the lexically oriented intuitions of the layman. It is worth adding here that recent work in lexicography also shows that the word can be a very efficient core for a whole constellation of grammatical information – we might note the increasing amounts of morpho-syntactic information being provided by dictionaries in general and the computerised techniques of collocational analysis which underpin the dictionaries produced by the COBUILD project (1987, 1988) in particular.

The success of our activity chain seems to us to have a further implication for pedagogical grammars: they should help learners to approach their target language system inductively. As we noted above, most traditional approaches to pedagogical grammar offer generalisations about the structural relations between words; that is, they require to be used deductively. However, when learners approach a foreign language deductively they are immediately confronted with two sources of uncertainty: how *exactly* are individual words governed by the rules? and how do the rules interact with one another? By contrast, our activity chain proceeds inductively, beginning with specific words and the problem of arranging them in correct and appropriate semantic as well as syntactic relations.

It seems clear to us that both induction and deduction have a role to play in developing learner competence both in its analytic and in its automatised dimensions. We have argued elsewhere (Little and Singleton, 1988) that learners need information of various kinds about the target language, not only to enhance those processes, skills and strategies to which conscious knowledge can contribute, but also to help make input comprehensible and thus facilitate unconscious inductive, internalising processes. This means that pedagogical grammars should contain much more information of a social, socio-linguistic and pragmatic kind than has traditionally been the case; and it seems to us that they might also usefully include some basic information about language learning and language processing. At the same time, however, pedagogical grammars need to be organised in such a way as to promote inductive learning processes as well as deductive analysis. This means developing a systematic approach to complement the random relationships that are thrown up by work on authentic texts.

5   Some practical proposals

The question then arises, how can these and similar arguments be turned into actual fixed support for language learners? Our answer is to devise a manual for users of *Authentik* that provides a wider than usual range of information about language learning and language use, and organises information about the target system in ways which coincide explicitly with the 'words in context' approach prompted by work with authentic texts. The intention is to encourage learners to compile much of the target language grammar for themselves, since achieving a degree of autonomy as language learners should increase their capacity to behave as self-reliant and efficient language users.

The first part of the manual was published as a 24-page supplement to the September 1989 issues of *Authentik*. In a series of two-page spreads it

– provides information about first and second language acquisition;
– shows how discourse precedes sentence grammar in naturalistic language acquisition;
– explains the importance for language learning of world and discourse as well as grammatical knowledge;
– provides information about how we store words in memory and offers suggestions for vocabulary learning;
– illustrates a way of observing words in action that derives from the concordancing technique used to compile the COBUILD dictionaries (phrases containing the item under consideration are collected and listed one under another, with the item in a central column);
– suggests that when composing in a foreign language learners should take a 'words first' approach, devising the broad semantic structure of their text before concerning themselves with issues of grammar at and below sentence level;
– shows how authentic and simplified texts can be used as a quarry for grammatical examples and information.

The processes and techniques under discussion are illustrated with worked examples in English, French, German and Spanish; and the centre spread offers (i) four diagrams that can be xeroxed and used to analyse any authentic text and prepare for various kinds of productive activity, and (ii) a blank map of Europe that learners can annotate with information gleaned from the *Authentik* newspapers and cassettes.

We hope to publish the second part of the manual, which will deal with the central concerns of traditional pedagogical grammars, in the autumn of 1991. It is still very much at the embryonic stage. We shall of course adopt the strong lexical orientation required by the arguments we have rehearsed in this paper, though we shall not follow Hudson (1984) in abandoning the usual distinction between grammatical rules and lexical entries – in strictly pedagogical terms it seems to us an essential aid to generalisation, which in turn is an essential aid to learning. However, our approach to issues of morpho-syntax, word order, tense and aspect, and so on will always be from within a constellation of meaning.

In syntax there is an obvious ascending order of difficulty from the NP (noun phrase), through the PP (prepositional phrase) to the VP (verb phrase). The specific notions that form a substantial part of some language teaching syllabuses tend overwhelmingly to be nouns and adjectives, which refer to material and abstract realities but do not of themselves generate the structural relations on which the articulation of meaning depends. The PP embodies a limited set of structure–meaning relationships, but it is the VP that is the engine of linguistic structure. In this connection Harley (1986: 59) quotes Palmer's 1974 view that 'Learning a language is to a very large degree learning to operate the verbal forms of that language . . .', and refers to research findings which suggest that if the VP is in order, competence generally will also be in order. Accordingly, within our general lexical orientation we shall give particular attention to the verb and the VP. If naturalistic language acquirers typically progress from individual nouns and adjectives to an increasingly differentiated command of the verbal system, and if this progression can be matched by effective pedagogical measures, that is a further reason for putting the VP and the verbal system at the centre of pedagogical grammars. We envisage presenting the semantic and syntactic relations of the VP in the form of tables, charts, and diagrams that learners can extend for themselves by using them as tools for the analysis of authentic texts.

The success of our pedagogical experiments has reinforced our conviction that grammar as traditionally conceived and Language Awareness as more recently invented are inseparable from one another and should be taught inductively as well as deductively; and recent developments in linguistic theory support the strong lexical bias that we wish, in the light of our experiments, to give to pedagogical grammar. It remains to be seen whether what makes sense to us at a theoretical level and is easily sketched in outline can be turned into a tool that is genuinely useful to language learners.

Note

1. Further information about the *Authentik* newspapers and cassettes can be obtained by writing to: Authentik Language Learning Resources Ltd, O'Reilly Institute, Trinity College, Dublin 2, Ireland.

10 The potential of Language Awareness as a focus for cross-curricular work in the secondary school

Jim Anderson

1   A context for language learning

Language Awareness begins with teacher awareness. As specialists in English as mother tongue, English as a second language, community languages, classical languages or (as in my case) foreign languages we tend to think within our subject compartments, to reflect the structure of the education system and to transmit that structure to the minds of our pupils.

Why should this concern us? First, because there tends to be little dialogue between these various teachers, little attempt to gain an understanding of each other's perspectives on language, and little consideration of whether what the one may be doing is being enhanced or undermined by the other or whether there are common concerns to which all should be devoting attention.

Second, because the view of language that comes across to pupils is a highly fragmented one. The opportunity to demonstrate all that different languages and different experiences of language learning have in common is lost.

Third, because the low status of bilingual pupils is reinforced due to the fact that community languages commonly appear as being irrelevant to the main business of the school. What is more, those teachers who support bilingual pupils are generally not viewed as having an important contribution to make to the planning of courses.

Language Awareness, if it is to come near to achieving those aims which it is commonly held to pursue – i.e. deepening understanding, fostering tolerance and increasing receptivity to new linguistic experience – must begin by seeking to provide a broad context for language learning and this can only be done by breaking down some of those barriers so effectively maintained within schools.

What do I mean by a 'broad context' for language learning? I mean very definitely something that will be different for each school. Different because within each school and within each local community a distinct range of languages and dialects are likely to be spoken. Different, too, because teachers will bring different viewpoints on language learning depending on their experience both personally and professionally. This said, I would describe a broad context for language learning as one where each language or language variety is seen to have an importance and a value, where language is recognised as being an expression of culture and identity, where the linguistic resources of the school and the local community are drawn upon, where difficult issues to do with racism, sexism and classism are confronted honestly and common policies are arrived at.

It may be felt that this is to confuse Language Awareness with a school language policy. It is not. Rather it is to say that a cross-curricular approach to Language Awareness offers a practical means of carrying out certain important aspects of a language policy or indeed of raising awareness that such a policy is needed. The great value of Language Awareness is that it provides such a useful focus for opening up a dialogue with colleagues because the topics and issues which it deals with quite evidently cross subject boundaries. The study of languages spoken in the local community, for example, can be viewed from a variety of perspectives – social, cultural, historical, political as well as purely linguistic. A cross-curricular approach in fact opens up a wide range of possibilities and brings many advantages for teachers and pupils, but most importantly it establishes a context through which understanding is deepened and interest and enthusiasm are stimulated.

2   From theory to practice

There are undoubtedly many who would share the view that there is a need for a cross-curricular approach to language. The Bullock, Swann and, most recently, the Kingman Reports all argue along these lines. The Kingman committee (DES, 1988a: 43) states explicitly that:

> It should be the duty of all teachers to instil in their pupils a civilised respect for other languages and an understanding of the relations between other languages and English. It should be made clear to English-speaking pupils that classmates whose first language is Bengali or Cantonese, or any other of the scores of languages spoken by the school population (over 160 in inner London alone), have languages quite as systematic and rule-governed as their own.

One of the recommendations of the report (DES, 1988a: 69) is that:

> . . . all subject departments concerned with the teaching of language in secondary school (including English whether as a first or second language – and foreign languages, ancient or modern) develop a coordinated policy for language teaching.

Unfortunately, none of the reports has seriously considered how the theory can be translated into practice, how a constructive exchange of ideas leading to new approaches in the classroom can practically be brought about. In this section I wish to outline how just such a development is taking place at the John Roan School in south-east London where I am currently teaching.

John Roan is a mixed comprehensive school with just over 1000 pupils of whom 96 are bilingual. Of the seventeen languages other than English spoken by pupils at the school, Punjabi has the highest number of speakers, although there are an increasing number of Turkish-speaking pupils as well. At present, there is no language policy in the school, nor is there a language coordinator. English and Languages are two separate faculties; within Languages are included foreign languages (French and German), community languages (Punjabi and Turkish) and English as a second language. Punjabi is taught on the mainstream in the fourth and fifth years, Turkish is taught as an after-school class serving pupils of primary and secondary age in the Greenwich area.

As far as Language Awareness work is concerned a short unit was introduced for first-year pupils during languages time from September 1986. Informal discussion took place within the languages faculty and with some colleagues from the English faculty about cross-curricular work on Language Awareness, but it was not until February last year that a first formal meeting was held, attended by some members of the Languages and English faculties and including the head teacher, who is an English specialist.

The meeting centred largely around what we each understood by Language Awareness, but there was obvious interest in pursuing discussion and it was decided to arrange further meetings to explore topics of relevance to both faculties. It immediately became apparent that the scope for an integrated approach was quite enormous, but that the time and effort required to do things properly would also be very great, all this at a point when morale generally was not at its highest.

There was also, very importantly, a question of management and procedure. Because of my previous experience in the field and the strong commitment I felt to developing Language Awareness work at John Roan it was tacitly assumed that I would take on the coordinating role. The fact that, as head of languages, I was regularly involved in meetings with other faculty heads and the senior management was clearly an advantage because it enabled me both to consult with and inform those involved in curriculum issues of what we were proposing and to keep Language Awareness on the agenda as far as the school development plan and INSET requirements were concerned.

However, although it fell to me to create the conditions in which Language Awareness work could develop, the process of devising and implementing the scheme has been very much a collaborative effort. The group we have formed is composed of teachers of English, foreign languages, community languages and English as a second language and includes a language specialist from the local language resource centre.

Much time has been and continues to be spent on defining our aims and gaining a deeper understanding of the different perspectives that we each bring to issues of Language Awareness. Assumptions that we make about each other – e.g. the view English teachers have of foreign languages teachers, and vice versa – have needed to be challenged and explored. Moreover, the way in which our work might be received by pupils, parents and colleagues has constantly had to be borne in mind.

In terms of the topics that we wished to focus attention on initially and which we felt would lend themselves to a cross-curricular approach there was broad agreement fairly early on. These were

TABLE 1   Varieties of Language

English	Languages
Language variation – an introduction	Views about language
Development of baby language	Discovering languages
	Major world languages
Different ways of talking:	Languages of the UK
(a) accent	
(b) accent prejudices	Languages of Greenwich and John Roan
(c) dialect	
(d) slang	Focus on the Indian subcontinent:
(e) playing with words	(a) location
(f) inventing a language	(b) five major languages
(g) language and gender	(c) scripts
	(d) cultural background
	(e) Punjabi taster
	The value of being bilingual

varieties of language, language growth and language learning. Table 1 gives a rough outline of the first of these units, showing which aspects are covered in English and which in Languages time.

Essentially what we are doing in this area is to explore the different forms of language used within the school and the local community. The many aims are to broaden pupils' perspective on language, to examine attitudes to different forms of language and to create an atmosphere in which pupils feel confident in their own use of language. In order to highlight the interconnections between work being carried out in each subject the English and languages parts of each topic are taught as far as possible simultaneously. Clearly, it is important throughout the course for teachers to discuss frequently with each other in order to be able to draw on each other's experience with the class and to reinforce positive developments. Other ways in which it is possible to highlight integration in the pupils' eyes are through assemblies conducted jointly by members of different faculties, through combined display work and through a progress sheet made up of course elements from each faculty area. The progress sheet for the Language Awareness unit of the GAML (Graded Assessment in Modern Languages) scheme provides a useful model to work from.

Even more important though than achieving consensus on what topics to teach is to establish basic principles with regard to methodology. It seemed to us essential to our aims that we should pursue a child-centred approach, drawing very much on the linguistic experience of our pupils and building from it. Thus, as far as possible, our lessons are centred around activities where pupils are working collaboratively and are then encouraged to reflect on insights they have gained. Because we as teachers have been working together sharing the knowledge and ideas that we have each acquired within our different specialisms and from our different experiences, the lessons we have prepared have been made richer and more imaginative and, equally significant, the task of preparing them less arduous.

At the same time as working on Language Awareness as a group and sharing our teaching experiences we have had to be careful not to isolate ourselves from other colleagues who have felt uncertain and possibly threatened by our proposals. Thus one afternoon of INSET last term was devoted to a presentation of our work to other staff within the languages and English faculties and we have spent other INSET sessions training colleagues to take on Language Awareness work. In the course of last term interest was expressed by several members of the humanities faculty in becoming involved in the scheme and potential contributions were immediately evident.

Clearly, in considering any kind of collaborative work between colleagues it would be naive to assume that personalities do not matter. There must be a basis of trust and respect and common understanding. What is obvious though is that once a spirit of teamwork has been established the excitement and feeling of confidence that it engenders is real and infectious. As far as teachers of English as a second language and community languages teachers are concerned, it establishes their place, their status and their contribution to what the school is about.

It is worth pointing out also that Language Awareness is more likely to establish itself on a permanent basis within a school when a team of teachers is actively involved. There are too many instances of positive developments fizzling out when one or two key individuals leave to take up posts elsewhere.

3   Ways forward

On the basis of our experience at John Roan it is clear that a cross-curricular approach to Language Awareness is both possible and in many ways desirable. But the development I have described represents merely the beginning of a process that has to be built upon if it is to achieve what it has set out to achieve, namely that broad context for language learning.

One way it certainly could develop is horizontally to include a wider range of subject areas. In a school where I taught previous to my present post a Language Awareness scheme was implemented which included every subject area. At that school Language Awareness then proved very valuable as a focus for establishing links with local primary schools.

The scheme must also develop vertically because the issues raised at first-year level need to be expanded and explored in greater depth as pupils move up the school. Unless this happens there is a danger that the effects of experiences in the first year will be transitory and insubstantial.

Equally important, however, it has become extremely clear that Language Awareness work is most meaningful when set within the context of a carefully conceived school language policy – not a policy which is a mere paper exercise, but one which involves all staff in an active process of reassessing their own attitudes to language and of developing positive strategies to support the learning of all pupils. Through such a policy the place of Language Awareness work within the curriculum would be validated and strengthened.

Looking forward beyond the bounds of the school walls it would be encouraging to see greater efforts within colleges of teacher training and at advisory and inspectorate levels to break out of the straitjacket of narrow subject-based thinking and to appreciate how much there is to be gained on all sides by greater understanding and cooperation.

11 Switching off: learners' perception of the appropriacy of input

Elizabeth Toncheva

1 Introduction

Recent studies of learners' conscious efforts to master a second/foreign language have had two main goals: (1) to make teachers and materials writers aware of the types of behaviour learners use to facilitate their own learning, and (2) to identify successful learning strategies which could be taught to less competent learners with the aim of promoting the development of their proficiency in the target language. (For an extensive review of existing research on language learning strategies, see Oxford, 1989.)

Various researchers have come up with different lists of learner-applied strategies (see, for example, Naiman *et al.*, 1975; Stern, 1975; Rubin, 1987; Oxford, 1990) which, however, seem to be reducible to four basic categories: (a) metacognitive; (b) cognitive; (c) affective; and (d) social strategies.

The purpose of this paper is to take a close look at a learner behaviour which, surprisingly, has received little, if any, attention so far. It is what I would like to call the SWITCH-OFF strategy.

2 The switch-off strategy

Foreign language teachers, as well as teachers in other subjects, have often complained about their learners not paying attention to their instructions and/or not participating actively in the classroom activities. 'They simply switch off!', teachers say. I would like to claim, however, that we should distinguish between two essentially different types of switch-off. The first, commonly practised by good and poor learners alike, is usually prompted by constant or incidental lack of interest or motivation to learn in a particular class. It can also be explained by the learner's current psycho-physiological state, e.g. tiredness, anxiety, emotional unrest, etc. The second can be defined as *the behaviour good language learners consciously employ with the aim of providing for themselves better learning opportunities than those offered by the teacher-directed instructional activities in a particular teaching/learning situation.* It is this second type of potentially constructive learner behaviour that I shall refer to as the SWITCH-OFF strategy.

As it is concerned with self-regulating and self-monitoring, SWITCH-OFF can be classified as a *metacognitive strategy applied in a formal setting and definitely aimed at self-directing learning.* Its successful application necessarily involves:

(a) the learner's awareness of his/her wants and needs (both target and learning) and his/her perception of the aims and objectives of the teaching/learning situation;

(b) the learner's awareness of his/her learning style preferences and matching teaching techniques;

(c) the learner's self-evaluation of the progress he/she is making in relation to other learners in the class, the demands of the teaching/learning situation and his/her self-perceived target aims and objectives;

(d) the learner's assessment of the effectiveness of the teaching methodology for his/her own learning process;

(e) the learner's intuitively correct judgement of his/her ability to provide for him/herself new, presumably better, learning opportunities than those offered by the classroom instruction;

(f) the learner's willingness to take greater responsibility for the management of his/her own learning;

(g) the learner's appropriate choice of self-initiated activities to engage in, instead of wasting valuable learning time;

(h) the learner's ability to eliminate the distracting effect of teacher talk, other learners' talk, noise, etc., and engage in self-directed activities for a sufficient length of time;

(i) the learner's ability to consciously control his/her switching off and back again on to the teacher-directed classroom activities, at the right moment, without being noticed by the teacher.

Why do learners choose to use the SWITCH-OFF strategy in the first place? I believe that even the keenest observer would not be in the position to produce an exhaustive list of reasons. It seems, however, that SWITCH-OFF is most commonly prompted by some current needs the learner is aware of at a certain point in the process of learning, for example:

(a) to analyse a certain language item and then form, test, and confirm or reject his/her own hypotheses about the structure and rules of the target language;

(b) to revise or consciously activate knowledge that was part of previous linguistic input;

(c) to check some aspect of his/her current proficiency in the target language;
(d) to avoid being involved in what he/she considers unnecessary reinforcement of already acquired language items and do (a), (b) or (c) instead, or learn some new item which was not part of the classroom input;
(e) to use learning techniques which he/she considers more suitable to his/her learning style than those required by the teaching methodology applied;
(f) to fight boredom induced by some aspect of the learning environment, e.g. teacher, materials, fellow-learners, etc., and make foreign/second language learning more enjoyable.

The learner's awareness of his/her current needs is very often prompted on the spot by planned, focal input from the teacher or by incidental, non-focal input either from the teacher or the learner's peers. It may, however, be suggested by learning activities the learner was previously engaged in, either in or out of the classroom.

Being a metacognitive learning strategy, SWITCH-OFF has the potential of indirectly contributing to the process of learning. By employing it, the learner hopes to provide for himself/herself appropriate opportunities to engage in some cognitive memorisation, planning or practice activities, which would be beneficial to his/her learning, and thus compensate for the deficit of such opportunities in the teacher-initiated classroom activities.

Many factors tend to influence the choice of the SWITCH-OFF strategy, as well as the scope and frequency of its application. Among them the most important seem to be the following:

2.1 Age

As this factor correlates with previous learning experience, i.e. experience in learning other subjects and possibly other foreign languages, it seems reasonable to assume that adult learners are more likely to apply SWITCH-OFF than young learners. However, the SWITCH-OFF strategy is by no means an adult learner prerogative. During a visit to a French class at the Ripley St Thomas Church of England School in Lancaster, England, I was surprised to discover that the 11-year-old schoolgirl who was sitting next to me was actually applying SWITCH-OFF with amazing dexterity. While the teacher was conducting a controlled practice activity nominating the learners to provide answers to questions in a predictable order, the girl managed to check up a number of words in her dictionary, read the explanations about a grammar rule and apply the rule successfully as she did a couple of exercises in the textbook ahead of the teacher's instructions. She also demonstrated a brilliant ability to be in tune with the right moment to switch back on again when it was her turn to answer the teacher's question.

2.2 Language being learned and language proficiency

The SWITCH-OFF strategy can be applied to the learning of any foreign/second language and in fact it is not confined to language learning. The learner may venture into employing it as soon as he/she feels enough self-assurance to direct his/her own learning. It seems probable, therefore, that learners will be more likely to apply SWITCH-OFF when acquiring language systems that are closer to their own mother tongues, as in that case they will find it easier to feel less dependent on their teachers and indulge in all kinds of self-initiated learning activities.

As far as level of proficiency goes, Tyacke and Mendelsohn's (1986) diary study showed that lower level learners are generally much more dependent on their teachers and on the linguistic code than higher level learners. Research done by Chamot *et al.* (1987) has suggested that metacognitive strategy use rises with the increase of level of proficiency in the target language.

Speaking from my personal experience as a teacher of English to adult non-native speakers, I can claim that advanced learners who have entered the phase of 'desatellisation' (see Stern, 1983) tend to employ SWITCH-OFF much more frequently than beginner or intermediate learners.

2.3 Task requirement

Good language learners often feel undertaxed if the learning task set by the teacher is too easy in relation to their current linguistic/communicative competence. Therefore, they may apply the SWITCH-OFF strategy and engage in activities which are both cognitively and linguistically more challenging. A similar phenomenon has been described by Rivers (1983) as the process of 'time sharing'. This can occur whenever the learners are expected to engage in a mechanical, non-meaningful activity which does not require much processing capacity – 'just enough to mimic, more or less accurately, and make minor adjustments, which are discarded as rapidly as they are produced' (p. 97). However, unlike 'time sharing', which is a way of getting detached from the learning process, SWITCH-OFF is employed with the aim of facilitating learning and making it more effective.

The learners may choose to 'switch off' also when the task is unrealistically demanding, sometimes to the point of having a demotivating effect on learning. In such cases, however, it would be hard to predict a SWITCH-OFF as constructive learner behaviour.

2.4 Learning style and teaching methodology
Learners in general, and especially adult learners, usually have their own ideas and beliefs about language learning and the ways in which they personally learn best (see, for example, Wenden (1986b)). Therefore, they may employ the SWITCH-OFF strategy when they become aware of a discrepancy between their preferred style of learning and the teaching methodology applied in the classroom.

Let me take an example from my own teaching experience. I was conducting a pair-work communicative activity with a class of intermediate adult learners, when I realised that one of my students had 'switched off' and was working on an exercise from the textbook. As I was confident that the activity I had spent hours to design was a 'sample of teaching ingenuity', I was both puzzled and annoyed. I managed somehow to curb my emotions and asked him to explain why he was not doing what the rest of the class seemed to be enthusiastically involved in. 'I learn much better when I work on my own. Besides, I may pick up my peer's errors if I work with him!', was the reply. Obviously, that learner was aware of his preferences in terms of learning style and was reluctant to try a new learning technique. (It should be mentioned, however, that later the same learner was able to enrich his repertoire of learning techniques and to use it with greater flexibility.)

Preferences for a particular learning style presumably depend to a large extent on the learner's educational background and previous classroom learning experiences. So it may be that a learner coming from a translation-dependent background will tend to 'switch off' and continue to use word-for-word translation out of habit and/or 'awareness' that that is the best way to learn. Research done by Reid (1987) and McGroarty (1987) throws some light on the variables which significantly influence learning style preferences.

2.5 Personality type
Naiman *et al.* (1978), Ehrman and Oxford (1989), etc., suggest that there is a close relationship between the learner's personality type and the choice of learning strategies. Self-reliance, self-confidence and perseverance are among the learner personality traits which seem to be most important to the choice and application of SWITCH-OFF. The uninhibited, challenge-loving learner who is not deterred by risk-taking, will not be discouraged by the lack of appropriate learning

opportunities in the classroom. Moreover, he/she will try to provide such opportunities for himself/herself and make his/her learning easier, more effective and more enjoyable.

2.6 Self-image

This factor is of particular relevance to adult learners, as they are normally aware of their own learning abilities in general, and their foreign language aptitude, in particular. A learner who perceives himself/herself as 'hopeless at learning languages' will naturally be reluctant to take any risks by trying to self-direct his/her own learning. He/she would much rather leave to the teacher the responsibility for decision-making and managing his/her learning.

On the other hand, the learner's self-image is closely related to the social role he/she performs outside the classroom. As adult learners are generally reluctant to give up their well-established social identity, it seems quite plausible that a self-important manager, for example, will be more likely to avoid teacher-dependence and loss of adult status by employing the SWITCH-OFF strategy than a learner who is, say, a 'humble' housewife.

I remember a rather unpleasant, discouraging episode from the beginning of my teaching career: one of my learners, a middle-aged managing director, kept 'switching off' the classroom activities because he thought I was too young and inexperienced to teach him. And I felt both dismayed and annoyed to see him continually consulting textbooks, grammar-books and dictionaries, pushing his way through to a basic level of proficiency in English.

2.7 Motivation and learning goals

Since the Gardner and Lambert (1972) research on attitudes and motivation in second language learning, investigators have repeatedly emphasised the priority of motivation among factors which directly affect the learner's active personal involvement in language learning. Highly motivated learners will take up any learning opportunity offered by the classroom that meets their individual learning 'standards', i.e. ideas, beliefs and expectations, as to what should be learned and how. If, however, they find the teaching methodology inadequate or disappointing, they will tend to 'switch off' and look for better paths to their learning goals.

To illuminate this statement, I would like again to quote an example from my own teaching experience. I was using a text in the target language with the aim of developing my learners' reading skills. The text itself was full of technical terms which, according to my initial plan, were not to be taught, and therefore, not to be learned, either. I had finished the reading-skills activity and had proceeded with another activity, when I realised that some of my learners were not following at all. As they were engineers by profession, they were interested in some of the technical terms I had intentionally neglected and were busy looking up words in their dictionaries. Obviously, they were intrinsically motivated to supplement the teacher-provided input with linguistic knowledge that would serve their long-term aims.

2.8 Teachers' attitude

SWITCH-OFF is not only one of the most frequently employed learner behaviours in the second/foreign language classroom. It is also the behaviour learners are most secretive about. They take all precautions not to be spotted if they decide to deviate from the 'orthodox' teacher-designed route to learning. Teachers' conventional reactions to SWITCH-OFF are disapproval, scorn or annoyance, as they are generally unaware of the fact that SWITCH-OFF can be a constructive learner behaviour. Besides, in spite of recent appeals to promote self-directed, autonomous learning, most FL/SL teachers are still flattered to believe that they are the omnipotent influence in the classroom. Therefore, many learners either avoid using SWITCH-OFF altogether, or apply it less frequently than they would like to, for fear of inviting confusion, embarrassment or even punishment.

2.9 Socio-cultural background

The conventions of the community to which the learners belong will inevitably influence the choice, scope and frequency of application of learning strategies. Research done by Politzer and McGroarty (1985), O'Malley *et al.* (1985), etc., has investigated the relationship between the learners' ethnic origin and the strategies they tend to employ when learning a second/foreign language. Reid (1987) and Houghton *et al.* (1988) have suggested that attitudes to independent, autonomous learning vary substantially from culture to culture. Therefore, it could be claimed that the application of SWITCH-OFF will vary, depending on ethno-cultural and educational conventions.

3 Conclusions

Research on learning strategies has suggested that it is possible to train learners to use better, more effective ways and means of acquiring a second/foreign language by:

(a) teaching them how to evaluate their own learning strategies;

(b) making them aware of the possibility of using a larger, more varied repertoire of learning strategies;
(c) encouraging them to be more flexible with the learning strategies they apply to different learning tasks in different learning situations.

The SWITCH-OFF strategy is undoubtedly among the learner behaviours most frequently employed in the classroom. It has great potential to contribute to successful learning by preventing boredom and providing better learning opportunities which suit the learners' needs, wants, learning styles and goals. However, it would be unreasonable to expect that we could encourage or train our learners to apply it effectively in the same way as we can train them to apply other successful learning strategies. Therefore, it seems that research on the application of SWITCH-OFF would have implications for teacher training, rather than learner training.

First, teachers should try to be more realistic and admit that '. . . unless negative attitudes toward learner self-direction are changed, no amount of training in better strategies will have a sustained effect on learning strategy use' (Wenden, 1987: 12).

Second, teachers should be persuaded that, as a constructive learner behaviour, SWITCH-OFF can be just another item on the learner's repertoire of potentially successful learning strategies.

Third, teachers should try to believe that SWITCH-OFF can be yet another sincere attempt the learner makes to self-direct his/her learning and by doing so he/she means no offence to the teacher's professional abilities.

Once teachers have adopted a more tolerant attitude to their learners' strategies in general, and the SWITCH-OFF strategy in particular, they might be able to get more effective feedback on the learners' perceptions of the suitability of the 'imposed' learning opportunities. Then, perhaps, through a joint effort, teachers and learners will be able to eliminate the atmosphere of insincerity in the classroom, most aptly expressed by Rivers (1983: 12):

> . . . pride in status and superior knowledge on the one hand, and on the other, defensive attempts to please, to succeed by doing and giving what the authority figure wants, to hide one's weaknesses and one's real feelings.

12 Learners' awareness of their learning

Nicholaos Chryshochoos

1 Rationales

1.1 Learners and their needs

In this paper I present and compare the findings of two surveys carried out in 1987 and 1988 aiming to identify the needs of 'general' learners of foreign languages. The first was a study of two classes of English pupils learning French. The other was a survey of Greek learners of English.

The starting point for both surveys was the hypothesis that if learners had identifiable needs, then syllabuses might be designed that are sensitive to those needs. In the existing literature, however, doubt is expressed whether the 'general' learner has identifiable needs (Alexander, 1976). Some of these doubts originate from a careful examination of the initial motivation of learners who are taught foreign languages in various settings (Foldberg, 1977; Abbott, 1981; Rogers, 1982); some others relate to target situation analysis (Chambers, 1980) and/or the identifiability and predictability of needs (Robinson, 1980; Brumfit, 1981) while some others are based on the difficulty of identifying any foreseeable or immediate learner purpose for language use, that could, in some way, be taken into account in syllabus design (Lee, 1969; Harding *et al.*, 1980: 9; Byram, 1982). The surveys in this study are based on the assumption that needs *always* exist, since they derive from the learner's exposure to the target language. However, needs cannot be perceived in a vacuum (Brindley, 1984: 33) since they are created from the interaction between individuals and their environment (Rousson, 1975). Therefore, needs identification should always be practised as a catalyst for needs expression.

Learners' awareness of their needs is a prerequisite of the learner-centred classroom. Current practice, however, applies this criterion mainly to Languages for Specific Purposes (LSP) courses, where the learners' professional or academic orientation is likely to increase the possibility of their defining and predicting their own needs (McDonald and Sager, 1975; Richterich and Chancerel, 1978; Richards, 1985: 6), however restrictively the needs of learners are defined in the above sense (Holec, 1980). This is why, for example, the distinction between ESP and General ELT persists, despite the fact that it cannot be substantiated beyond registerial differences of lexis and structure (Candlin, 1978). Mere *existence* of needs is insufficient to sustain the ESP/General ELT distinction. *Awareness* of needs is crucial here (Hutchinson and Waters, 1987: 53). This argument fundamentally contradicts Richterich's view (1984) that the existence of needs automatically implies one's awareness of them. The latter reinforces my argument for the interrelationship between needs and individual awareness of them, indicated in my definition of learner need as: 'the dynamic manifestation of learner awareness of lack of language ability, in contexts which provide the learner with such an awareness' (Chryshochoos, 1988b).

Although, in practice, awareness of needs is given considerable prominence in LSP, what about 'general' learners of languages? The dominant view on this issue is clear and epitomised by Wilkins (1983), who rejects both the value and the feasibility of detailed needs analysis of 'general' learners while recommending the enterprise in the case of LSP students. This lack of exploration in the 'general' learners' world provides the motivation for this paper. It is worth while, then, examining the issue of learner awareness in line with the principles directly derived from the definition of needs, and from this perspective to analyse the role of the context for the fostering of learner awareness. By examining different types of learner awareness, it is possible to check whether, and to what extent, valid information provided by learners might help us to formulate suggestions for syllabus design.

1.2 What is learner awareness?

We must initially decide what we precisely mean, when using the term 'learner awareness'. Brumfit (Paper 2) clearly distinguishes between an explicit knowledge of the target language system and an implicit individual projection towards the language system, as the language is being acquired during the learning process, metalanguage-like. In this work learner awareness refers to the latter as overall – explicit and implicit – knowledge defined in learners' terms, reinforced by some input from previous language use experience. Hence this paper focuses on learners' ability to:

- specify and rank their learning difficulties and difficulties in language use with reference to the four language skills;
- state which factors are important for effective learning; and
- make realistic recommendations to improve the situation.

The above issues are viewed as fundamental for the foundation of a needs rationale, since, as Richterich (1983) claims, needs formulation is based upon the learners' conceptions of language, language use, learning and teaching the language, which, in turn, are compared with and related to what the learners observe, discover, experience and feel at the actual time of learning the language. A needs analysis focusing on the learning process itself can create conditions of heightened learner awareness, reinforcement and assessment (Watzlawick, 1972: 127; quoted in Richterich, 1975) necessary for learners' adjustment to a course of study, their awareness of capabilities and needs, as well as for their suggestions and definition of the learning strategies and content which suit them best (Richterich, 1975; Chryshochoos, 1989). It is worth mentioning some earlier works on 'good language learner' characteristics (Rubin, 1975; Stern, 1975), which also marginally touched upon the issue of learner awareness, in the sense that insights into learner strategies can help learners to take control of their learning. This is positive because the exact identification of the learners' current level of awareness will promote its further increase and development through the teacher's intervention within the parameters that contribute to, or conversely neutralise, the formulation of a certain awareness favourable for foreign language learning. Learner awareness and foreign language learning can be seen as inseparable, because it seems that the latter largely depends on the ability to take charge of one's own learning (Holec, 1980: 3), while it can also be argued that learners' explicit beliefs about learning languages may influence what they actually do to help themselves learn (Wenden, 1986a; Horwitz, 1987).

2 Method

2.1 The target groups of learners
One survey was carried out at Framwellgate Moor Comprehensive School, Durham, involving two different groups of French learners:

- a class of 27 beginners (age group 11–12), and
- a class of 20 intermediate level learners (age group 14–16).

French was the first foreign language for both groups, but the intermediate learners could also choose German. All the learners came from middle-class and lower-middle-class backgrounds.

The survey conducted in Greece involved eleven classes of English learners at the 15th High School of Piraeus, as follows:

– four Form 'A' classes (age group 11–12), totalling 132 beginners;
– three Form 'B' classes (age group 12–14), totalling 90 post-beginners; and
– four Form 'C' classes (age group 14–15), totalling 102 intermediate level learners.

English was a compulsory subject for all the Greek learners, who did not have the option of another foreign language. They all came from working-class or lower-middle-class families.

In this paper, we shall examine data concerning beginners (first year of instruction in the foreign language) and intermediate level learners (third year of instruction).

2.2 The surveys

The basis for comparison of these nationally and socially different groups of learners derives from (a) the common aim of the surveys, i.e. to collect information about learners' needs, and (b) the means of needs identification which were used (similar questionnaires). However, the purpose of each study differed. The pilot study consisted of a single survey by questionnaire, so much of the supplementary information about the learners was based upon their teachers' reports. The Greek survey allowed a more extensive study, involving:

(a) preliminary meetings with officials (advisers and academics);
(b) study of the existing English syllabus;
(c) discussions with language teachers about the syllabus, their problems and suggestions;
(d) survey of the pupils by questionnaire;
(e) classroom observation and evaluation of the teaching tasks and learning activities using the high-inference TALOS observation scheme (Ullmann and Geva, 1984)[1];
(f) discussions with learners, mainly about their progress and motivation.

To ensure that as much information as possible was collected the questionnaires were written in the learners' mother tongue (with one exception discussed below) and structured so as to facilitate the learners' self-expression. The latter is crucial, as I have argued elsewhere (cf. Chryshochoos, in preparation). Sequences of closed questions followed by open questions were avoided, because of the strong influence of the former on the latter in such sequences (Clark, 1979).

Specifically, the questionnaires investigated a wide range of issues regarding learners' abilities and needs (see Appendices 1, 2 and 3). In this paper, we focus on those findings pertinent to the learners' awareness, defined as their ability to specify their needs, lacks, learning difficulties and difficulties in using the language, factors affecting their learning, and their recommendations concerning potential improvements to the classroom situation.

2.3 Learner awareness

2.3.1 Awareness of difficulties
The first issue (specification of their difficulties) was addressed in order to find out what learners lacked and also to give some indication of their current stage of language proficiency. All learners stated whether in the past they had made some use of the foreign language outside the classroom. All the Greek learners were questioned about what they were able to do with the foreign language, but this question was not put to the English beginners, simply because we knew their answers would be uninformative. The Greek beginners were a different case because only *some* of them were absolute beginners.[2] Many of them had been attending English courses for several years at private schools and part of the aim of the survey was to identify constraints on the learners' development due to mismatches between the learners' current competence and the target competence which the existing syllabus aimed to achieve, independently of other considerations such as the learners' current proficiency in the foreign language. There was also a provision to check the language ability of the English intermediate level learners, by initially giving them a questionnaire in French, and, immediately afterwards, the same questionnaire in English. Our intention here was to test the validity of their answers concerning their ability in language use.

All the learners were asked (a) to rank their difficulties with reference to the four skills, and (b) to specify them if possible. This approach is based on those used in earlier studies of non-general learners, reported, for example, by Brindley (1984) for immigrants in Australia, Faern and Shillaw (1986) for science students in Hong Kong, and Tarantino (1988) for ESP students in Italy. All such studies have, justifiably, as their concrete target the exploitation of the findings for teaching and learning purposes. However, they do not give any clear indication of the degree of the learners' awareness or where to ascribe their awareness of difficulties or why. This is extremely important because an understanding of the sources of learner awareness can guide our attempts to increase awareness. Since the purpose of accessing awareness is pedagogic, exploiting any potential for teacher intervention to influence it must be a prime concern. One step in this direction is teacher action accounting for information provided by learners in principle, accompanied by a study of the context within which learner awareness is formulated in practice.

2.3.2 Awareness of effective language learning

The second issue under examination concerned the factors that the learners considered the most important and favourable for effective language learning. The learners were given four options they could mention and rank. They could also express their own opinion if it was not included among the following four options:

- the language teacher;
- frequent contact in their own environment with people speaking the target foreign language;
- extensive use of the foreign language in the classroom;
- the natural linguistic environment where the foreign language is spoken.

2.3.3 Recommendations to improve the situation

The third issue was meant to indicate if learners had some idea of effective language teaching and learning. They were invited to suggest what was missing from the language sessions. As the question was open, learners' answers covered a wide range of recommendations on how to improve the classroom situation.

3 The findings

3.1 Learners' awareness of their difficulties in language use

The learners had four options and the following results represent all their mentioned options proportionally (Table 1). The percentages refer to the total number of the subjects questioned. The relative increase indicates the changes observed from beginners to intermediate level learners.

The more advanced learners (English and Greek) were found to use the foreign language more frequently outside the classroom than the beginners, according to other data not reported here. The significance

154   *Nicholaos Chryshochoos*

TABLE 1   Learners' difficulties in foreign language use

	GB	GIL	% Change	EB	EIL	% Change
(a) Specified their difficulties	29	67	(38)	66	100	(34)
(b) Ranked their difficulties with FL use	65	90	(25)	100	100	(0)
(c) Ranked by skill						
Listening	36	52	(45)	56	75	(34)
Speaking	27	52	(90)	26	70	(169)
Reading	19	23	(13)	82	60	(−37)
Writing	19	20	(7)	74	85	(15)

GB = Greek beginners   GIL = Greek intermediates
EB = English beginners   EIL = English intermediates

of the above findings as related to learners of their first foreign language, is, therefore, as follows:

– learners' awareness of their difficulties in language use is proportional to their competence and frequency of language use;
– the more learners' competence in the foreign language develops, the more aware they become of their difficulties in oral communication and the more they can specify these difficulties.

Despite the fact that the Greek learners used the foreign language more frequently, it was the English who ranked and specified (apart from one-third of the beginners) their difficulties more readily than the Greeks. This makes us very sceptical as far as the Greek learners' awareness of their language ability is concerned. It is widely acknowledged in the Greek state school system that the existing teaching mistakenly aims to develop some language skills which the vast majority of the learners have already acquired. This has certain consequences for the learners' perception of the target language system used in the teaching context, as opposed to the target language used for communication in the outside world. The learners have false illusions about their competence, and in some cases this leads them to claim that they can do things with the language well beyond their current competence. This is a case where teaching conditions do not help learners to develop their awareness of difficulties.

3.2 Awareness of effective language learning

The learners were asked to mention which factors in their opinion could affect their learning drastically and enable them to overcome their difficulties. The findings are given in Table 2.

The learners' awareness of effective language learning is proportional to their existing language ability and is manifested by the relative emphasis they lay on two learning factors:

- *The linguistic environment.* The higher their ability, the more important they consider the authentic linguistic environment to be for developing proficiency.
- *The role of the language teacher.* The higher the learners' language ability, the less they consider their development depends on their language teacher.

A closer look at these findings reveals the following: the English learners believe that the most effective way to learn a foreign language is to live in the country where the foreign language is spoken. We can observe a slight weakening of this belief from the English beginners to the more advanced learners. This can possibly be explained with reference to other responses not reported here, such as the development of a slight negative attitude towards French accompanied and perhaps caused by their belief that English is a *lingua franca* and should be learnt

TABLE 2   Factors affecting foreign language learning

	Greek			English		
(All answered)	BEG.	INT.	(% Change)	BEG.	INT.	(% Change)
(a) Ask the language teacher when problems arise	64	53	(–24)	33	35	(6)
(b) Have frequent contact with people who speak the FL	54	64	(16)	37	55	(49)
(c) Live in a country where the FL is spoken	37	55	(44)	67	60	(–12)
(d) Speak the FL exclusively in the classroom	34	48	(37)	26	40	(54)

by all, or by their experience of meeting French people talking back in English.

The Greek learners see themselves as more dependent on their teachers than the English learners do. The degree of this perceived dependency falls remarkably as we move from the Greek beginners to the more advanced learners. At the same time all the other factors ((b), (c) and (d)) related to the natural linguistic environment or promoting oral communication become more important as the learners' competence in the foreign language develops.

3.3 Recommendations from learners

The learners were asked to suggest what they thought could improve the foreign language sessions. The findings are given in Table 3 for the English learners.

Both groups of English learners of French (beginners and intermediate level) emphasise personal interaction through their involvement in language activities. Beginners prefer games while the more advanced learners prefer role-play and a high proportion of them would prefer to communicate with French people in the classroom. Furthermore, the latter specify a different type of involvement at the decision-making level: they want to decide what to do and learn as well as how to work.

The intermediate level learners' suggestions also correspond to their expressed difficulties and needs with reference to the four language skills, which were ranked as follows: oral communication (speaking and

TABLE 3   The English learners' suggestions

All answered			
Beginners	(%)	Intermediates	(%)
More games in French	59	French visitors in class	45
French people in class	22	Films, videos, slides	40
More writing	19	French magazines	25
More films	15	Role-plays	20
Changes in the sessions		Exchange/visits to France	15
(shorter sessions,			
learn different things		Learners to decide	
each time, not go over		– what to do/learn	
things too much)	15	– how to work	15
More talking in French	11	Information about France	10

listening), reading, writing. This is not the case with the beginners, who ranked their reading and writing difficulties first.

The Greek learners' suggestions are given in Table 4.

TABLE 4   The Greek learners' suggestions

	Greek beginners	Greek intermediates	
	(71% answered)	(98%)	(% Change)
Equipment (videos, slides, films) and different teaching materials	27	69	(84)
Different classroom organisation	6	8	(0)
To keep quiet	15	0	(0)
External changes to occur (different teacher)	8	10	(–10)
Different lesson procedures	20	46	(68)
Additional topics of interest	0	15	(0)

Comparing the Greek beginners with the more advanced Greek learners, we observe the following: the more competent the learners are, the more they want changes in the teaching materials and lesson procedures. Comparing the Greeks with the English learners, we should mention this similarity following the increase of learner competence. We should also not lose sight of a major difference: the Greek learners did not mention English visitors in class or exchanges with England. At the same time the urgency for equipment and teaching materials is underlined more by the Greek learners than by the English. Moreover, the Greeks' suggestions do not correspond directly to their expressed priorities as regards the language skills they wanted to develop.

4 Discussion

In this comparative study of Greek and English school-age pupils we shall not discuss which are the best foreign language learners. This is something to be tested in practice and is not easily settled by argument. However, their expressed beliefs support those of us who argue that there must be certain criteria according to which a truly learner-centred classroom can be established. First, the insights we gain from information provided by learners into their needs are valuable. Porcher (1983), referring to needs in a broader sense, characterises as such all the information, of whatever kind and whatever source, that is relevant to setting-up a learner-centred teaching process.

Second, this information must be confirmed, and this is why the issue of learner awareness should be examined. In every respect, however, we cannot ignore learners' beliefs mainly because this would undermine their motivation (Horwitz, 1987). Third, this information must be compared with our beliefs of the learners at hand. Allwright (1982) rightly argues that language teachers should organise things so that learners can first perceive their needs, and then pursue them. The findings here support the extension of this view in the direction of the teacher's perception of learners' needs. The learners involved in the surveys, especially the English (Chryshochoos, 1988a), view language learning largely in line with current learning theories in which the role of the authentic linguistic environment is emphasised. Consequently, we should examine their suggestions from a new perspective that necessitates a revision of our initial position as practitioners. If institutional limitations do not allow French people in class or do not provide up-to-date equipment appropriate for foreign language teaching and learning, then why do we characterise such constraints as 'learner illusions'? Furthermore, the information provided by learners and then compared to teacher plans creates a necessary condition for initiating and signalling negotiation procedures.

Finally, the consequences for our teaching of the development of learner awareness should be examined. Our responsibilities arising from our action specify certain contexts within which learner awareness arises. Some of the differences emerging from this study of Greek and English learners could be ascribed to the social framework in which they live. All different types of learner awareness in which our target groups differ from each other derive from the learners' position in different environments, each with its own characteristics.

To sum up, there seems to be a correlation among learner competence, language use and learner awareness. Learners' competence and frequency in language use define the degree of their awareness as regards their abilities to (a) specify their learning difficulties and difficulties in language use, (b) understand what helps them with their own learning, and (c) make their suggestions accordingly, in agreement with the learners' priorities.

All the above concern each individual's development. However, this is not the case when comparing individuals with different backgrounds and this should be considered by language teachers who largely influence the formulation of the teaching/learning context. Although the teacher role is important, the relative dependence of the foreign language learners on their teachers can be ascribed to cultural and/or educational differences.

A finding related to different degrees of learner awareness due to individual conceptualisation in given social and educational contexts is that frequent language use does not seem to facilitate the specification of difficulties in the foreign language when it is not accompanied by an awareness of how a foreign language is best acquired. In this respect, the findings pose a strong challenge to the widely accepted view of Campbell *et al.* (1985) that the reliability of information concerning self-assessment reports is related to the degree of exposure and proficiency in the foreign language. This is why the Greek learners, who for various reasons used the foreign language more frequently than their English counterparts, do not believe to the same extent as the latter that effective language learning requires a natural linguistic environment. However, this belief develops during the learning process, as can be seen from their recommendations for improving the situation.

Furthermore, the whole issue of learner awareness raises many questions which cannot be answered merely from a linguistic point of view, given that individual awareness derives from individual interaction with one's social environment. This interaction provides individuals with the idea of what is feasible and what is not. For example, as exchange visits between Greek and foreign pupils never occur, we should not expect them to include such exchanges in their recommendations. Alternatively, if such exchanges were actually mentioned, this awareness should be ascribed to input from social experience, as in the case of the resource for teaching and learning purposes mentioned in their recommendations. Moreover, when the Greek learners state that living in England is not the most effective way to learn English we should examine whether they are in the position to contemplate the possibility of doing so.

Notes

1. The high-inference Target Language Observation Scheme (TALOS) is an observation instrument to measure Teacher–Learner–Programme variables related to the second language learning and teaching process in classroom observation, and aims to discover the characteristics of, and interrelationships between, process and product variables, in order to assess the effectiveness of the programme (Ullmann and Geva, 1984). The variables examined in this study with the help of TALOS were:

   – use of L1, use of L2, teacher talk time, task orientation, personalised questions and comments, enthusiasm (of the teacher);
   – use of L1 on task, student talk time on task, initiate problem-solving, attention, participation, personalised questions and comments, positive affect (of the learner);
   – linguistic appropriateness, content appropriateness, integration with general curriculum (of the programme).

2. The proportion of the Greek learners who were also enrolled in private foreign language schools was extremely high (82 per cent), given the financial status of their families. This fact underlines the will of people to face current demands and learn English at any expense.

Appendix 1: Questionnaire A to the English pupils

Name:
Age:
Sex:
Class:

1. Have you ever used French? When and where?

2. Did you have any difficulties when you used French in the past? Please list some of these difficulties.

3. Do you want to use French now? (NOT in the classroom.) For what reason?

4. Do you want to use French in the future? For what reason?

5. What is more important for you to do with French? To speak, to listen, to write or to read? (For more than one choice, please number your priorities.)

6. What are the most important things you would like to discuss with a foreigner who speaks French? (Please number your priorities.)

Appendix 2: Questionnaire B to the English pupils

Name:
Age:
Sex:
Class:

1. Do you think you have more difficulties in (NOT in the classroom –
    please number priorities)
    – understanding when people speak in French?
    – speaking French?
    – writing in French?
    – reading in French?
    – all?

    ⟶ only in: . . .
    ⟶ specify some of the difficulties: . . .

2. How do you think you can overcome your difficulties in French?
    – by speaking only in French in class
    – by having frequent contact with French people
    – by asking my teacher
    – by living in France

    ⟶ other: . . .

3. What do you wish to read in French? (NOT in the classroom.)
    – magazines   – newspapers   – stories
    – novels   – information brochures
    – anything   – only my school French textbook

4. What do you wish to write in French?
    – stories   – letters   – fill in forms
    – poems   – take notes   – send messages

5. How could French lessons at school be more interesting, in your
    opinion?

Appendix 3: Questionnaire to the Greek pupils

Name:
Age:
Sex:
Class:

1. (a) If you use the English you learn at school, what is the reason you
        use it for, and why do you think English is useful for you?
    (b) How often do you use it?

2. (a) Do you want to learn English because you have a specific reason,
        or future target to do so? In what sense can English be useful
        for you?
    (b) Can you specify your reason/target?

3. Did you use English in the past? Was it when
    (a) you went abroad to a country where people speak English?
    (b) you met English-speaking people here in Greece?
    (c) you wanted to communicate in English in a different way?

If you never used English in the past, go on to Question 5

4. (a) How often did you use English?
    (b) What was more difficult for you?
         (i)   to understand what you were told
         (ii) to say what you really wanted to
               to read
               to write
    (c) Can you specify some of the difficulties you had?

5. How do you think you can overcome these difficulties?
    – by speaking English exclusively in the classroom
    – by having frequent contact with English-speaking people
    – by asking my teacher whenever a problem arises
    – by living in a country where people speak English
    – other ways . . .

6. Do you attend English lessons at a private school, too? If yes, which form do you attend at the moment?

7. Do you take private lessons at home? If yes, then what is the reason for this?

8. What is more important for you?
    – to speak and understand when people speak English
    – to write in English
    – to read English

9. Please refer to some of the things you can do in English.
    – to say correctly
    – to understand
    – to read
    – to write

10. What topics would you like to discuss with an English-speaking person (e.g. TV, movies, sports, friendship, issues concerning the two sexes, specific human problems, adventures, trips, etc.)?

11. What would you like to read in English (e.g. magazines, stories, newspapers, novels, commercials and prospectus, only the school book, etc.)?

12. What would you like to write in English (e.g. letters, messages, stories, poems, to fill application forms, etc.)?

13. Is there something you are taught and you do not really need it? What is it?

14. Do you really need something which you are not taught? What is it?

15. In what way, in your opinion, can your English lessons at school become more interesting?

Section Four: Language Awareness at tertiary level

The papers collected in this section deal with the implementation of LA at the tertiary level: work is reported from universities, polytechnics and colleges of higher education in the UK and overseas. The first three (Clark and Ivanič; Hedge and Gosden; Holmes and Ramos) are from the English for Special (including Academic) Purposes field, while Silvester's concern (Paper 16) is exclusively with English-speaking students of modern languages in a British setting. The work that Scholfield describes in Paper 17 involves British and overseas teachers of EFL as well as students of linguistics, and thus has both an 'academic' face and a special purpose face.

In Paper 13, Clark and Ivanič describe the background rationales to a specific illustrative activity for raising awareness of the writing process, an activity that serves as an introduction to and a reference point for their extensive study skills course. Central to their view of Critical Language Awareness (CLA) is Fairclough's (1989) model of language, which, unlike Kingman's, integrates form, process and socio-historic context. Thus, in their view, any text requires to be approached from three perspectives: its form (as a product); the socio-cultural forces that directed the process of that text's coming into existence; and the socio-historic context in which the text was conceived, including the discourse conventions of the culture that the text represents. It also follows that the writing of a text must be sensitive to forces emanating from these three perspectives. They show how students, native as well as non-native speaker–writers of English, can be led to raise relevant questions about writing that they never before had the courage to raise. As the questions are raised, so are the students' levels of awareness about the writing process. Two basic methodological principles arise from their work: the first is that, to be successful, such LA work must be able to make use of fully open feedback channels between students and teacher; and that writing, even for academic purposes as in English for Academic Purpose (EAP), has an indispensable interpersonal dimension. Affective and social forces are at work at the same time as the cognitive ones that usually receive priority in classrooms.

Hedge and Gosden's paper (Paper 14) is in some ways a counter-weight to the article by Clark and Ivanič: the former choose to focus on the *cognitive* strategies deployed in writing and reading for academic purposes. They insist on giving product as much attention as process in their search for ways to identify and evaluate the language-using strategies that such students are equipped with. They also suggest that students are not uniform in their strategy preferences and we should be prepared to encounter learner variation, the first step being that of identifying the three major recurrent types of learner styles. They are, however, in total accord with Clark and Ivanič (C&I) in their desire to raise their students' learner-ego, seeing *task-awareness* as the most obvious means to this end. The course they are developing therefore is one which '. . . is designed to let the students into the secrets of their own learning'. Like Clark and Ivanič they also raise the question of where to start when it comes to confronting the target language and the texts that embody it: at the discourse end (top-down) or at the grammar end (bottom-up)? They see one positive advantage to the sentence grammar approach: it gives the learners confidence in their own abilities and eventually prepares the way to a natural and authentic concern for discourse. As for the question of how to organise work on discourse, Hedge and Gosden (H&G) propose a genre-based approach, referring in particular to Swales' (1981) analysis of introductions to scientific journal articles as comprising four moves: establishing the field; summarising previous research; preparing the reader for present research; introducing the present research. We might add that such applied genre analysis is not limited to ESP contexts: as Swales (1985) has pointed out, there is a huge range of 'real life genres' waiting to be exploited in LA work, such as recipes, testimonials, newscasts, annual reports, sermons, to name but a handful.

Holmes and Ramos' (H&R) work (Paper 15) is, like that of the other two groups, concerned with the identification and subsequent refinement of learners' language using (literacy) strategies; they report the feedback gained from Brazilian students of psychology writing summaries (in their L1) of English texts in psychology. It is instructive to compare the data-collecting techniques used by these three groups (C&I, H&G and H&R): C&I talk about a WORKSHOP in academic writing; H&G used a QUESTIONNAIRE to help learners to identify their learning orientation; H&R have developed a CHECKLIST of reading/summarising/writing strategies culled from the literature on strategies, from teacher observation of the writing process enacted in group work (and in L1, which has certain clear advantages), and from scrutiny of the finished products (the summaries themselves). Of this method, H&R say that it '. . . owes more to ethnomethodology than to cognitive psychology'. Again and again we see how researchers, and then researchers turned teachers, rely more and more on the learner for sources of insight into the processes of language use and learners' control, through LA, of these processes (see Toncheva (Paper 11) and Chryshochoos (Paper 12)). The LA movement is reinforcing earlier trends towards taking the teacher from the centre-stage of the learning process and assigning the teacher a different role.

The checklist of available strategies becomes a reference point for the learner-user to identify, then evaluate, his/her own 'preferred' strategy selections for any given reading/writing task. It is a catalyst for awareness 'building' as H&R term it. They list ten practical uses for the checklist and even claim to be able to *quantify* changes made by individual learners in their deployment of strategies as the course progresses. This is an interesting claim, since quantification is nowadays thought by some to be a *sine qua non* in educational evaluation. Note that, by contrast, H&G go to some trouble to justify NOT offering a quantitative evaluation of their approach: they argue instead that qualitative evaluation can be just as reliable as quantitative in the social sciences.

Silvester, in Paper 16, is also concerned with methodology: in her account of the initial failure of a linguistics component in some earlier modern languages Area Studies courses and their eventual replacement by a more 'humane' Language Awareness component in such degree schemes, she raises the question of what it means to try to 'demystify linguistics' or to call LA a 'linguistics with a human face'. At the seminar the question was raised whether LA : linguistics equals nature study : biology, i.e. is the former a simplified and concreticised version of the latter? So, what was wrong with the old-fashioned teaching of linguistics in colleges and universities that could be put right in LA? Translating this to the wider context of language work in our schools, we could ask what was wrong with the 'grammar grind' that could similarly be put right when teachers come to put LA into practice?

Silvester identifies three shortcomings of the earlier linguistics in early Area Studies courses. The first is the absence of relevance of the former for the latter. This is not surprising when we see that early linguistics was largely microlinguistics, limiting itself to description of the language code at the levels of grammar, phonology and lexis. Since that time linguistics has come of age, now encompassing the study of language in use and in context. Certainly code-based linguistics can have no illuminating relevance to Area Studies, since such courses must involve students in evaluating the cultural, historical, economic and social substratum of the area in focus; it is the very *ideology* of such cultural entities that must be subjected to scrutiny, and knowing what a morpheme or affricate are will not be much help. One feels that what Silvester is really seeking is a wider and more culturally relevant model of language with which to contribute to Area Studies: would perhaps Critical Language Awareness, such as Clark and Ivanič outline in Paper 13, satisfy the requirements? Such a reorientation might solve her other problem of whether and how to teach linguistics metalanguage; this problem is still with us today, and remains a potential problem in LA work. Ability to master linguistics jargon must not be confused with understanding of language use. The third drawback was that students entered higher education with a very wide range of skills in their respective foreign languages: the solution for the new LA course was clear – to make the mother tongue, English, the basis for discussion, then make provision for insights gained here to be transferred to the study of the foreign language.

We feel, however, that the main and overriding cause of dissatisfaction with the 'old' linguistics was the methodology whereby it was (and in some places still is) taught. The methodology to which it seems all protagonists of LA subscribe is essentially inductive, introspective, experiential and interactive. We see this tacit assumption being made time and time again. The question that arises is perhaps uncomfortable: could it be that LA is not a new body of knowledge for learners to consume but a new way of mediating old knowledge to users as well as learners of language? So it is not a matter of demystifying linguistics but of making its methodology well and truly learner-focused: this is the lesson Silvester's illuminating case study has to offer.

Scholfield's paper (Paper 17) has much in common with Silvester's despite their differences in focus, his being on computers in LA work and hers on LA in Area Studies. The commonality is that both are concerned with awareness of language 'in its broadest sense': they address the relationships between LA, FL proficiency and the teaching of linguistics. The papers are also similar in that Scholfield sees the main value of computers in language education in the learner-centredness that they promote: he describes a program where the student learns by teaching the computer something, which must be the ultimate in learner-centred learning! He similarly points out that it is not so much the 'rightness' of any particular solution that matters as the language and cognition called upon by learners giving their *reasons* for making the choices and decisions they have made: in this Scholfield strikes a chord with Holmes and Ramos, for whom the awareness of their strategy choice is what should matter to learners and language users. There is also an element of Critical Language Awareness with Special Purpose in Scholfield: he reveals that when postgraduate EFL teachers see some Computer Assisted Language Learning (CALL) programs, they tend to criticise them for their linguistic content: language teachers may be in great awe of the expertise that gets programs into the computer, but these same humble teachers feel confident enough to evaluate the language-analysis as well as pedagogical decisions recorded in such programs. Here then the teachers are also the learners, thus enabling us to demonstrate both claims: LA is learner-centred, LA starts with the teacher.

13 Consciousness-raising about the writing process

Romy Clark and Roz Ivanič

1 Introduction

In our previous work (Clark *et al.*, 1987; Ivanič, 1988) we outlined the view of language which we believe should underlie Critical Language Awareness (CLA) in the classroom. We also discussed the relationship between awareness and action: how critical knowledge about language can contribute to the development of confident and socially responsible language use. Here we want to show how this critical approach to Language Awareness has informed our own classroom practice in helping learners improve their academic writing.

First we shall briefly summarise the view of language which underlies our work and discuss how CLA relates to language use, identifying three principles for CLA. Then we shall describe what we mean by consciousness-raising about the writing process, one setting in which we have introduced it, and the procedure we have evolved. We shall discuss the value of the activity, drawing on student evaluations during one of the courses on which we have used it. Finally we shall discuss how this classroom procedure accords with the three principles of CLA with which we started.

2 Some principles of CLA

It is essential to be explicit about what we mean by 'language' when we talk about 'Language Awareness'. Other contributors to this seminar have taken up this point: Mitchell and Hooper (Paper 3) have shown how different groups of teachers operate with different views of language: heads of English focus on 'socio-linguistic KAL (knowledge about language)', heads of modern languages focus on 'syntactic KAL' and primary school language consultants focus on 'the technicalities of the writing system'. Our view of language is the one proposed by Fairclough (1989), which integrates form, process and socio-historical context in a single model. Figure 1 is a simplified version of the model; for a detailed explanation, see Fairclough (1989).

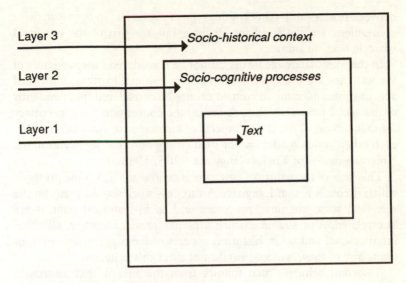

FIGURE 1   A critical view of language

This model of language provides a way of analysing any sample of naturally occurring language. It accounts for both the production and interpretation of spoken and written language. Here we shall explain it in terms of writing. Layer 1, 'text', represents the aspect of language often also termed 'product': the audible or visible 'form' of language, in grammatical 'patterns' at sentence level and beyond. We see 'text' as carrying two interwoven types of meaning: what Halliday (1985) calls 'ideational' (ideas or content), and 'interpersonal' (reader–writer relations). These meanings in the text derive from Layer 2 of the model: the socio-cognitive processes in the writer's head. (For simplicity we are describing this from the point of view of the writer only. From the point of view of the whole discourse the meanings in the text are also dependent on the readers' processes of interpretation.)

Layer 2 of the model represents what people do with language: the way they use its resources to convey particular meanings to particular readers in particular social contexts. 'Socio-cognitive processes' are the reader–writer relationships (socio-) and the thoughts (cognitive) which are encoded in text.

Layer 3, 'socio-historical context', represents the way in which discourse conventions for particular types of writing are shaped by dominant views of the nature of knowledge and the assumed relations between readers and writers of this type of discourse. In our view, these conventions are not fixed for all time, but are part of the continual struggle over meaning.

In this view, language forms cannot be considered independently of the way they are used to communicate in context. Further, individual acts of communication in context cannot be considered independently of the social forces which have set up the conventions of appropriacy for that context. That is why aspects of language are embedded within each other in this model (rather than strung out in sequence as in the Kingman model of English language (DES, 1988a)).

This view of the nature of language is central to CLA. One principle which it entails is that Language Awareness work should focus on the way text, socio-cognitive processes and socio-historical context are interrelated. A programme which presents formal, cognitive, affective, interpersonal and socio-historical aspects of language in isolation, or omits any of these aspects, would not meet this criterion.

A second principle that follows from the first is that awareness should emerge from the production and interpretation of real language; contrived examples could not possibly provide insights into Layers 2 and 3. For example, learners can only hold the conventions of academic discourse up for inspection when they are struggling to use them to express their own meanings.

As well as a model of language, those of us concerned with Language Awareness need a view about language learning; that is, a view about the relationship between KAL and developing language capabilities. The Kingman Report (DES, 1988a) takes it more or less for granted that explicit knowledge about language can help learners speak and write more accurately and appropriately. We are very dubious as to whether it is an acceptable or even a viable aim to help learners use language more accurately and appropriately without examining critically the origins of the conventions for accuracy and appropriacy. We suggest as our third principle that CLA should help learners to become confident and socially responsible language users, and to empower those who do not usually have the power to offer alternative conventions.

We shall summarise what we mean by this here; for a more detailed discussion see Ivanič (1988). CLA can help to develop confident language use by focusing on the learner's own language, his or her experience of how it is valued and the attempts to express ideas, making him/her conscious of his/her identity as a speaker and writer. S/he should develop self-awareness as a member of one or more particular discourse communities, of any conflict which this causes when s/he attempts to operate in other discourse communities, and potential ways of resolving that conflict. Language Awareness should above all help the learner to recognise that s/he is an active part of language – it is not a system which exists without him/her. CLA can also help to develop socially responsible language use. This means, first, making learners aware of how their discourse affects their interlocutors; writers need to learn how to anticipate readers' reactions and expectations. Second, they have to be aware of how their discourse affects the people they write about. Language labels and evaluates: language learners need to become aware of the effects of these labels and evaluations on the people they are describing, and take conscious responsibility for the language choices they make.

In our view, CLA would be an extremely pessimistic enterprise if it were not integrated with purposeful language use. For example, if CLA leads learners to realise that some of the most deeply rooted conventions of academic writing result from an objective view of knowledge which they do not share (see Martin, 1989: 26f), they may give up in despair. However, if they have the opportunity in parallel to explore ways of expressing a subjective approach to knowledge, the result may be positive not only for the writers themselves but also in helping to shape the conventions for future generations.

The practical example of CLA which we are going to describe arose initially out of a different strand in our work. We shall first describe the genesis of the procedure and later discuss how it seems to accord with these principles of CLA.

3 Awareness of the writing process

While working on these principles for CLA, we were members of the Teaching of Writing Group at Lancaster University. In 1987 the group decided to develop its own model of the writing process. We did not want to accept uncritically the models currently available (such as Flower and Hayes' model, 1980). We felt that there are more components to the process than such models represent, and we felt intuitively that the process itself is more varied and complicated than any diagram we had seen in the literature. We devised a procedure for raising our own consciousness as teachers. One member of the group prepared some cards on which were written such things as 'planning' and 'considering the reader'. We then discussed these as a group and attempted to build up a model with them on a large sheet of paper, adding arrows to show relationships when necessary. We used blank cards to add other aspects of the writing process which we thought of as we proceeded.

The resulting model is not of particular importance. What matters is that the discussion around it was extremely rich and illuminating for all participants. We had shared personal anxieties about writing, each discovering that s/he is not the only one to prevaricate and feel inadequate as a writer. We had realised that there is no one simple solution to how to write: different people do it in different ways in different circumstances. We discovered that it is not wrong to go backwards and forwards from one bit of text to another, or to start planning all over again when you are half-way through a draft: the writing process is of its nature recursive. We were theoretically aware of most of these points from reading the literature on the writing process (e.g. Beach and Bridewell, 1984; Rose, 1985), but discussing them in relation to our own experience brought them into full focus.

One member of the group (Anne Marshall-Lee) suggested that this consciousness-raising activity would be valuable for students too. Since then Joan Allwright and others have experimented over a period of two years with consciousness-raising about the writing process with different groups of learners. We saw this activity as an opportunity to put into practice the CLA principles we outlined above. It provides a starting-point for making our view of language available to learners who could use it to improve their writing. In order to do so, however, it needed to be integrated into a course in which they were writing for real purposes. In the next section we shall describe one setting where we have attempted to meet this criterion.

4 Subject-specific study skills provision

In-sessional study-skills support for overseas students at Lancaster is provided on a university-wide basis. There are general classes with such titles as 'Academic Writing' and students from a variety of departments enrol in them together. This is unsatisfactory for at least two reasons, well known to study skills teachers. The extra work, especially for writing, places an extra burden on students already pressed by their course requirements. The general advice seems only indirectly relevant to the particular demands of different departments.

One solution we are currently attempting is also to provide some classes tailored to the needs of particular groups of students. We offer workshops and tutorials in which the students can work on assignments set by their department, so there is no extra language homework. The tutor can offer support which is specifically geared to the demands of the course and the discourse conventions of the particular discipline. 'English Study Skills' becomes an integral part of the course, valued by the subject staff and validated by appearing on their course timetable, instead of being an optional extra. Of course, this way of working depends on there being a viable number of overseas students on the same course, and on cooperation from subject departments. In particular they need to be convinced that collaborative writing workshops in which the tutor and students all work together on assessable work do not amount to 'cheating'. We once attempted to avoid allegations of 'collaborative plagiarism' by devising a special unassessed practice assignment for the study-skills course. However, students did not tackle this with the same seriousness as the others, and one did not even attempt to finish.

A big disadvantage of this type of provision is that the only students who can benefit are those in participating departments. However, it does mean that some students in some departments at Lancaster University are getting appropriate provision, and among these are the Diploma and MA students in the Department of Politics. In the first year this provision was only available to overseas students; this year the department did not want to deprive anyone of a good thing, and the study skills support was offered optionally to all postgraduates in politics, whatever their language background.

We introduce the consciousness-raising activity about the writing process in the first session of the course to make good use of the time before any assignments have been set. However, it is far more than a mere introductory exercise. It sets an agenda and acts as a core for the rest of the course, providing a reference point for work on later assignments. We shall explain how the course is structured to integrate awareness of the writing process with collaborative writing workshops and explicit, critical awareness of linguistic resources and conventions after we have described the activity itself.

5 The consciousness-raising activity

As a result of the work of the Teaching of Writing Group we have chosen seventeen components of the writing process for the students to discuss.

5.1 Components of each act of writing
− Accumulating knowledge, opinions and feelings.
− Establishing goals and purposes.
− Analysing the 'assignment'.

- Planning.
- Drawing on familiarity with types of writing.
- Considering constraints of time and space.
- Making the neat copy.
- Drafting.
- Formulating your own ideas.
- Revising.
- Experiencing panic, pain and anguish.
- Clarifying your commitment to your ideas.
- Establishing your identity as a writer.
- Considering the reader.
- Experiencing pleasure and satisfaction.
- Deciding how to take responsibility: whether to mask or declare your own position.
- Putting your knowledge of the language to use and developing this knowledge.

Some of these, for example 'Establishing goals and purposes', are well-attested components of the writing process. Others, for example 'Clarifying your commitment to your ideas', reflect our own view of the importance of the interpersonal aspects of language use. In general, we have tried to add affective and social aspects of the writing process to the more familiar cognitive aspects. We do not want to suggest that this is a definitive list: just that these seventeen components seem to stimulate wide-ranging discussion about the writing process. If anything, we would like to reduce the list as in some circumstances it is difficult to find time to discuss each component fully. At present, however, we feel that dropping any component would remove access to an important area of discussion. We write each component on a separate card. The cards are written by hand and we encourage students to reword or add to them if they find a different formulation gives a better expression of what they have been talking about. Anything else the students think of can be added on blank cards.

We make up several sets of seventeen cards. This is how we use them in class:

(i)   We divide the class into small groups, so that the participants have greater opportunities to talk.
(ii) We provide each group with a set of seventeen cards.
(iii) The students discuss each card in turn in terms of what they think the card means and any comments they might have based on their own experience; the tutor only intervenes to guide

students towards the meaning when they cannot work it out for themselves or have grossly misinterpreted it.

(iv) We provide a large sheet of paper (A1 size), some blutack and a pen to each group. The students use the cards to make a representation of the writing process as they see it – this involves a lot of negotiation between different viewpoints. Students are encouraged to rewrite and add cards. They can also leave cards out, as long as they can justify discarding them. All the groups we have worked with so far began by trying to build a linear model but soon found that it was impossible to agree on the order of the elements. In our experience those most reluctant to abandon a linear model are practising teachers! At this point the tutor would intervene and pick up two closely related cards (for example 'planning' and 'considering the reader') and ask the students if they see any connection between them. This is usually enough to get the students looking for connections and ways of showing those connections. After sufficient discussion, the tutor encourages the students to stick the cards down on the paper with blutack and draw in arrows where necessary.

(v) The groups compare representations and discuss the reasons for their decisions.

(vi) The whole class compare their representations with the one we produced (in the Teaching of Writing Group) and discuss the similarities and differences. Where connections between elements in our representation are not clear to the students we explain and give examples. The value of this has been that it legitimates the non-linear, untidy models, and loops and arrows the students have produced by showing that so-called authorities on the subject – teachers and researchers – recognise that this is the nature of the writing process. It also gives us the chance to discuss relationships we think are important which may not have been included in models produced by this class. In the future we may also show the best of previous students' models at this stage (for example, the one reproduced in Figure 2).

(vii) The whole class discuss what they have learnt from the exercise and what implications they see for their own writing.

Most classes spend at least two hours on the whole task – some have spent much more than that. No two models are ever the same and the content of the small group and class discussions varies enormously. An important focus of discussion is the difference between conscious and subconscious activities – often different interpretations of the same

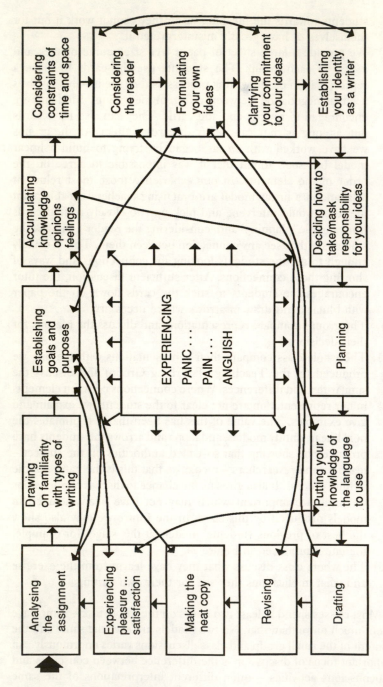

FIGURE 2   A model of the writing process produced by students

prompt card. For example, there is the conscious activity of writing a provisional plan, and also the subconscious activity of, say, planning how to weigh two ideas in relation to each other. We encourage discussion of this sort and suggest that the students use the blank cards to represent such distinctions. In order to give a flavour of the outcome of this activity, Figure 2 shows a model of the writing process produced by a group of students recently.

This activity is the introduction to two terms' work (two hours per week) in which students will be discussing their own assignments with the tutor and each other. As a result of this collective consciousness-raising about the writing process they have a shared reference point and a minimal metalanguage in common for talking about their work in progress. Figure 3 (see page 178) shows how the course is structured to integrate awareness of the writing process with collaborative writing workshops and explicit, critical awareness of linguistic resources and conventions.

In Figure 3, arrow 1 represents the way in which the consciousness-raising activity helps students feel less anxious about writing and embark more confidently on writing tasks. Arrow 2 shows how problems which arise in students' own writing feed back into the on-going discussion of the nature of the writing process. Arrow 3 shows how generalising about what you are trying to do in writing leads to talking about the linguistic resources and conventions available for achieving these ends. Arrow 4 shows how students can feed the explicit discussion of linguistic resources back into their own writing. In the next section we shall outline our reasons for concentrating on consciousness-raising about the writing process, both as an activity in its own right and as the core component in the whole course.

6 The value of consciousness-raising about the writing process

At first sight the consciousness-raising procedure we have described will seem very different from other activities which have been presented at this seminar under the label of Language Awareness. For example, the activities presented by Tinkel (Paper 7) and Wright (Paper 5) have very different aims and content from ours. Here we shall outline what we see as the advantages of our approach to Language Awareness, including some comments by the students who took the course in 1988–9.

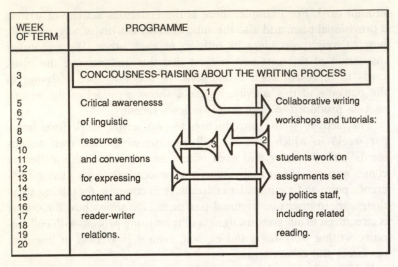

FIGURE 3   Consciousness-raising about the writing process in study skills course structure

6.1 It relieves anxieties about writing

This activity helps people to overcome fears and worries and to realise that everyone finds writing difficult: they are not alone: 'I had no idea writing was so complex – no wonder I find it difficult' and 'It's difficult for everyone, not just for me'.

6.2 It dispels misconceptions

The writing process is something most students have never thought about before. It is often mystified, misrepresented or ignored. Those students who have learnt anything about it have probably done so by trial and error and may well have picked up some inhibiting 'rules', such as having to write the introduction first. Most learners take it for granted that a good writer can produce perfect text straight from the pen.

The consciousness-raising process helps to disabuse them of these misconceptions. They discover that pre-writing, drafting and revising cannot be separated from each other into neat stages. They realise that writing is not a mere medium for expressing perfectly formed ideas, but is actually part of the thinking process. 'I'm glad I don't have to be linear because I can't do it!'

6.3 It puts important aspects of writing on the agenda

Students discover that there's more to writing than they had assumed. If they have been taught anything at all, it is usually the conscious processes, such as 'make a plan'. What they discover from this activity is the subconscious processes which are often responsible for tying writers up in knots and making them feel 'stuck'. 'I'd never thought about the effect of language choices on the reader before; I'd no idea it was so important.'

In particular students pick up on the interpersonal aspects of writing. When they start discussing such things as 'Establishing your identity as a writer' and 'Considering the reader' they find out that these are in fact the causes of a lot of their writing difficulties. 'It's really interesting. I'd never really thought about my identity as a writer or my responsibility before but now I will be more aware.'

6.4 It provides a framework for students to reflect on their own experience

As Donmall points out (Paper 8), an important characteristic of Language Awareness is that classroom activities should help to make the implicit explicit: help learners to become consciously aware of aspects of language they already know. This activity helps students to bring out into the open their experience as writers and this helps them to put on the agenda aspects that bother or interest them. From the discussions generalisations can be made, turning personal experience into meta-cognitive awareness.

6.5 It sets in motion a process of unlearning bad practices

Becoming aware of what's involved in writing is the first step towards taking a new approach to their own assignments. This is a slow and often difficult process for many students and they have to try out alternatives, such as leaving the introduction to last, or personalising their writing by using the pronoun 'I', before they feel totally confident that they can 'break the rules' without being penalised in some way.

6.6 It provides a backdrop for all future writing activities

The tutor can always say 'remember when we talked about XXX?' and refer students back to what was said during the initial consciousness-raising; this is often a very swift and efficient way of reminding students of particular aspects of writing which have slipped out of focus momentarily under the pressure to finish an assignment.

It also serves as a useful reference point for the students, helping

them to make sense of their experience later. Here is an extract from
a letter from a student, seven weeks into the course:

> Do you remember our first session that we have drawn the 'elements of
> an assignment writing?'? We had designed a continuous loop of/circle
> of essay/dissertation writing . . . And, this happened to me! At the end
> of my essay, after reading an article, I completely changed my mind
> about the construction of my essay! I found out that I missed some
> very important and interesting arguments!

6.7 It treats language as meaning in context

Our approach focuses on 'languaging' as a process, not language as an
object. By this we mean that instead of starting from language patterns
(e.g. the language of comparing and contrasting) in the abstract, we
focus on the ideas that the writers are struggling to express, the best
ways to express them, the relationship between the writers and their
reader(s), and the social context in which they are writing. In other
words, we focus on Layer 2 of Fairclough's model of language.

6.8 It leads into talking about HOW

As the learners become more aware of what they are trying to do with
language, they can key in to learning about the choices available for
achieving these ends. In terms of Fairclough's model of language,
discussion can move from Layer 2 to Layer 1. Here are some examples
of how awareness of socio-cognitive processes in writing can lead to
awareness of the resources of the language.

Focusing on establishing the identity of the writer helps learners to
become aware of the way they appear through their writing choices:
verb choices which make them sound more or less arrogant; modification which makes statements sound more or less categorical.

If a student is aware that s/he faces a decision about whether to
mask or declare his/her own views, it is an easy step for the teacher
to introduce expressions of degrees of commitment: hedging, modality
and evaluative language. Similarly, if the tutor reads drafts where the
students seem to constantly mask their own views – making it difficult
to see where they stand on a particular issue – the tutor can ask why
the students do this and raise it as an issue for the whole class to
consider.

Workshops make considering the reader become a reality: by acting
as readers for each other – or with the tutor as reader – they begin to
see the importance of such things as discourse markers as signposts
through a text, because when they read something that has no markers
they recognise the difficulties readers have when they have to 'work'

too hard to establish connections between ideas, etc. Similarly, the purpose and content of introductions in academic essays, the need for explicitness and examples become much more meaningful as a result of sharing drafts with the tutor and/or with each other. (Questions such as 'What do you mean exactly?', or 'Can you give me an example, I'm not sure I understand this?' or 'Do you think you have demonstrated that you really understand this point?' are very fruitful.)

When learners are personally committed to conveying the meaning they are discussing, they can make sense of some of the most difficult aspects of English grammar. For example, one student learnt how choices in the tense system affect meaning. He discovered that you can give the wrong impression about historical events if you use the inappropriate forms of the past (in this case giving the impression that an event was still on-going when it in fact had finished by the time a second event happened and therefore setting up a false relationship of causality). This provides an excellent opportunity to spend some time talking about the difference between the past tense meanings – and it is infinitely more meaningful because it grows out of a real attempt to produce meaning which 'went wrong'.

Layer 2 also makes the link to Layer 3. When discussing familiarity with types of writing, students can move on into questioning where particular conventions come from, who has easiest access to them, and how far they identify with them. For example, when first discussing academic conventions in writing, one group asked to look at a 'typical' essay. The essay we examined contained a large number of quotations and no obvious traces of the student writer's identity or position. Many of the students were critical of this 'hiding' behind the appeals to authority, leading to a fruitful discussion of the role of 'evidence' and support for arguments in student writing together with the problems of the status of opinions and criticisms coming from 'just students'.

6.9 It introduces terminology

We are not referring to conventional grammatical terminology such as 'noun' and 'verb', but rather terms such as 'taking responsibility for ideas', 'to mask responsibility', 'signposts for the reader', 'overt markers of connections between ideas'. That is, it generates an intuitive sort of metalanguage for all to draw on – metalanguage which has grown out of experience: a genuine need to 'label'. It is the terminology for what you want to do with language rather than 'the naming of parts' so common in learning about language as an abstract system.

6.10 It is a catalyst for a student-driven syllabus

The introductory activity gives students a way of talking about writing. They are then in a position to say 'We want to know more about XXX', or 'We want to know how to do XXX', or 'We want to know why XXX is like this'. This is a very practical way of putting the students in control of their own learning.

One participant at the Bangor seminar asked what we do if the students only ask 'trivial' questions or do not raise certain important issues at all. First, in our view, students never raise 'trivial' questions. The fact that they raise them means that they have some importance for at least the person who raised them and so need to be dealt with and, if necessary, put into perspective. Second, it seems likely that during fifteen weeks of work on current assignments, everything salient for that particular group of learners is likely to arise. It is questionable whether anything that doesn't arise is really essential to those learners at that stage in their development. Finally, the tutor can always 'get' issues on to the agenda by a bit of prompting and by using the students' drafts as a basis for raising issues. A student-driven syllabus does not mean only issues which are directly raised by students; it can include issues arising from the students' own language practices.

6.11 It helps learners become more self-assured, responsible and critical writers

Nearly all the students (in the end-of-course evaluation forms) commented on the fact that they felt much more confident in their writing as a result of the opportunities to discuss their writing in the ways we have tried to describe. One student – a native speaker of English – said that no one had ever commented on his actual writing before and so he found the course really helpful. Another native speaker said that he had read the essays of other English and American students and that, although they had really interesting ideas, they did not come across very effectively and they would have benefited from our course. We believe this confidence is not just to do with being better at playing the game. First, the students learn not to be demoralised by getting stuck with writing, and instead to view it as a necessary part of thinking through writing. Second, they seem to learn reasons for writing in one way or another and the ability to choose responsibly and critically between alternatives. For example, they will do their best not to mystify the reader by using a passive, or they will know that writing 'I am not sure' may be truthful, but unacceptable to their tutor.

6.12 It can serve as a useful research tool

In the Bangor seminar, it became apparent that classroom activities which are good for consciousness-raising are also good for research – both 'action research' leading to improvements in a particular teaching situation and research which leads to generalisations of wider interest (see also Hedge and Gosden, Paper 14).

There is potentially an interplay between the three aims, as represented in Figure 4.

Once students start talking about their own perceptions of something, a responsive teacher can treat that information as a 'needs analysis' and use it in designing provision for that class (see 6.10). To gather more permanent data, teacher and students can keep careful records of these perceptions by tape-recording the discussions, keeping the students' representations of the writing process, and keeping diaries. They can then analyse these data to make some generalisations about students' perceptions of the writing process for wider dissemination. In this way students are involved in the production of knowledge about writing processes and can also get credit for it. (This principle is being developed in the Research and Practice in Adult Literacy Group at Lancaster University.)

Finally, we need to explain why we use this approach with learners of English as a second language. Some teachers assume that second language learners do not need to learn about the writing process as part of their course, because they will have learnt about it in their first language. In some cases this may be true, but we think there are often good reasons for focusing on the process with second language learners

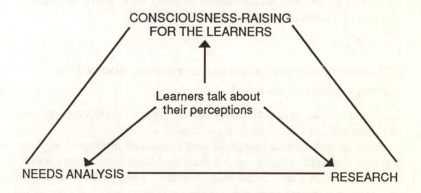

FIGURE 4   Potential aims of consciousness-raising activities

too. Not many school systems in the world teach anything about the writing process; the focus is usually on the product and often in fairly prescriptive terms. Even if they have had some explicit advice about what's involved in writing, many learners find that they have to do more complex writing tasks in English than they ever had to do in their first language. Particularly, many people all over the world who are literate in their first language have to learn English for educational purposes. This is often the very time when it becomes necessary to understand the complexity of the writing process.

Our students' comments have persuaded us that consciousness-raising about the writing process is well worth the time we spend on it. We are hoping that the same sorts of procedures would bring similar benefits to children in secondary and perhaps even primary schools. Work on the National Writing Project (1986, 1987) has shown that children as young as nine years can talk about writing and benefit from it. The activity we have described could help extend such work.

While some of these benefits accrue from the activity in isolation, the full value of it can only come from the interaction of awareness and developing confidence in language use provided by the whole programme. However, we would not want to give the impression that this approach is problem-free. In our experience the biggest problem is when students do not bring actual writing with them to the workshops – or not enough do. This means that the tutor always needs to have something 'up his/her sleeve' just in case. In reality, the tutor can always prepare activities in the light of earlier discussions with students. Another solution we have adopted is to treat the workshops as 'drop in' sessions where students only come if they have writing to work on in some way or if they have things they particularly want to discuss or do, such as brainstorming an essay topic with colleagues or discussing a particular reading text.

7 Conclusion: consciousness-raising about the writing process as CLA

In conclusion, we shall outline how far this procedure puts into practice the principles of CLA which we discussed above.

First, we believe that this procedure stimulates interest in all three layers of the model of language we presented. The introductory activity itself focuses on Layer 2: the socio-cognitive processes of writing. In this respect it differs from many other activities which concentrate on form. It seems to us appropriate to make the processes the starting point. Once the students are involved in the socio-cognitive processes demanded by their own assignments, discussion can move to Layer 1 and Layer 3, as described above.

Second, the way the consciousness-raising activity is integrated into subject-specific study skills provision means that CLA develops around texts the students are actually reading and writing for the urgent purpose of succeeding on their course. Language systems and choices are not discussed in the abstract: they are always related to real texts and their authors' purposes. (On the study skills courses we are describing we include critical study of the texts the students are reading too.)

Third, open discussion of the particular components of the writing process on our list, alongside writing workshops, has the potential to help learners develop confident and socially responsible writing. In particular, focusing on establishing the identity of the writer helps learners to become aware of the way they appear through their writing choices.

Finally, we believe that our students develop a sense of personal worth through critical awareness of the writing process. This awareness helps them to operate creatively in a medium in which they felt they had many obligations but few, if any, rights.

14 Language Awareness and EAP courses

Nicki Hedge and Hugh Gosden

1 Introduction

This paper focuses on the role of Language Awareness (LA) activities in academic writing, reading, and study skills programmes designed for overseas postgraduate students. The LA activities described here exploit both product- and process-oriented approaches to teaching, and they should be seen within the context of an overall programme designed to raise learner consciousness in terms of task, text and purpose. Implicit within this approach is the requirement to estimate and raise the 'learning ego' of students undertaking pre-sessional and concurrent EAP courses.

The paper reports on research in progress and as such should be viewed as an 'interim' report of the procedural issues currently being faced by the tutors/researchers involved with this project. The research is thus, at this stage, exploratory and largely phenomenological in nature, yielding results which aim to provide access to the activities of learners involved in academic reading and writing tasks.

2 Students' initial perceptions

The majority of overseas postgraduate students studying on EAP courses in the UK enter their courses with certain expectations and preconceptions of the 'sort of English' they require. Although students describe rather different previous learning experiences, and these experiences inevitably colour their expectations, most students tend to describe their objectives and hopes in general terms. The 'I just want to improve my English' response by learners is common and appears to highlight both a lack of metalanguage, whereby communication of needs might be facilitated, and the 'learned helplessness' described by Fanselow (1987) that, in this instance, suggests an inability to frame needs in specific terms, according to specific linguistic and communicative requirements. Students already involved in postgraduate research or taught courses are, generally, better able to focus on specific areas of English that they would like to improve. However, even at this stage, comments by students are frequently vague and conceivably do not reflect the student's 'actual' needs. Horwitz (1987) suggests that a systematic assessment of student beliefs might greatly facilitate learning in the ESL class, and, this accepted, it follows that an EAP class might also benefit from such systematic attention to student beliefs and perceptions. This paper reports an attempt to combine systematic pre-course assessment of learners with attention to the learners' evolving needs and beliefs, throughout pre-sessional EAP courses. Such an approach is influenced by, and dependent upon, the notion that consciousness-raising (both in Rutherford's (1987) sense, and the more general sense used by Scott (1986)) will enable learners to assume greater control and understanding of their own learning and that this control will, in turn, both enable, and be aided by, an increased sense of 'Language Awareness'. This awareness will clearly be genre related, task related, and level related but, in addition, it is the basic tenet of this paper that it should be firmly grounded in individual learners' approaches to learning, their expectations of language learning in general, and of their current course in particular, and of either or both their preferred and 'adopted' style of learning and operation in specific tasks for specific purposes.

3 The research programme

The research reported here is being undertaken by staff concerned with the teaching of academic reading, academic writing and study skills in particular, although it should be noted that similar CR activities characterise other components of the EAP courses at Liverpool. Motivation for this research project came from students' writing and what they were telling tutors concerning the difficulties they had writing Academic English, from students' reading and the problems they were having processing texts, and from Study Skills sessions which required them to use and reformulate information from a variety of sources in order to produce a well-written review of literature in their subject area. The staff involved were concerned to exploit both product and process in their courses and this dual orientation was seen to be initially dependent upon the development of instruments which would allow both staff and students to access the learning strategies, the learning approaches, and the pre-existing and evolving learning procedures and habits of individuals. The product emphasis of eventual course design was seen, at this stage, to require both an understanding of student perceptions and previous experience in, for example, L1 academic writing, and an investigation of 'potential evaluator/reader' requirements. Thus, in addition to genre and sub-genre discourse analysis, it was considered necessary to undertake a more qualitative, subjective investigation of reader (in our case, academic supervisor) requirements, judgements scales and standards. This paper will discuss the development of the research programme thus outlined and will focus on investigative methodology and results to date in the fields of academic writing and reading.

4 The starting point: stimulating discussion

In order to examine students' attitudes towards learning and to focus attention on their study patterns and habits, a questionnaire, originally devised by Entwistle and Ramsden (1983), was adapted for use with overseas postgraduates. As suggested by Lewin (1979), critics have deemed questionnaires '... a quick and dirty research instrument: cheap, easy to administer, but providing superficial, invalid, artificial data'. The use of questionnaires was, however, thought to be appropriate within a research project intentionally exploratory in origination.

It is not within the scope of this paper to discuss the lengthy theoretical arguments for and against the use of qualitative data. However, it should be noted that a phenomenographic approach relies upon the notion that learning, and language learning in particular, is open to variations in interpretation, which in turn have a bearing upon our students' performance, aims and objectives. In addition our students will have inherently multifaceted views and beliefs which underpin these interpretative variations (see Rommetveit, 1988); and this particular approach seems to offer a rigorous, systematic and appropriate investigative framework in which to explore these variations. Saljo (1988) suggests that the concrete praxis of phenomenography implied that a limited set of categories, usually between three and five, might account for all the variations in forms of talking about a particular phenomenon. The questionnaire, semi-structured interviews and text exercises in this research do not result in a composite score for any individual; rather it is the aim to suggest 'trends' or a limited set of categories into which individuals might 'fit'. It is this notion of 'fitting' that becomes theoretically difficult to justify if we consider the inevitable criticisms levelled against introspective data of this nature. In addition, the 'fitting' itself is only the first part of the tailoring and is viewed as the starting point for discussion with students, the introduction or clarification of the metalanguage of language learning and learning in general, and the initiation of a programme designed to afford both learners and tutors the opportunity to value and understand the learning process.

Students complete the Study Approaches questionnaire in a time-tabled Study Skills session. Following completion of these question-naires students' responses are blocked into three basic orientations (see Entwistle and Ramsden, 1983) as follows:

(i) *Meaning orientation* – including Deep Approach, Relating Ideas, Use of Evidence, Intrinsic Motivation.

(ii) *Reproducing orientation* – including Surface Approach, Syllabus-Boundness, Fear of Failure, Extrinsic Motivation.

(iii) *Achieving orientation* – including Deep or Surface Approach, Organised Study Methods, Positive Attitudes to Studying, Achievement Motivation.

Depending upon the level of the students, the questions are taken either one by one with explanations and limited discussion during their completion, or students simply request help with certain questions as required. Whichever method is used, the completion of the questions is followed by a group discussion on learning and, in particular, on the problems and perceived constraints of learning in English. Thus the questionnaire forms the introductory component to a study skills course which aims to increase students' self-awareness of studying in English. If we accept Saljo's view that 'access to the *learner's perspective* on the activities of teaching and learning is essential for understanding educational phenomena and for improving education' (Saljo, 1988: 32), then we should also, we believe, couple to that an appreciation of the difficulty of gaining such access. Learners from a variety of cultural and educational backgrounds are, themselves, unfamiliar with the notion that self-awareness may be the crucial first step to improving inefficient, and capitalising on effective, study skills and learning strategies. Indeed, many students who have now completed the study skills programme described here say that this has provided them with their first ever opportunity to think about how they execute certain academic tasks and how the use of certain cognitive strategies when they are using English as the medium of communication may differ from or resemble the enactment of similar tasks in their first language. We shall differentiate between cognitive styles and cognitive strategies and thus view the latter as decision-making regularities that at least in part are a function of the conditions of particular strategies. Discussion with students lends support to the hypothesis that having, for the most part, adopted an effective range of strategies for tasks in their L1, they then tend, at least initially, to adopt quite different strategies for learning in their L2. It is our contention that the L2 strategies used by many overseas students are not consonant with their preferred cognitive strategies. Clearly the use of English for study increases, and alters, the demands made on students, but it appears that in some instances 'perceived' difficulties with language incline students towards the adoption of inappropriate and/or inefficient learning strategies. Messick (1976) has suggested that, as cognitive strategies alter according to different learning conditions, they might be amenable to change through training under varied conditions, and it appears feasible that overseas postgraduates embarking on pre-sessional EAP courses have a perception of their ability to function effectively or not as the case may be when studying in English. This perception will almost always be influenced by the students' 'learning ego' in addition to their 'language learning ego' (see Douglas Brown, 1980), and one of the aims of the questionnaire and ensuing discussion is to examine whether or not students are, in fact, adopting certain cognitive styles in response to actual or 'imagined' linguistic variables. Within the area of 'imagined' variables we would include students' strategies that have been encouraged by previous teaching and learning in addition to their own perceptions. The extract below, taken from the protocol of an Iranian postgraduate (S), illustrates the point. Five of the questionnaire items ask students to consider whether or not they relate ideas when reading. This student's questionnaire responses indicated that he tried to do this but he had written 'I just try to read because sometimes that is enough before trying to relate topics'.

> S: If I read a topic . . . if I read a particular piece of information once and I now read a topic . . . the same topic . . . which is related now . . . the new topic is related but one is general I will start for example I should remember that once start link them together and try to help myself to create an the reason.
> T: So you link topics together when you're reading?
> S: That is the problem . . . I would like to do it this way but because this is not my first language I can not do it so I read it very carefully . . . very slowly . . . and try to concentrate on the thing that I am reading but I can not to relate the other thing . . . the thing from before . . . because it takes a very long . . . very long time to read the one thing so then . . . when I have understood all of it . . . then maybe I can try to relate the thing to get the reason . . . to link the topic.
> T: Tell me what happens in your first language.
> S: Then it's not this problem . . . then I read and I link the topics together but I read not the same . . . not slowly not carefully like in English so I can do it . . . together I mean.

In this extract and the remainder of his protocol he describes an approach to reading that suggests his perception of the task has led him to adopt a surface approach to reading, as part of an orientation to study described by Entwistle and Ramsden (1983) as a Reproducing Orientation. The student's protocols suggest that he would prefer to adopt an approach more in accordance with that of the learner inclined towards a Meaning Orientation, using a deep approach to reading texts, using evidence critically and relating ideas logically. This initial 'talking about learning' stage of the C-R programme has, we suggest, a vital role to play in the more global 'Language Awareness' emphasis of a course designed to equip such students for independent study in English. Until the learner is aware of the approach he/she takes, the perceptions of language and language learning he/she has, and the cognitive strategies he/she uses (be they 'chosen', 'imposed', or largely 'unconscious'), then Study Skills courses designed to improve the student's ability to cope with the linguistic demands of reading and writing in English will not be of optimum long-term benefit.

The student who shows a flexible, effective range of reading strategy utilisation in English classes but who later returns asking for help to read more quickly, bemoaning the impossibility of reading critically, 'confessing' to attempts to read 'word-by-word', and admitting to plagiarising large sections of texts, is all too familiar to many EAP teachers. 'Language Awareness', in this programme, therefore tends to be subsumed under a 'learning awareness' approach which deems the exploration of learners' ideas, beliefs, strategies and preconceptions an essential prerequisite to long-term language improvement. Rubin argues that in order in help students build on what they already know '. . . it is essential for students to be able to assess their own knowledge' (Rubin 1987: 17) and she supports Smith's view that consciousness-raising is '. . . not a time-wasting procedure' (Smith, 1981: 165).

5 After the questionnaire

It is far from adequate, but all too easy, simply to pay lip-service to an exploration of student beliefs concerning their learning by asking them to complete questionnaires and by following this with a discussion of 'results'. If we examine recent debates arising from Kingman (DES, 1988a) and Cox (DES, 1989b) we notice that although both reports have emphasised the importance of learners having knowledge about language, neither report has much to offer in terms of clear guidance to teachers concerning the means whereby this consciousness-raising might come about. Linguistic objectives are, we contend, far easier to specify than the methodological bases which might facilitate the attainment of these objectives. Thus, having initiated student discussion of learning and encouraged, for some students, their first ever 'self-conscious' appraisal of 'how' learning works for them, we then embark upon a programme of academic reading and writing which aims to synthesise form-focused activities with genre-based activities in an approach which attempts to raise both task awareness and learner ego.

Individual and class discussion pertaining to learning, the individual remediation of problems, and the negotiation of specific objectives are seen as important elements of the course. It is interesting to note that students rapidly improve their willingness and ability to talk about their learning and their needs as they realise that they will not be penalised for discussing the fact that perhaps certain 'good practice' techniques and suggestions do not work for them. The extract below exemplifies the shifting of students' comments, from very general to rather more specific reporting after having completed the study questionnaire. The second extract is taken from the same student in a writing session in Week 2, and the third extract was recorded during an academic reading class in Week 3 and does, we believe, show his willingness to challenge what is now being taught and to explain what he thinks he needs.

Pre-questionnaire
It's grammar . . . it's the biggest problem for me to learn . . . in all things.

Post-questionnaire
Grammar in the writing for me it's the biggest problem and . . . in the speaking is a problem . . . yes . . . but not so much . . . it's the writing we must write like this for the academic style . . . so the thing I need it's the grammar especially for writing the long sentences . . . yes and the way how to join these sentences it's hard for me . . . 'however, moreover, on the other hand, therefore' . . . the grammar for this and the words for these things.

Week 2
I think confused now . . . the passive . . . the active . . . in my country we are told to use the passive . . . this writing . . . academic writing . . . but now I have to use them both . . . so it's confused for me . . . to choose . . . I used passive only . . . it's wrong I think now . . . before it was more easy to use the passive . . . only the passive for academic writing.

Week 3
I understand why we look at the introductions but I understand
now . . . so I can understand the '4 Moves' [see Swales, 1981] . . . so I
think it's useful for me . . . for us . . . but I know it now so now I want
to know why sometimes they use it like this and why sometimes they
do not . . . this paper uses it but different . . . it writes . . . they write
Move 4 in the beginning so why do they do this? I think there has to
be a reason . . . I do not know . . . how will I decide if to write 1, 2, 3,
4, or 4, 3, 2, 1? I think is important this so I would like it if we look at
these things.

6 Combining product and process in reading and writing activities

Swales suggests that a 'literature-utilisation' approach to teaching the
English of research papers might activate and develop the formal
schemata required for the genre, and that these schemata will serve
'not so much as rigid templates against which all texts are forced to fit,
but rather as *caricatures* which self-evidently simplify and distort certain
features in an attempt to capture certain identity' (Swales, 1987). He
also maintains that in such an approach it is *early* in a course that
students need to be sensitised to the recurring rhetorical structures
of specific genres. Although not all of the students on the course
described here were from the hard sciences, where introductions seem
most frequently to take a four- or five-part form, the four-move form
suggested by Swales (1981) has been used successfully as an introductory 'caricature' for students. Indeed it seems particularly appropriate
within the approach described to introduce learners to one model of
rhetorical structuring which can be seen to occur in *some* research
papers but not in *all* papers. (For further discussion of the information
structure in introductions, see Crookes (1986), Cooper (1985) and
Swales (1986).) The notion that writers working within the accepted
conventions and 'rules' of the 'academic game' have to make choices
from a limited, but complex, range of rhetorical and lexical possibilities
is an essential idea to convey to students. Although, for example, the
selection of tense and modality is clearly not wide-ranging in itself,
the distribution and patterning of such choices at certain stages of
the discourse is, potentially, an added complication for students. In
an attempt to combine both product- and process-oriented approaches
to EAP, classes in academic reading are based upon the analysis of
academic texts that students themselves, often in consultation with
their research supervisors, select on a specific topic. Essentially there
is a significant degree of 'repetition' between the reading and the

writing classes, and in timetabled study skills sessions the aim is to bring together aspects of these courses in order to arrive at a finished product: a review of literature in the students' subject area. The 'repetition' present in the courses ensures that students are using a shared form of metalanguage to discuss their global learning orientation and cognitive preferences for task execution, in addition to the type of language used to discuss micro-level structural points that arise as they are working. It should be noted that students are not required to use this metalanguage themselves if they do not wish to; teachers working with them, however, endeavour to be consistent in *their* terminology.

The academic writing course focuses on text-level aspects of discourse functions – for example, on knowledge 'about' writing conventions and linguistic realisations – and on sentence-level remediation of mechanical errors in English in an attempt to eradicate learners' fossilised written errors. An important aim of the course is to encourage a greater awareness of the dynamic nature of grammatical choice in academic discourse composition, and it is interesting to note the role that awareness of writer-motivated choices and their consequences appear to play in the development of the learner's self-esteem as a writer. Inevitably students who respond negatively to study questionnaire items and interview questions that give an indication of self-confidence need rather more encouragement, and possibly greater micro-level support, with writing tasks demanding author-motivated choices. Gosden's (1988) work with overseas postgraduate writers suggests that focus on sentence level grammatical elements gives much needed 'moral support' to all students, and not surprisingly we have found this to be an essential element of the course, especially during the early stages. However, in contrast to work on higher order discourse structures, it appears that sentence-level work with immediate feedback improves student writing only during the confines of the classroom (see Gosden (1988) for further discussion).

Attention to overall text organisation, specifically to topic choice and cohesive linking or given/new information, was a major concern for students, and to date learners have viewed LA activities which focused on typical discourse features of the genre as being 'the right sort of language support'. Subjects' own comments confirm Weir's (1988) study that, generally speaking, rhetorical organisation was rightly considered as a criterion for judging the quality of their work, whereas minor grammatical errors were not. Students have, in fact, expressed irritation and confusion when supervisors corrected 'minor' mistakes that were not thought by the students to affect understanding. Typically students tend, at least at the start of their course, to view 're-writing' tasks simply as an opportunity to 'clean-up' their texts by word-based error hunting, although they maintain that attention to higher level discourse features is important. There appears to be an almost fatalistic resignation to lack of control over the finished written product, as if there were 'external' forces at work over which they, as non-native writers of English, had little or no control. Kaplan (1984) has suggested that contrasting cultural thought patterns may play an external role, but it seems likely that the tight conventions of academic writing may supersede these. In order to try and increase learners' self-esteem, it has been necessary to make time to 'listen' to students talking about their writing problems during writing classes and to focus their attention on the role of the writer during reading sessions. Within the traditions and practices of teaching writing, models of written products have played a significant role and the reading course described here does, in some senses, draw upon the use of product models. However, we have tried to steer away from the dangers of over-emphasising the written product, which tends to be the finished version of an 'expert', usually native-speaking, writer and as such allows only a hypothetical discussion of the cognitive processes involved in the arrival at the finished product. In terms of Flower and Hayes' (1981) model, there is a need to pay more attention to the writing task environment; to the 'emerging text'. As a means of achieving this Rutherford (1987) suggests the use of Propositional Clusters – verbs plus associated noun phrases – as a basis for raising the grammatical consciousness of the learner. These semantically related clusters attempt to encourage a synthesis of interacting aspects which focus learner attention on the grammatical process. Our use of these clusters aims to stress:

(i)   the effects of certain topic choices and the idea that this is not a random selection but has an effect on what follows and precedes, and relates to consideration of theme and rheme;

(ii) the consequences of writer selection on language internal choices, e.g. the use of active versus passive voice;

(iii) text cohesion as a natural, rather than a contrived, 'add-on' feature, e.g. the use of discourse markers;

(iv) the recursive, non-linear nature of composition, with its cycles of establishing goals and sub-goals, planning, generating ideas, revising and evaluating.

The writing course currently on trial at Liverpool follows from Davies' (1988) research into the potential of a genre-based syllabus. In an attempt to combine awareness of conventions in academic writing with an investigation into how a text 'emerges' as a result of writer choices, clusters have been used as a means of revising and discussing the order of 'moves' in academic articles, theses and essay introductions, by recognising lexical, grammatical and evaluative signals which can be associated with each move. Clusters are subsequently expanded, both individually and as a collaborative exercise, and finally drafted to produce a coherent and cohesive paragraph.

The following example illustrates the use of clusters, printed for ease of manipulation on separate file cards. This particular set has been used after students have studied their own texts in the reading course and decided whether or not the '4 Moves' (Swales, 1981) are realised in their introductions. The clusters are presented to students, drafted, consequently expanded and/or reformulated and then, as necessary, redrafted.

- write – essays/theses – overseas students – challenging demand
- report – 'overseas students – feeling of inadequacy – organisation of ideas' (Sharwood-Smith, 1981)
- research – few studies – most effective academic writing support
- investigate – this paper – EAP needs – overseas students.

The following is a third draft written by one student for the cluster above:

> For overseas students, the writing of essays and theses is a challenging demand. A report by Smith (1981) suggests that they often have feelings of inadequacy especially about how to organise their ideas efficiently. However, there have been few studies about what is the most effective type of academic writing support. The aim of this paper is to investigate the EAP needs of overseas students.

For the writer, and the teacher/researcher, the most rewarding part of such an exercise is the process and stages therein that the writer follows from first decisions and drafting through to a final version. Students are encouraged to discuss possibilities and alternative selections with teachers and peers and, at sentence level, are thus provided with an opportunity to 'take charge' of their writing. The use of the word-processor in the classroom has facilitated the re-writing of drafts, enabling an easier manipulation of texts and a more 'presentable' final version than handwritten drafting. As a consequence, students to date show a greater willingness to make more radical changes to larger units of text, with an increased attention to discourse features, in addition to the 'cleaning up' of mistakes.

7 The continuing research

At the beginning of this paper we suggested that learners need to focus on their existing and evolving cognitive strategies employed in a variety of writing and reading tasks in English. The use of questionnaires as a stimulus for student–teacher and student–student discussion initiates the consciousness-raising programme, while reading sessions encourage the analysis of both the texts studied in students' disciplines and the processes and strategies which might be applied to the comprehension and information selection of texts. This selection, with emphasis on learner decision-making and individually determined purposes for reading, is 'echoed' and reinforced in a writing course that builds upon the 'model' use of texts from reading classes with the aim of encouraging a greater awareness of the dynamic nature of discourse, of the cognitive processes underlying the writing activity, and of the linguistic realisations that enable students to 'take control' of their writing.

The collection of introspective data, the recording of class and individual discussion in reading and writing classes, and the storing of student writing at all stages of the process, will continue to be analysed within categories currently being developed by the teachers/researchers. Behavioural validity checks on the data, such as those suggested by Grotjahn (1987), will continue as part of the research design itself, but equally importantly, as an essential feature of EAP courses designed to let the students into the 'secrets' of their learning as part of a general aim to foster greater Language Awareness within an overall consciousness-raising approach.

15 Talking about learning: establishing a framework for discussing and changing learning processes

John Holmes and Rosinda Ramos

1 Talking about learning

Recognising and diagnosing one's own learning problems is an important step towards changing and improving one's own learning. However, just as the average patient is unable, without training, to identify the causes of the symptoms that are felt, so the learner cannot spontaneously name the causes of his or her language learning problems. We believe that in order to help learners to assume greater control over their own learning it is important to help them to become aware of and identify the strategies that they already use or could potentially use.

This paper reports part of a study of strategies used by students in completing language learning tasks in an EAP Study Skills course. The aspect covered here aimed at helping students to identify the strategies they used in performing the tasks and helping them to discuss their procedures and those of their colleagues. We shall also examine the consequences of this self-reporting for students' own learning procedures and the teachers' own insights into classroom processes.

We did not set up our research project with the sole aim of helping students to identify and control their own strategies, but this became an essential part of our methodology when we found out how useful and revealing this was to us as teachers and to our students. The wider research project that we refer to in this paper is aimed at investigating the study-summary as an evaluation instrument in EAP reading comprehension with Brazilian postgraduate students of psychology. A description of the evaluation process and an analysis of the strategies used by the students in carrying out study summaries is given in Holmes and Ramos (1990).

In this paper we shall be concerned with describing how our framework for talking about learning was arranged. This took the form of a checklist based on classroom observation and was subsequently refined with student feedback. We shall evaluate the various advantages which this framework brought to both teachers and students and possible ways in which this could be adapted to other contexts.

2 Assumptions

We took several decisions when constructing our framework. We wished to enable students to talk about their own learning as a means to an end and not an end in itself. During our research and in our work as teachers we also made other assumptions:

(a) Learners do not spontaneously analyse their learning strategies in depth. They need explicit help in order to be able to name the strategies they are using and compare them with possible alternatives.

(b) The first step in identifying possible learning strategies must come from observation of learners engaged in and talking about language learning activities. In this way we begin with what learners do in the real world and not what they should do according to theory. While theoretical insights from cognitive psychology and language learning theory should inform the selection of items for the checklist, they should be a corollary to the strategies that learners really use, and not the foundation of the framework.

(c) In observing learners we should focus on language learning tasks that are meaningful to the learners and relevant to their needs. In this way we focused on the way in which students go about preparing study summaries rather than their strategies for completing 'artificial' exercises or tests.

(d) Once these strategies have been identified by the teacher, they can be presented to learners in the form of a checklist and form the basis for discussions on the learning processes used and reflection for any changes deemed necessary by the learner.

In our discussion we shall be focusing on a specific clientele. They are Brazilian students of psychology at the Catholic University of São Paulo, at present in the MA programme in educational psychology or related subjects such as social psychology. The English course aims specifically at helping students to read and do research using sources in English in their area of study. The course lasts for 30 hours spread over 15 weeks and the evaluation is carried out by means of a summary, written in the students' L1, of an article or chapter of a book written in English. The course, given the time available, does not aim at teaching spoken English, and the language of the classroom is the native language, Portuguese. As researchers we enjoyed the advantage of being able to converse with our students in their native language, and all discussion of learning strategies or procedures took place in Portuguese.

3 The problem of self-diagnosis

Our first premise is that learners do not, unaided, analyse their own learning effectively or diagnose their own problems successfully.

In the past the diagnosis of learners' language learning problems was left to the language teacher, in the form of correction of written or spoken production. The classic example is that of the 'correction sheet' often painstakingly crafted to give feedback on the learner's essay. The teacher indicates mistakes such as grammar, punctuation, vocabulary, spelling and so on. The learner is then supposed to reflect on the pattern of errors and take steps accordingly: brush up tenses, use the dictionary more often, simplify the language to be within his or her own capacity for expression, and so on. In real life this type of diagnosis and feedback has a dubious effectiveness, and too often the most important feature of the correction process is always the teacher's grade. After noting the grade the student seldom glances at the essay again.

During the 1980s increasing emphasis was switched to learning strategies and to helping students gain control over the strategies they used. In the area of reading comprehension, which is our present concern, the initial publication of books for teachers on reading strategies was gradually extended to books for students which explicitly mentioned reading or learning strategies and how to use them. There are numerous examples, such as the materials produced by the Brazilian ESP project, as mentioned in Celani *et al.* (1988), or published textbooks such as *Reading on Purpose* (Dubin and Olshtain, 1987). The spirit of this awareness-building is conveyed in Scott's (1986) paper on *'Conscientização'*.

However, in many ways the role of the teacher does not change radically. The strategies and the objectives are presented by the teacher, and the diagnosis of learning problems is made by the teacher, using the teacher's knowledge, training and expertise. To some extent the teacher can also attempt a solution: some kind of 'remedial' activity if a problem is common enough, or an individualised activity for the student to do, by going to a resource centre and tackling relevant material.

We make two criticisms of this type of diagnosis. First, it is made by the teacher and even though students are encouraged to self-diagnose or self-correct, they do not have the background or experience to do so effectively. Second, the language of the diagnosis is that of the teacher and reflects the approach or method in vogue at the time.

In our experience, Brazilian postgraduate students of psychology find difficulty in diagnosing their own problems in reading and understanding English texts and also have limited means of naming and discussing their problems. In Ramos (1988) students in protocols identified their reading comprehension problems chiefly in terms of vocabulary and sometimes grammar. The following quotations are typical:

> What I found most difficult here . . . really my difficulty is vocabulary which bothers me most . . .
> Informant: Lena, p. 49 [Our translation]
>
> It's getting difficult here; the vocabulary! I don't know a thing!
> Informant: Paulo, p. 86 [translation]
>
> It's because I don't know many terms that I stay at a kind of vague level . . . a lot of sections of the text were very vague . . .
> Informant: Mara, p. 49 [translation]

In one particular protocol it was established that although the informant said his main problem was 'vocabulary' he in fact only failed to infer the meaning of three important lexical items in an 800-word article.

Thus we would contend that students need help to analyse and identify their own learning problems. The first step is to set up the checklist of learning strategies which comprises the framework.

4 Identifying the learners' strategies

In setting up a checklist for learners how can we identify the component strategies? We have two approaches: first, to search the literature and note the strategies observed in previous research of a similar nature, or, second, to note what our own students do and say when they work together on a learning task.

The first approach may fit in more closely with course design, in that very often reading comprehension courses are designed around a supposed hierarchy of skills: moving from skimming for general meaning to lexical inference, for example. However, we were concerned that the teacher's classification of strategies might result in omission of strategies which actually were activated. For example – to anticipate our findings – some students use a classroom strategy called 'copying', which does not appear in the literature on cognitive psychology but is something which most teachers have observed in their classes!

Thus we opted for the second approach. Our students work in groups, do a lot of talking as they go about their tasks, and we as teachers had excellent conditions for carrying out classroom observation in fairly authentic situations.

Students were observed while carrying out 'meaningful' tasks and not in 'language exercises'. As Holmes (1989) points out, the feedback from these two types of activity can be different. During any language course, students evolve specific strategies to cope with the demands of teachers and textbooks. Many of these strategies reflect an increased sophistication in language learning, but some are evolved only in order to deal with the immediate demands of the classroom activity or exercise. We can call these 'classroom-coping strategies' as opposed to language learning or reading or summarising strategies in our case.

An excellent example is the case of the 'test-taking strategies' which Nevo (forthcoming) identified in students taking reading comprehension tests. She identified strategies which were specific to the test situation and which in real life would have been useless to help the students comprehend a text more effectively. For example, the strategy of looking at the questions then scanning the text for the right answer is obviously not valid in real life, when texts are not accompanied by questions.

In this case, observing students on such an activity would have resulted in a set of strategies not very close to the real-world needs of students in terms of reading strategies for coping with academic text.

Accordingly we took the decision early on in our research to observe students taking part in completing tasks that were as near to 'real life' as possible. In practice this meant gathering data from students' summarising tasks, where students worked in groups to prepare a summary, in the form they themselves chose (prose, diagrams, notes, etc.) of a text taken from a learned journal or relevant textbook. Thus we hoped that our data from the classroom would be relevant to the real world needs of our students.

5 Gathering data

Our initial framework for discussing strategies was drawn up from three sources of data. First we obtained process data by observing the students working in groups in the classroom on the reading and summary-preparing tasks. Then, after completion of the task, we obtained more process data by analysing the finished product and the intermediate stages such as drafts, underlinings in the original text, etc. For example, in analysing the product we were able to identify cognates which had been recognised in the original text, or if students added information which they previously possessed but was not in the original text. Finally, we analysed the finished product to obtain data on the summary itself: the format, mistakes, the relation between important and less important information and so on.

To us the most interesting and novel type of data came from the observation stage. Since students worked in groups and used their mother tongue, they talked about the task and how to perform it in a way which reflected their own attitudes and experience. Thus we obtained an ethnographic analysis of the stages involved in reading and summarising an academic text.

We should mention in passing why we did not use protocols to obtain data on the students' strategies. Our previous research (Holmes, 1986; Ramos, 1988) gave us important insights into the way students read in English in the area of their specialism. However, we were concerned about the cognitive overload on students who, during a protocol, must read, summarise and think aloud at the same time. In the classroom situation we have students working in groups, with the opportunity of monitoring and going back over initial guesses. This monitoring occurs far more frequently when students are working in groups than when they are giving think-aloud protocols.

6 Observation

The observation took place as follows: students were observed carrying out summarising tasks, working in the classroom and using source materials relevant to their areas of specialisation. The observation was simply carried out by noting the behaviour of students as they worked in groups, or singly, on the tasks. Since the students were spread out it was not possible to obtain recordings of each group discussion. During the task the teacher was often asked for advice and used this as an extra opportunity to obtain data.

The task would begin with the teacher issuing an instruction sheet for the preparation of the summary, similar to that given in Holmes (1989). The text to be studied was then issued. At later stages in the course students would bring their own texts to work on and would dispense with the specific instructions for the summary.

As the session began there would be a squeaking of chairs and students would begin to form groups of two to five students. The teacher would note the disposition of groups, and the inevitable individuals working on their own, and note how they began the task. Some groups would begin with everyone reading silently; others would begin with a collective reading or collective consultations when unknown vocabulary was encountered; while others would plan by saying 'Let's look at the first sentences in each paragraph' or 'You read the first paragraph, I'll read the second'.

The task-completing process continued with the teacher circulating, observing and answering any questions. Students discussed procedures and problems in many different ways. Sometimes they named the reading strategies that formed part of the course content; they would say 'Let's skim the text' or 'Look at the context; what can we infer about the meaning of this word?'. At other times it seemed as if all our work on reading strategies had never taken effect, and the students would plunge into a word-by-word translation of the text which would result in inevitable problems of time distribution later on. Students rarely used a specific order of strategies, but went back and forth from macro-structures to lexical items, reflecting the real nature of the task of understanding a text.

The result of this observation is a checklist which owes more to ethnomethodology than to cognitive psychology. The strategies noted were those that students used, said they used or could use in the task situation.

7 The checklist: analysis of the process

The strategies observed in the first series of observations formed our checklist in the following manner:

(a) *Preliminary stage*

- Planning
- Sub-tasks

The students decided how to go about the task. They could deliberately divide the text among members of the group, for example. They could take decisions such as to look for the source data and make a few guesses as to the content. Also decisions to work in groups or to work alone on the whole of the task.

- Skimming.
- Individual reading.
- Collective reading: as the students got under way it was clear that some groups decided to read the text at the same pace, while other groups split into individuals for the reading of the text.
- Diagramming: setting out the ideas in the form of a diagram or schema.

- Note-taking: noting down the ideas in the text.
- Underlining/highlighting: as the students read the text they carried out different actions, relatively easy to observe. Some underlined or highlighted words in the text – either important words, or difficult words – others noted on separate sheets of paper the main ideas of the text, in note form or as a diagram.
- Previous knowledge.
- Specific knowledge.
- Personal experience.

These categories seemed complicated to us, but students were anxious to distinguish between them as they crucially affect text comprehension. *Previous knowledge* refers to general world knowledge applied to understanding the text. *Specific knowledge* refers to specialised knowledge of the topic, as in the case of a text in the area of psychology, where psychology students will naturally make use of this knowledge. *Personal experience* is the connection the individual makes between the text and his or her personal life. Those who observe the students are always hearing comments like 'This reminds me of a film I saw' or 'Something like this happened to a friend of mine' even with the most 'academic' texts. These three items in particular came from suggestions by the students who amplified a category we had called 'previous knowledge'.

(b) *As the summary takes shape:*

- Crossing-out (micro)
- Crossing-out (macro)
- Changing wording

As the notes began to gather shape towards the summary, the students began to go back over what had been previously noted down. Thus, crossings-out began to appear, sometimes of single words, sometimes of whole sections. Other changes would take place as wording was changed (in the L1).

- Translating sections
- Abandoning sections
- Identifying known ideas

During the formation of the summary, some sections of the text were treated differently. Sometimes a difficult section was translated word for word, at other times it was abandoned either because of difficulty or because of its lesser importance.

 – Clarifying doubts
 – Copying

Interaction with others varied from simple consultation on vocabulary or ideas, and looking up in a dictionary or (very rarely) a grammar reference book. Some students felt so insecure that they would copy whole sections from colleagues, or let some dominant member of the group tell them what the text meant.

In the above sequence we should emphasise three important points:

(i)   The strategies do not carry value-judgements. Our instinct as teachers and our own students' traditions often led us to try to think of some strategies as inherently 'bad'. Thus, we might regard 'abandoning sections' as tantamount to a breakdown in comprehension, and equivalent to what Faerch and Kasper (1984) call 'reduction strategies' as opposed to 'realisation strategies'. In fact, it could also be a sensible decision to economise on time in some situations. Similarly, we often thought of 'planning' as 'good', but as students became more accustomed to dealing with certain text types – such as reports of experiments – they needed to spend less time at the beginning in deliberately thinking about how to go about the task.

(ii)   There was also a temptation to regard the checklist as a list of procedures in chronological order. We give the list in an order approximating the way in which the individual strategies can be conveniently observed, but the order in which individual students make use of the procedures can vary. The checklist must not become a recipe.

(iii) We tried to arrive at a reasonable number of strategies so that students would be able to recognise a half-dozen or so which they already used as well as recognise strategies that they did not use. We applied Occam's razor in keeping our number fairly low, but this meant that some categories could be a little vague. For example, in underlining the student could be underlining known words and terms that were recognised at first sight, or difficult words that would be referred to in the dictionary, or key words and concepts in the text.

8 The checklist: analysis of the product

When the finished summaries were handed in we analysed the product for further evidence of the strategies used. This gave us the following elements:

- Source references
- Metastatements

Any summary must mention details of how to find or quote the original text, and it helps to include information which we call 'metastatements' such as 'This text is a survey of recent research', 'This text is a reply to X's paper'.

- Diagram
- Notes
- Prose

These refer to the form of the summary when it is handed in. In order to fulfil the criteria for a 'study-summary' (Holmes, 1988) the summary must be accessible to other readers and the summary writer at a future date, but the final form can vary.

- Inclusions of 'important' facts
- Exclusions of 'unimportant' facts
- Translations
- Extra information

Ideas from the source text are conveyed to the summary in various ways. The summary writer must take a decision as to what facts to select and whether to paraphrase, translate or explain at greater length.

- Structure

The structure of the summary often reflects the structure of the original text. It could be on a paragraph-by-paragraph or section-by-section basis.

- Criticism

The summariser opts for including his or her own opinions on the text.

- Stylistic problems

Translation problems reveal incoherences in the reading comprehension. For example, in one group, the word 'swing' was confused with the word 'swim' in a phrase 'Brazil is now swinging to the left . . .'. Stylistic problems appeared when the summary of one student said 'Brazil is swimming to the left' in the midst of a text on political changes and voting patterns. Another produced 'Brazil is sailing to the left' while a third fell back on the context and said

'Brazil is drifting to the left'. The first two examples would be 'stylistic problems' where, judging by the context, there is clearly something wrong. (Remember the students are writing in their L1.)

9 Applying the checklist

The complete checklist is given in the appendix in a translation from the Portuguese original. To many it may appear a strange hodge-podge of different items: reading strategies, group decisions, ways of working, and details of the finished product. We as teachers had to make a decision between presenting neatly categorised lists of different types of items and the aspects of the task which concern students who are carrying it out. More important, these items reflect the preoccupations of the students when carrying out such tasks. Students do not often say 'Right, which reading strategy do we use now? OK, now what kind of surface features shall we note in the text structure?' The students go from one category to another, and often go back and forth, taking decisions as to which is more useful, sometimes making mistakes, but in general taking a variety of decisions that switch from planning strategies, to single vocabulary items to questions of format and grammatical items. This is the way in which human problem-solving takes place, and the checklist is a reflection of this, not a potential computer program!

The checklist was used in two ways:

(a) Immediately after handing in the completed summarises the students marked in the checklist the strategies they had used while the task was still fresh in their minds. Thus the teacher obtained quantitative data on what students said they did. At the beginning we asked students to give a pseudonym to preserve anonymity but later we found that it made no difference if students wrote their real names.

(b) In the following lesson the checklists were returned and the summaries were handed back, corrected and commented on by the teacher. The students are asked to discuss the task briefly in class. The following questions oriented the discussion:

'What strategies did you use?'
'Were they successful?'
'Would you use the same strategies the next time?'

In this way students comment:

We didn't really plan our time very well, and so we rushed the last part.

We got stuck on the first sentence in the third paragraph, which didn't make sense until we compared it with the first sentence in the first paragraph, which we'd forgotten because we were reading word by word. Next time we'll go through the topic sentences of the paragraphs first.

We entrusted too much to Sonia, who was very secure, but she made some mistakes and we didn't check on them in the context.

I should have prepared my summary in note form like Emerson, then I wouldn't have spent so much time writing out drafts.

During the course, students' strategies change, not simply as a result of trial and error or intuition, but as a consequence of reflection on learning processes and deliberate attempts to change them.

10 The value of the checklist

Some of the uses of the checklist are as follows:

10.1 Talking about learning

For the classroom teacher the checklist is of inestimable value in providing a framework for talking about learning. Students can recognise the strategies they use and consider others, as well as hear from colleagues who use different procedures. Although some strategies are more frequently mentioned than others and are easier to identify during the course, students cease to mention with such frequency factors such as 'vocabulary' or 'grammar' and analyse their own learning more profoundly.

10.2 Feedback for the teacher

The teacher has explicit evidence of the strategies that students use, or say they use. Clearly the checklist reflects only what the learners perceive, but this is an enormous advance on the previous state of knowledge. It is interesting to observe, for example, how difficult it is for some students to change their reading strategies, and that often even after several weeks of a course dedicated to helping students use top-down strategies looking first for gist, the group or the individual will settle down to word-by-word reading. It's healthy for the teacher to check if all the work on strategies and building learner awareness is really changing the way that students learn.

Although this is no place to give a detailed quantitative analysis of the way in which students' strategies change during the course, simply by 'eyeballing' the completed checklists we could perceive changes in the strategies during the course. Some clear examples:

(i)   Planning and the use of sub-tasks increased from practically zero at the beginning of the course to being reported by almost all students in the later stages.

(ii)   Underlining/highlighting at first was of unknown lexical items, and later of important or key sections.

(iii) The use of personal experience and negotiating format was dependent on the topic of individual texts and not on the students' expertise.

Thus, in relation to the choice of materials we can also obtain insights for future course design. Certain text types seem to produce certain patterns of strategies; for example, a chronological account provokes less negotiating format than more argumentative texts, and texts which do not provoke personal experience seem to motivate students much less.

10.3 Feedback for the student

By discussing the task openly the student has a means of evaluating his or her own learning and diagnosing his or her own problems. Self-diagnosis does not take place in a vacuum, nor is it purely a product of the teacher's feedback or awareness building. It also comes from individuals working with colleagues and comparing their own strategies with those of other members of the group and other groups. The group work component of the tasks was of crucial importance not just in the data gathering but also in students' self-evaluation.

10.4 Research: a source of quantitative data

In the area of Language Awareness it is difficult to make comparisons or gather data in a quantitative way. A great deal of data come from students' protocols or interviews, which is of necessity qualitative. In collecting data from a students' checklist it is relatively easy to apply statistical tests of significance to the phenomena under investigation. Thus this is a powerful research tool for the classroom teacher.

11 Limitations

There are limitations to the technique. As in all work on awareness building it is easy to fall into the temptation of talking about learning at the expense of actually doing some learning. The advantage of the checklist is that it is quick and simple and need not take up an excessive amount of class time. The discussion of task procedures on handing back the summaries to students takes much less time than the traditional going-over of students' mistakes in a remedial session.

We were at first concerned that students may simply have ticked items in the checklist at random, or even worse, ticked items they thought the teachers would approve of. However the students' own feedback was consistent with our observations of the groups in the classroom, and was often against the expectations or recommendations of the course programme. Our students were far more honest and sincere than we had given them credit for!

12 Conclusions

The use of these checklists is still in its infancy, but clearly this instrument seems to reflect the ways in which students think about their own learning and provides a way of voicing what students feel implicitly as well as drawing their attention – and that of the teacher – to aspects of the learning process that may have gone unnoticed.

We must emphasis the ethnomethodological aspect of the checklist: that it must reflect what students do and say they do, as well as what the teacher has taught. Thus the checklists have already varied depending on the group, and we are constantly adding and scrapping different categories. It is up to each teacher to work out a checklist which is appropriate for a particular class, pilot it, and then negotiate any additions or omissions from it.

To us it has been an interesting experience: first because we have solved the problem of the students who say 'Oh it's because of my inadequate vocabulary' and also because we have a powerful tool with which to continue classroom-based research into our students' learning and our own classroom practice.

Appendix: Checklist for preparing a study summary

1. **Working with the text**
    Planning
    Sub-tasks
    Skimming
    Individual reading
    Collective reading
    Diagramming
    Note-taking
    Underlining/highlighting
    Previous knowledge
    Specific knowledge
    Personal experience

2. **Preparing the summary**
   Crossing-out (micro)
   Crossing-out (macro)
   Changing wording
   Translating sections
   Abandoning sections
   Identifying known ideas
   Clarifying doubts
   Copying

3. **Analysing the product**
   Source references
   Metastatements
   Diagram
   Notes
   Prose
   Inclusions of 'important' facts
   Exclusions of 'unimportant' facts
   Translations
   Extra information
   Structure
   Criticism
   Stylistic problems

16 Language Awareness on area studies degrees

Lindsay Silvester

1 Background

If one traces the development of language degrees in universities and polytechnics in this country during the last two or three decades, one finds that the rationale and planning of the linguistic element (by which I mean language and linguistics) to some extent lags behind that of the more 'academic' content of such degrees. In traditional language degrees, course philosophies addressed themselves primarily to the study of literature, and language study had a somewhat subservient role. For example, in my own degree, language study, even diachronic language study (which was the only form of linguistics recognised at the time), was secondary to the literary purpose of reading poets such as Goethe, Rilke and Walther Von der Vogelweide. Even prose translations had literary or philosophical content, and I presume were supposed to increase our knowledge of and ability to handle German literary criticism.

More recently, as literature has been superseded by other disciplines in 'area studies' courses, degree rationales have addressed themselves to the reasons for the change in emphasis from literary study to the geographical, sociological or economic, etc., study of a given area, before addressing any change that might have occurred to the less central and less 'academic' linguistic element, which has remained secondary.

Area studies and European studies degrees – 'those courses which have attempted to replace the study of literature in whole or in part with ... an interdisciplinary combination of historical, sociological, political, and cultural studies' (Bell, 1979: 269) – tend to view language as a more prestigious element, one which gives a student not only insights into the way that the various disciplines relate to the 'areas' of study, but also a degree of competence in using the language as a communicative tool. There is still considerable debate, however, about the precise relationship between the language element and the other disciplines. Should one aim for native fluency in the language? Should one aim for a reading knowledge? Should one use as language material only examples of the foreign language used in the study of the other disciplines? In an article on the place of literary study in area studies courses, Findlay (1980: 3) finds that language is viewed in two ways:

> sometimes it is seen as the expression and product of a given
> society, what we might call *symptomatic* language, and sometimes it
> is considered to be simply a practical tool used to gain entry to that
> society – *communicative* language.

He goes on to say that the two views coexist, but this ambivalent view of the nature of language concedes the potential of the language element to have a life of its own, its own rationale as well as a role which may be secondary, albeit supportive, in relation to the other disciplines.

2 The role of linguistics in 'area studies'

During the 1970s and 1980s, as the 'area studies' concept became more consolidated and accepted as a valuable alternative to the literary language degrees, linguistics as a discipline was seen as a worthwhile study, certainly in its synchronic form, complementary to the study of a foreign language or foreign languages. Its role was therefore bound up with the role of the foreign language in relation to the area studies. What did not seem to result from the inclusion of linguistics was the recognition that it might be a discipline in its own right, equal to the other disciplines and contribute to the study of a particular area. At least, with very few exceptions, this was never made explicit.

Taking Portsmouth Polytechnic as an example of an institution where area studies degrees were developed from the early 1970s, we can trace the development of the degrees themselves and the role of linguistics on those courses. To begin with, we created a number of single honours degrees, having been freed from the constraints of the external London BA degree structure: French studies, Russian studies, German studies, Spanish studies, focusing on single 'political' areas; Latin American studies, which focused on a geographical unit. Each regarded the language element as a core element, though the amount of time given to language teaching, and the ratio of receptive to productive skills teaching, varied from degree to degree.

Concurrent with the growth of area studies was the acceptance of a more systematic approach to the teaching of language – the abandoning of the grammar translation method, the embracing of the language laboratory as a vital teaching aid, the implicit acceptance of behaviourist theories of language learning, which used, for example, minimal pair and structure drills to produce accuracy in pronunciation and fluency in speech production. Linguistics – the academic study of language – was father to the new approach: it was by relating language teaching to linguistics that the foreign language syllabus writer and producer of the new technological language teaching aids raised the teaching of foreign languages from what I would call the doldrums of subservience to the teaching of literature to a position whereby it could aim to provide students with a live tool. This tool was for use both in the study of a particular area and in the outside world where jobs existed for linguists as well as experts in French culture, German history, etc.

Linguistics as a separate subject for study was introduced largely to aid the language learning process: it aimed to provide the student with an understanding of language systems, which would help him or her to learn the foreign language and to perceive the rationale behind the language teaching programme. Of particular importance were the study of phonetics and syntax, as the ability to listen and speak was based on the theory that we decode and encode on the two levels of grammar and sound.

3 Content of linguistics course for first-year students

A typical syllabus would include:

- What is linguistics?
- What is language/what is a language?
- Phonetics/phonology
- Morphology
- Syntax
- Register/style
- Semantic universals (synonymy, homonymy, etc.)
- Discourse

It was also recognised (by the people who taught it) that the study of linguistics was 'good for the soul' inasmuch as it made students aware that there could be a scientific study of a language from which there emerged sets of descriptive rather than prescriptive rules. Preconceptions were questioned, and prejudices exposed. Another by-product of the study of linguistics was the educational benefit it supposedly afforded – that of instilling a little discipline and rigour into students who were non-scientists, who had until then encountered 'waffly' subjects such as literature, or a rudimentary area studies type component of their 'A' level course. Linguistics became the acceptable face of a language teaching component in the eyes of those who frowned on the elevated role of language learning – a mere skill – on an academic degree course.

It followed that linguistics should have its own academic integrity: those who taught it saw it as discrete discipline, in much the same way as the sociologists, historians, etc., initially viewed their own subjects as discrete, to be applied to the particular 'area' under examination. Linguistics, like those other disciplines, had its own framework of investigation, and, what was most distressing to the students, its own jargon.

4 Foundation course in linguistics at Portsmouth Polytechnic

At Portsmouth Polytechnic, for example, we attempted to formulate the ideal 'Foundation Linguistics' course. It was a core course, in the same way that there was to be a core economics course, a core history course, etc. We included the topics listed above, though not always in that order. A group of us taught it as a team, in the form of a series of lectures, which formed the general and mostly theoretical introduction, and a series of back-up seminars in which the theoretical concepts were applied to individual languages. In other words, we taught what we considered to be the most relevant concepts of linguistics and, in the seminar time, discussed them and taught the skills associated with the concepts, which would provide the analytical framework for the efficient study of the language in question. To give you an example: the lectures on phonetics and phonology included auditory and articulatory phonetics as a background to the study of a particular phonology; the concept 'phoneme' was introduced, and examples given of vowel charts, etc. In the seminar, the terms of articulatory phonetics were explained again and used in the description of the sounds of French, German, Spanish, etc. The phonemic symbols were also taught and used in the phonological transcriptions of the various languages. The transcription of a language was seen as a way of helping a student to pronounce the language. There are still teachers who would stake their life on this belief, even though no real evidence has come to light as to its validity.

4.1 Problems encountered on the foundation course
The course continued for many years, but each year there were heated debates between the staff, who represented all the language

degrees, on the relevance and therefore the content of the foundation programme and on the order in which concepts should be introduced. There were also complaints from students who failed to see the relevance of the first-year linguistics programme until their fourth year, by which time the new concepts and terms were fully internalised. But the complaints ranged from the very general 'What is the relevance of the linguistics programme?' (in its entirety) to the very particular 'Why do we have to have examples given to us of languages that we don't know and may never study?' The foundation course, therefore, underwent annual modifications to try to respond to the criticisms from students and to the dissatisfaction of the linguistics and language staff, and annual post-mortems were held to consider the success or otherwise of the enterprise.

The problems seemed to arise from three separate sources: first, the assumption that there is a fixed body of linguistic knowledge that everyone who is on an area studies course ought to have, whatever language is being studied; second, the assumption that the lecture/seminar method is the best way in which to impart this knowledge; and third, the students' backgrounds.

4.2 Reasons for the problems

4.2.1 Relevance

To explain the first problem, one has to look at the reality of area studies degrees. In our case, no one area studies course has exactly the same structure, emphasis or even philosophy as any other. For example, students on the Spanish studies degree can follow a linguistics pathway through their undergraduate career: in their first year, they attend a diachronic linguistics course in addition to any core linguistics course that is offered, and in the third and fourth years (they go abroad in their second year) linguistics is a major option for those who have chosen that pathway; students on the German studies degree, on the other hand, follow a core course in linguistics in their first year, and can opt at a later stage to do 'translation theory and practice' as a 'minor' option. Linguistics on this degree, therefore, is seen as having a supportive role, whereas it is studied in its own right on the Spanish studies degree.

Another major difference between the degrees – and this must be seen as a major factor contributing to the debates about the role of linguistics in a foundation year – is the level of language attained by the incoming first-year students prior to entry to their degree course: French studies, for example, receives students with a high level of competence in the French language; Latin American studies students are mixed ability – some have 'A' level Spanish, others have 'O' level or below; Russian studies students rarely come with any prior knowledge of Russian. French studies students are therefore happy to learn about such concepts as dialect and accent and to discover the various dialects of France, and are competent to consider French as an 'object of study', while *ab initio* students of Russian and Spanish are in the position of having to grapple with the metalanguage of Russian or Spanish grammar, etc., and the newness of a foreign language, at the same time as considering the universality or otherwise of the term 'definite article'.

The attempt, therefore, to dictate a core set of linguistic items to be learnt by every student was somewhat idealistic, and however dogmatic one might like to be about this, if the relevance is questioned by both the providers and the receivers of a course, some radical rethinking has to take place.

4.2.2 Method
With regard to the second problem – that of the teaching format – the difficulties of the lecture/seminar structure relate to some extent also to the attempt to standardise. As is by now well documented, although the lecture format is theoretically the most economical in terms of staff, and large chunks of information can be conveyed in a short amount of time, from the students' point of view, it is only effective if time is provided afterwards for reinforcement and explanation of the material presented in lecture. So the seminar time, for us, was always taken up with the explanation of the concepts and terminology used to explain linguistic phenomena. The whole purpose of the follow-up seminar, as far as the given aim of the linguistics course was concerned – that of *applying* the concepts to the foreign language, to facilitate the learning of that particular language – was necessarily not fulfilled. There was no time.

4.2.3. Student backgrounds
The students themselves also presented problems during seminars. I have already indicated that, for example, a French studies student knew more French than a Latin American studies student knew Spanish. This is still the case. Even within the same degree course, however, there is a mixture of language abilities in the same cohort of students. Some students come with an excellent ability in the spoken language, but scant written knowledge; others have the reverse. Some

are bilingual up to a point, but their knowledge of the language in question may be restricted to one or two registers.

Students' ability to handle linguistic concepts also varies, and not necessarily in proportion to their competence in the foreign language. For example, so-called bilingual students are often unaware of the range of language not yet part of their competence, and may develop a defensive attitude when challenged on an aspect of the language which they think they know. Similarly, foreign nationals find themselves exploring aspects of their own language never encountered before, and this fact can shake their confidence where perhaps they thought that they had an advantage over the British students in the same group. While the reassessment of one's own knowledge and contribution is a worthwhile aim, when it happens in *the study of one's own language*, it is too close to home – the language is too much part of the expression of one's personality – and it takes a very strong person to view this reassessment as a positive process, at this stage. The result is often at best a negative attitude to linguistics and at worst hostility towards the linguistics lecturer and even a certain amount of animosity among the students.

This is not to say that all students face linguistics in this way. The subject appeals to some from the very beginning, and they go on to write fascinating and academically sound linguistics dissertations. But we have to design courses for the majority, not the enthusiastic few, though we must encourage those few while motivating the less scientifically minded majority. We therefore have to re-examine the role of linguistics, and therefore the content and approach of any linguistics syllabus, foundation or otherwise.

5 Re-examination of the role of linguistics

To do this, it is necessary on the one hand to return to the definition of an area studies degree and, on the other, to examine the development of combined honours or modular degree structures. Some regarded area studies as 'an interdisciplinary problem-orientated' activity (Cahm, 1980: 7), in which each discipline would contribute to an integrated study of a given area. Findlay articulated one of the initial difficulties encountered in the course teams – that of academic integrity, which was viewed by some lecturers as retaining their 'pristine disciplinary purity'. The refutation of this view of academic integrity on an Area Studies degree is expressed in the following extract:

But the underlying view of knowledge found here – that every
discipline has as its function the enquiry into a neatly fenced-off
section of the cosmos, and that its methods are drawn up in relation to
a fixed object of study – is, surely, a discredited one. Such a static view
of academic enquiry and its object completely overlooks two facts: that
the objects and enquiry are not fixed, but have a cause and a history;
and that 'disciplines' are not ends in themselves, but rather have the
task of meeting concrete needs in society. (Findlay, 1980: 5)

He goes on to view Area Studies courses as 'aiming to produce a
critical analysis of the evolution of a national consciousness in a
particular culture', which 'finds its most complex concrete expression
in the forms of language, which must now be viewed not only as
a practical skill, but also as an ever-changing register of ideological
signatures' (Findlay, 1980: 6).

We as linguists can learn two things from this conclusion: first,
students are not on Area Studies degrees primarily to learn a language,
or economics or sociology or linguistics. They are examining political, geographical and linguistic boundaries; political, sociological and
hence socio-linguistic problems; facts about integration, bilingualism,
etc. Second, students are learning the foreign language(s) of the
areas that interest them – the concrete expressions of the particular
culture(s). Some of them are bilingual. All of them know what it is
like to be language learners. These are the reasons that they are with
us and, by and large, these are the issues that interest them most.
Why not then devise a linguistics foundation course, the topics of
which relate very closely to the problems under discussion? Why not
enter into the interdisciplinary dialogue which is the essence of an
area studies degree? (Cf. Sager and Geake, 1981; Jackson, 1983.)

The first course to change direction with this in mind was Latin
American Studies. Only one hour per week was devoted to a language study element (other than straight language teaching) and this
developed into something akin to a Language Awareness course, but
centred on the problems of Latin America (see Appendix 1). The
course was called 'Language in Culture and Society'. It took certain
elements of the previous core course, but introduced other topics of
a more socio-linguistic nature and concentrated on the problems that
other disciplines would be looking at in the rest of the course. It was
well received by students and staff alike.

The next event that was to prove problematic in our continuing
with a very descriptive and language-oriented course was the development of combined honours degrees, in which German and French
could be combined, Spanish and Latin American studies, German

and Russian, and Hispanic and French. The combination of studies inevitably led to a more comparative approach to the areas of the single honours courses, not only across countries in a single continent, but across continents; not only across different political entities but across ideologies and worlds: Russian and German brought together two ideologies; Hispanic and French brought together the developed and the developing world.

The practical problems that would ensue from this development – the single honours degree structures still exist and are still well subscribed – would compound the two problems areas of relevance, hence content, and method, given that every combined honours student would receive exactly the same amount of time for the linguistics component as a single honours student.

Where time was short for applying the linguistic concepts to the single languages involved, it would be even shorter if we attempted to apply them to two or more languages – and teach the relevant skills in phonetic transcription, grammatical analysis, etc.

6 Solutions

The solution in theory would seem to be, therefore, to re-examine the role of linguistics and create a separate course for each degree; look at the problem areas to be central to each course and gear the linguistics component to participate in the interdisciplinary dialogue surrounding each problem area. Unfortunately, there is neither time nor staff for this approach. A better solution would be to look for the elements and issues that the area studies degrees – all of them – have in common, and design core elements that would be of relevance to each course, and then apply these to the language areas. We would then be considering linguistic issues across cultures.

The result of our own thinking was a linguistics syllabus which had much in common with the Language Awareness courses that feature in schools such as the Oratory School, but which, in the hands of foreign language specialists, took the concepts and issues 'abroad'. The mere change of title from 'Linguistics Foundation course' to 'Language Awareness course' alerted everyone concerned – students and staff – to the intention to demystify the subject as much as possible. The 'course' turned out to be a pool of topics together with a pool of materials which could be drawn upon by every member of staff concerned with a variety of language awareness (which perhaps in our case one would regard as linguistics with a human face!), and utilised if desired for his or her particular course.

6.1 Syllabus
This now includes:

(a) *The social context of language:* language functions; registers, styles, status of dialects and standard languages; diglossia, multiglossia; social context of meaning; language of persuasion, etc.
(b) *The learning of language:* first and second language learning/acquisition; bilingualism; student learning strategies, error analysis.
(c) *Language as a system:* phonological, grammatical and lexical systems and their structures; contrastive studies; semantic relations; textual cohesion.

6.2 Teaching format
The old lecture/seminar format has now disappeared. In its place lecturers can draw from a set of audio and video materials relating to language, some published and some broadcast (as educational material), and create their own courses. These materials they can arrange in any order to build a course which is coherent in its own right, and which relates most closely to the particular issues treated in the other components of the particular area studies degree on which they are working. One example of the selection of topics can be seen in Appendix 2.

This system allows for considerable flexibility in that, for the most part, two hours are still available, but the member of staff concerned, in negotiation with the students, can either present the material or require the students to prepare the material themselves, or create different material for a certain topic in preference to using that offered in the 'pool'. As indicated above, the material can be used in any order, because it is not dependent on the presence of a lecturer. Any of the material can be viewed, listened to, or read at any time by a student.

Thus, students who are absent from a particular presentation will not be disadvantaged; they can also have repeated access to it.

The two hours can then be profitably spent on the discussion of linguistic phenomena and the 'doing' of bits of linguistics that matter to them.

6.3 Materials
As can be seen from the syllabus, some of the elements of the old linguistics foundation course have been included; the foreign languages are still objects of study, and some courses, in particular French Studies and German Studies, require their students to carry out phonological, grammatical and lexical analyses as part of the raising of linguistic consciousness. But the general emphasis has changed.

First, most of the materials for presentation focus on *English*, which is the mother tongue of the majority. Linguistic issues can be introduced which draw on the direct experience of the students. Take, for example, the question of 'standard language'. Students are fascinated to learn that they have an accent which is different from the Portsmouth accent, and even more fascinated to learn they have one at all! One can obtain audio tapes dealing with Black English and other language varieties. Any of these will highlight issues surrounding dialects, accent and standard languages, but instead of presenting the subjects as chunks of information, with bits of terminology and their 'correct' definitions, these broadcasts tend to focus on linguistic phenomena in the flesh, as it were, and act as springboards for student discussion and investigation.

Second, there is an emphasis on the language learner, which was lacking in the old syllabus. Introspection is a popular activity, and we invite students to examine their own language acquisition, both first and second (and maybe third), before considering the wider issues.

Both the above examples would be regarded as issues that all area studies degree courses consider central. Other topics are: bilingualism and diglossia; the integration of non-native speakers of a given official language into a speech community; changes in political identity (which includes the study of political propaganda); informational, social and textual functions of language. And this is just a small sample.

6.4 Methods

The collection of a pool of materials has led to a much more student-centred approach to language awareness. As indicated above, the staff often select the topics for discussion in negotiation with the students. No one group of students is the same as another; no first year cohort is the same as another. With the exception of a core set of topics which is determined by the nature of the individual area studies courses, students under the guidance of their tutors can assess their own priorities and thus determine the kind of course that is most appropriate for them.

The methods of presentation are mostly inductive rather than deductive: students are able to investigate linguistic problems and discover solutions, or at least discover the necessity for learning the means by which solutions may be arrived at. Tasks are set; even role-play is used; students are invited to use each other's language as the 'object of study', even their imperfect German or Spanish. Bilingual students and foreign nationals become valuable assets to the teacher and monolingual British students alike, as they themselves become, for some topics, 'objects of study'.

7 Results

The solutions presented are not perfect. Not every student can adapt to an inductive or task-oriented approach, and nor can every member of staff.

The idea of 'popularising' linguistics, which is sometimes the view of the uninitiated, is 'degrading' to the discipline. The concept of a flexible core is still evolving and this type of resource pooling may be an interim solution; student and course needs may change.

The majority of students, however, enjoy the Language Awareness programme: they come out of group discussions still hotly debating issues of sexist language, or language learning methods; they even come to appreciate the ability they have acquired to use a foreign dictionary intelligently. With very few exceptions, students have not had to enquire as to the relevance of the course. Staff no longer have to explain the learning of linguistics in terms of its use to the learning of their second or third language. The course can clearly be seen as having a bearing on many aspects of their area studies, and their increased awareness of their own language has a beneficial effect on their ability to handle problems encountered in the foreign language or languages.

Appendix 1: Portsmouth Polytechnic School of Languages and Area Studies

LATIN AMERICAN STUDIES
SPANISH AND LATIN AMERICAN STUDIES
YEAR 1

LANGUAGE IN CULTURE AND SOCIETY

Aims of the course

This course is designed to complement students' acquisition of Spanish language skills in a manner comparable to the way the Social Theory course complements the examination of contemporary Latin America in the ICLA course.

It works on the assumption that 'culture finds one of its most complete and concrete expressions in the forms of the language, which must be viewed not only as a practical skill, but also as an ever-changing register of ideological signatures'. This is particularly important in the case of an area like Latin America, much of whose population is illiterate and so excluded from producing the kinds of written texts through which a culture is normally studied academically.

Taking this as a point of departure, the course will set students' personal experience of learning Spanish, the dominant language in most of Spain and Latin America, within a wider framework. Three main aspects of language in society, and of students' potential experience of it, will be considered:

1. The phenomenon of bilingualism/multilingualism in Latin American societies: how did it come about? how does it affect particular social groups? how can it be changed?
    Case study: Multilingual Nicaragua since the Revolution.
2. Language and thought, language and culture: language and meaning; how language refers to reality; classification systems and social norms; language and the socialisation of children into a culture.
    Case study: A significant Latin American word set – indio, espãnol, mestizo, campesino.
3. Learning a foreign language – becoming bilingual: some differences between learning a first language and learning a foreign language; expectations, learning strategies, rules and mistakes; language functions, and how different cultures realise them; meaning beyond words.
    Case studies: Reading foreign language texts; being polite in different cultures.

Teaching

Teaching will begin by exploring aspects of the topic in relation to English. This is followed by discussion in which students will be asked to analyse their own experience of language within a clear analytical framework, and then to draw analogies between this experience and the use of Spanish in Latin America. Further materials referring to the Spanish language will be introduced at appropriate stages.

Each section of the course will lead to a case study so that analysis can be applied to specific examples of language use, largely in Latin America.

A short bibliography to accompany each topic is chosen to enable students to consolidate on class-work and develop the necessary perspective to the case studies. It has been deliberately limited to short articles or chapters of books, selected for their accessibility to the non-specialist.

(Reproduced by permission of E.J. Freeland, School of Languages and Area Studies, Portsmouth Polytechnic.)

Appendix 2

GERMAN STUDIES
GERMAN AND FRENCH STUDIES
YEAR 1

LANGUAGE AWARENESS COURSE

Below are set out the AIMS and SPECIFIC OBJECTIVES of the course in Language Awareness. The aims are very general and implicitly represent our view of the role of such a course on an Area Studies degree.

The SPECIFIC OBJECTIVES are divided into two sections, section 1 detailing concepts and linguistic phenomena that we think students should be able to understand, section 2 detailing certain tasks which we consider students should be able to carry out by the end of the first year.

Aims

To develop students' awareness of
1. Language as a system
2. What is involved in language learning
3. The relation between language and culture.

Specific objectives

1. Students should be able to understand:
    (a) The relation between first and second language learning.
    (b) The concept of and issues surrounding bilingualism.
    (c) Language as interlocking systems: sound systems; structural and lexical systems; textual cohesion
    (d) The relationship between language and culture: register and style; communicative functions of language; relation between language and meaning.

2. Students should be able to:
    (a) analyse their own and others' errors;
    (b) produce a strategy future language learning;
    (c) write a broad phonetic transcription of spoken German/German and French;
    (d) analyse stress and intonation patterns in German/German and French;
    (e) use reference grammars and dictionaries effectively;
    (f) analyse language in terms of grammatical and lexical structures;
    (g) identify cohesive devices in language;
    (h) differentiate between a variety of styles of German/German and French;
    (i) identify informational and non-informational functions of different types of language, including socially determined linguistic conventions;
    (j) identify writers'/speakers' intentions and attitudes from the language used;
    (k) identify different aspects of meaning;
    (l) identify persuasive features of language.

17 Language Awareness and the computer

Phil Scholfield

How can the computer be used to help heighten someone's explicit 'awareness' of language, in the broadest sense? What issues arise in connection with computer use for this purpose? It is the aim of this paper to review some ideas on these matters and look at just a few suggestive examples of the use of computers in this connection: in short, I hope to stimulate awareness of computer-assisted Language Awareness tasks.

The present remarks are primarily based on the experience of this author at UCNW (University College of North Wales), and mainly relate to the use of some of the vast amount of software available for the BBC-B computer. In certain ways this is a limited machine – especially in the amount of internal memory – and is being superseded by much more powerful IBM-compatible micros for which more sophisticated next-generation software can be written, but BBCs in some form, and their associated software, probably will remain an important resource in the UK in many schools and elsewhere for some time.

The consumers of the computer activities I am personally involved with are native-speaker undergraduates doing linguistics courses, and postgraduate teachers of ESL/EFL. However, much of what arises for these I am convinced is relevant in some form also to computer-aided awareness heightening for native-speaker schoolchildren and FL learners generally. Hence, in what follows I shall use the vague word 'users' to refer to this full range of potential beneficiaries of computer-assisted Language Awareness work.

It is useful to identify three main sources of software which have some potential specifically to help stimulate Language Awareness – CALAH (= Computer Assisted Language Awareness Heightening), if one wishes to coin a new distinct label for it! Of these the largest is of course that created overtly for the purpose of Computer-Assisted Language Learning (CALL). However, there are also programs more dedicated to language research that have some awareness heightening potential, and a growing collection of software intended to teach linguistics. Let us look at just a few examples of these in turn.

1 Computer-assisted language learning software

Now clearly many CALL programs, especially for the ESL/EFL market, are aimed at somehow developing actual language competence and performance, rather than thought or talk *about* language, which is the present issue. Hence I am not concerned with those here: examples are the many 'simulation' programs such as *London Adventure* (British Council/CUP) and *Yellow River Kingdom* (Acornsoft), and adventure games, all of which lend themselves to acting as catalysts for purposive communication among a group of users. Many uses of computers linked to laser-disc videos are of this sort too. For fuller lists of CALL programs to examine for their awareness heightening potential, see for example Davies and Higgins (1982).

The first point to note is that in some language teaching quarters, particularly foreign language teaching in higher education, there has always been a belief in the value of talking *about* the language being learnt, often in terms of fairly traditional grammatical rules, which has endured through the years when others have eschewed anything of this sort, in the pursuit of a purely audio-lingual, communicative or whatever methodology. Hence, CALL software from this source often anyway has a strong metalinguistic element. An example would be a program which presents explicitly rules about the morphological shape of the past tense of verbs in French and goes on to provide gap-filling practice thereof, perhaps with the capability of analysing the user's wrong answers and referring him or her to the appropriate rule. This can be seen as much as teaching users *about* the French language (an awareness heightening activity) as improving their performance in French (a pure CALL activity). A number of the programs of this sort have been described at CATH conferences (= Computers and Teaching in the Humanities) and in the CTISS files (= Computers in Teaching Initiative Support Service) – e.g. Chesters and Gardner (1987) and WIDA (1989). Though presented as *language* teaching programs, they teach as much *about* the language.

However, many other CALL programs have strong awareness heightening potential that is less overt; for example, *Tree of Knowledge* (Acornsoft), which has some artificial intelligence features, can afford considerable stimulation for metalinguistic discussion used in various ways with the foreign learner of English or the native-speaker child. For example, if prepared by the teacher to deal with vocabulary in the semantic field of 'fruit', the program instructs the user to think of a word in that semantic field. Let us suppose he thinks of the word *lemon*. The program then makes the computer able apparently to ask a series of sensible questions of the user (e.g. *Does it have a stone? Does it grow on a tree? Is it orange in colour when ripe?*). In order to answer *yes* or *no* after each question the user has to think quite carefully about the detailed properties of the meaning of the word *lemon*. In the end the computer will apparently 'guess' and ask if the user was thinking of the fruit *lemon*, to which he responds *yes*.

If, on the other hand, the teacher had not included *lemon* among the fruit for which he had supplied information to the computer, the computer obviously will not succeed in guessing correctly. If we suppose the computer's guess is *apple*, the user's answer to the computer's final guess will be *no*. Another valuable feature of this program then comes into play: the computer asks the user, *What fruit were you thinking of?*, to which the answer is of course *lemon*. The computer then says, *Please give me a question to tell the difference between a lemon and an apple*: i.e. the user has to help the computer 'learn' new words to add to the ones it already has, and associated questions based on discriminating characteristics. This clearly again prompts more than superficial thought *about* the components of the meanings of the words involved, Indeed, in this way the user can readily be led to enter an entire 'field' of semantically related words with discriminating questions and get his teacher or peers to play the 'Think of a fruit (or whatever)' game with them.

This activity is clearly focused on a very specific area of language – word meaning – but can serve to draw explicit attention to a number of aspects of this in an amusing and useful way, for example the difference between defining and non-defining features of meaning, and meaning relations such as hyponymy and (near-) synonymy. It can be used with simple vocabulary as above, or with a much more taxing set of items such as technical terms from physics or a set like *experience, adventure, enterprise, encounter*.

One limitation is that the program only comfortably handles countable nouns or noun phrases: one rather clumsily has to embed anything else in a noun phrase to handle it. For instance, to deal with *happy, sad, dejected*, etc., one would have to handle them in phrases like *happy mood, sad mood, dejected mood*, etc. Another point is that the program is 'open': unlike the French tense program above, it cannot identify inaccurate information. If the user supplies the information that a good question to distinguish a lemon from an apple is *Is it blue?* to which the answer for *apple* is *yes*, that will be accepted. This means that the program is valuable as a stimulus, but the quality of the metalinguistic activity engendered must be monitored by the teacher, and perhaps controlled by having pairs of users working together and, having input a set of words with discriminating questions, getting other pairs to play the game and test them out. However, I think this is more than offset by the value of the discussion that may be stimulated, and the fact that the activity is more learner-centred: the computer plays the role of 'tool' or 'tutee' rather than 'tutor' (Canale and Barker, 1986).

CALL programs can also have awareness heightening use of a much less narrowly focused sort. For instance, a number of CALL programs are essentially text gap-filling ('cloze') tasks. They present a text on screen with gaps where certain words should be. The user types in a word that he or she thinks would fit, and the computer provides some feedback. If just done individually with an immediate right/wrong response supplied on each gap, this may not involve much awareness heightening; but such a task can have very valuable awareness heightening use *if* handled differently.

If three or pairs of users work together, with or without the teacher, and are focused *not* primarily just on guessing a word to fit the gap but rather on the *justification* for making one or another guess, then a very valuable discussion can arise which brings to explicit attention all sorts of features of text structure, lexical cohesion, pronoun cross-reference, the use of background knowledge and so forth – all the things that provide 'clues' to what a missing word might be. In the end, then, the user becomes aware of many of the key features of the normal competent reading process – prediction, exploitation of form and content schemata, etc. All this is also likely to improve the learner's ability to 'inference' the meaning of unknown words when reading in the future too. As an example consider the following simple passage (of course passages and deletions of various difficulty levels can be chosen):

> 'Oh, I'm so (1) _____,' said the Snowman. During the day the children had played happily round the Snowman, but they had gone inside hours ago for their tea. Now even the lights in the house had gone out. The Snowman was all alone in the (2) _____ garden . . .

Among the guesses suggested by a group for (1) might be *cold*. The focus is then on what *leads* to this suggestion. In the process of discussion it could emerge (not necessarily via the technical terminology I use here of course!) that the suggestion rests on first spotting that (1) is the complement of *I* in a simple copular construction (so (1) must describe *I* in some way). Further, *I* corefers with *Snowman*, so (1) is also a property of the Snowman. A snowman is made of snow, and from real-world (pragmatic) knowledge we know that a typical property of snow is that it is cold: hence *cold* is a justifiable guess for (1). But of course there are other possible guesses justifiable on other grounds, and in the end one might not think *cold* is the best . . . (I leave the reader to figure out other lines of reasoning).

Now the responsibility for making sure the right sort of discussion goes on lies mainly with the teacher, but it is worth noting that some programs do help with this more than others. Some provide straightforward feedback on the 'right' answer and are obviously geared to individual use (e.g. *Readamatics* from Longman). But *Divergent Cloze* (Questlar) comes with instructions which emphasise group use and encourages the thought and discussion aspect of the task by *not* in fact providing a definitive right answer. Rather it records what successive users of the program thought were good fillers and provides feedback of the type 'many people thought this was a good guess' or 'nobody has thought of that guess before'. This 'openness' again overtly throws the onus back on the users and encourages deeper thought.

In the preceding I was considering CALL programs which might be used directly as an important part of an awareness heightening task. A somewhat different activity is that of *analysing* and *evaluating* CALL programs critically for their linguistic content. I have done this profitably with teachers on our MA courses: it is of course a moot point whether or not this would be too dangerous an activity with learners.

A crude example is the *Entertaining English* program (Highlight Software) which ostensibly provides practice for the child (either native or non-native speaker) in producing simple subject–verb–adverb sentences in English. A character called Busy appears in animated scenes on the screen and the learner has to describe Busy's actions. The trouble is that the program only allows responses like *Busy runs quickly*, and rejects *Busy is running quickly*. This makes it an obvious focus for thought or talk *about* the meaning and uses of the present simple and present continuous tenses in English, and when each *would* be appropriate.

More subtly, *Tray* (MEP) and *Storyboard II* (WIDA) are both text reconstruction programs for the child or non-native speaker of English. In effect they are the ultimate cloze exercise: the user is presented with a screen showing a short text *entirely* blanked out: only punctuation and, in the case of *Storyboard*, an indication of spaces and the number of letters in each word remain on screen (each letter is replaced by a square block). The user, by 'buying' as little as possible in the way of words, letters, etc., and 'guessing' as much as possible, has to uncover the blanked out text.

This is best done by a group on a text of suitable level, and probably familiar to the users from prior work, to make the task less formidable. Also, again, to get the best awareness heightening value from it there must be emphasis on *discussion* of possible strategies to use. Then these programs provide ample stimulus for discussion of all kinds of features of language that one *would* want the users to become aware of. The fact that short words are often function words and that, being frequent, they are easier to guess and relatively 'good value' to buy is soon spotted. Also it is easy to bring out, if not spontaneously spotted, the dependency between function words and the part of speech of neighbouring words (e.g. once *the* is guessed, you have a good pointer to where nouns and adjectives may occur) – a valuable aspect of 'inferencing' to be aware of. However, against this, a *critical* discussion will reveal that awareness is also likely to be developed of strategies which are of use for winning the 'game', but have less language awareness heightening value – e.g. the user may become aware that it pays to 'buy' common letters like *e* early on (since if you buy a letter you get shown it wherever it occurs in the entire text), but this does not obviously resemble a strategy operative in real-life reading.

In fact almost every CALL program I have come across and discussed with teachers doing applied linguistics MAs raises some criticisms of a *linguistic* (including psycho-linguistic, etc.) nature. I shall just briefly cite some other examples.

Micro English (LCL) is a collection of exercises relating to aspects of what was the 'O' level English exam. However, in a number of places, especially in the punctuation section, the choice of answers allowed and disallowed can reasonably raise questions as to what the linguistic facts really are, and whether the program is not being a trifle prescriptive.

Rapid Reader (Synergy), among other things, provides a 'tachistocope' option which is supposed to improve users' reading habits by making them focus their eye-spans on stretches of text (which are flashed on screen for a brief period) rather than isolated words. However, the program selects stretches of text to flash up on screen on a purely quantitative basis, without regard for syntactic or semantic considerations, so can flash up a chunk like *even at their* followed by *best, these shows*. This may well prompt thought about the whole psycho-linguistic nature of the reading process and whether it is really likely that a proficient reader actually takes in chunks of text split up in this *arbitrary* way.

Wilt (Longman) provides one of the many computerised versions of the 'hangman' game that are available. This in itself can lead to overt discussion of the extent (or lack of it) to which this game brings into play the full range of different kinds of information about a lexical item that speakers actually need to possess in their mental lexical entry in order to be able to use the word appropriately. Can one play the game successfully without knowing the meanings of the words? Furthermore, *Wilt* provides an unusual form of help for the user, in the shape of information on letter frequencies in different word positions in English. This has interest in itself as metalinguistic information about English, but also raises psycho-linguistic questions of a more critical nature about whether native speakers exploit such information in the real-life lexical production process.

However, it must be stressed that in all these 'critique of CALL' examples the computer program is merely providing a talking-point. The activity is 'open' and it is entirely up to the user and his or her instructor to make sure that *useful* thought about language is generated. But a wide range of matters to do not only with language in the narrow sense but also with wider related things like the reading process can be brought into explicit focus.

Finally, before leaving CALL, mention must be made of certain programs used for CALL that are really content-free utilities used also in a wide range of activities outside CALL. An archetypal program of this sort is a word-processing program (WP) which of course can be used to write anything, but becomes a part of a CALL activity if used by the learner or native-speaker child to write in the language he or she is learning.

Those who have used WPs extensively with learners have reported that the ease of revision afforded by such programs, once the computing aspects of their use are overcome, does itself encourage users to get their peers and teachers to look at early drafts and comment more than otherwise. Hence more talk *about* their writing and the writing process than would otherwise arise is generated, and more drafts are gone through (Canale and Barker, 1986). Further, some WP packages incorporate spelling and style checking programs, and, within their rather narrow limitations, these obviously will automatically make the learner aware of certain nut-and-bolt aspects of his writing (mis-spellings, over-long sentences, split infinitives, etc.).

Two other content-free utility programs that we shall undoubtedly see more of in Language Awareness heightening uses are the database and the 'hypertext'. A database program is essentially like a filing system that enables the user to store and recall sets of connected bits of information in an organised way. *Wordstore* (WIDA) is a very simple program of this sort which enables the user to store any words he wants with, for each, a definitional paraphrase and an example illustrating its use. Clearly this is a facility which prompts the user to think overtly *about* such valuable matters as what words are worth entering, and what to enter about them. A fuller database program allows many types of information to be stored (not just three as above), and this can be accessed in systematic ways for study. For example, having stored various words at various times with information on their meaning and part of speech, etc., the user could call up, say, all verbs which have *go* or *move* in their definitions to examine them together as a semantic group. A ready-made resource of this sort is the *Oxford English Dictionary*, whose full-size version is available on laser disc for computer access in this way, though this particular dictionary would not be suitable for most school or foreign learner use.

A hypertext program essentially allows someone to enter text to which, at any point, notes can be appended which are stored separately from the text. The user who reads the text can, as desired, place the screen cursor on a word in the text and call up the notes associated with that point. This has obvious applications, e.g. in relation to reading difficult authentic text. The teacher can enter text and notes and when (and only when) the user feels there is a difficulty, he or she can summon up the 'help' that the teacher has stored hidden 'behind' the text. This could consist of information about difficult words, etc. (glosses, translations, etc.), or background information about content. Or most valuably it could give further 'clues' or questions to help the reader think about the language of the text in a constructive way to resolve the difficulty: the user could then call up a further level of help to get more explicit information if necessary (since these programs allow many levels of 'depth' of 'notes to notes', as it were). The great thing is that the learner is very much in charge of the pace at which he or she goes and the level of explicit help received.

2 Software designed primarily for language research

There are now a number of established computer uses in language research: computer concordance programs have been developed to go through corpora of text and count up various features of interest (for example, in stylistic and lexicographical research); statistical program packages are used by linguists doing all kinds of empirical work to analyse their results; computers are used to present stimuli and record responses in psycho-linguistic experiments; they are used to synthesise speech in phonetics; they are used to analyse the results of dialect surveys and draw maps; parsing programs are being written which automatically analyse the syntax of sentences; etc. These are very substantial activities at the frontiers of knowledge, and often require professional programmers and mainframe computers rather than the amateur working in BASIC on school micros typical of much CALL. However, a lot of this has obvious potential for use in the future development of CALL and especially Language Awareness heightening software, which we are beginning to see realised.

One simple example of the awareness-raising adaptation of such a program currently is the use of a concordancing program such as the *Oxford Concordance Package* (now available for micros). In essence the software scans text that is available in computerised form and picks out all the instances of some identifiable entity, specified by the user of the program, for display together – often a word with its surrounding context. As such it is a useful adjunct to various kinds of language study.

For instance, in vocabulary study it is obviously useful to be able to summon up a whole set of occurrences of a word in order to study and talk about its common collocates, or the exact range of constructions which follow it. For example, even from the not maximally 'friendly' kind of concordance output for *strikes* in various newspaper texts (see Figure 1), those instances can readily be spotted that relate to *strikes* in the sense of 'suspension of work', and the typical pre-modifiers of the word can easily be extracted. Each line in the figure gives part of the context for a separate occurrence of the word.

	strikes	
We have seen	strikes	in Yugoslavia, riots in
action is selective	strikes	at mail-processing centres
workers had staged 24-hour	strikes	
centre to direct air	strikes	into Angola within range of
created by the hunger	strikes	and the momentum generated
there have been 97 wildcat	strikes	in the Post Office.
of lack of rain and	strikes	by the Indians who work
A point that	strikes	an outsider is the durability

FIGURE 1

This same approach can be relevant in a more grammatical connection. Appropriate use of modal verbs is a well-known problem area for many learners, and would also have to form a part of a grammar awareness program for native English speakers. Again, being able to summon up in one list a lot of instances of, say, *may* or *can* from authentic text is a valuable resource for discussion. It could come in valuably as a follow-up to the presentation of some overt grammar-book statement about the meanings of the modals, in place of the conventional textbook exercise, as a means of testing the rule and users' grasp of it. Or it could be used as a resource for inductive work, where users are set (in group discussion perhaps) to try to *establish* a set of meanings for *may*, which will then be checked against a grammar book's statement.

Even certain text/discourse features can be approached this way. For instance, Tribble (1988) mentions how he was able to demonstrate to his EFL learners with the use of a concordance program how the usage of cohesive words like *however* in their own technical writing differed from that in authentic text. His learners turned out to be using them mainly sentence initially, while in authentic text they normally occurred mid-sentence between commas.

These examples illustrate further the important point that the computer can play a part in awareness heightening without those whose awareness is heightened being necessarily in direct contact with the computer. If necessary the teacher can obtain the output of the concordance program on paper from a distant computer, since in the uses of this section the computer's unique role is more in the output it provides than in any interactive activity in which it is involved.

There are, of course, some provisos on this use of concordance packages, however. For instance, someone has to have entered a sizeable amount of appropriate text for the concordance program to scan – a time-consuming task even with optical character readers (OCRs) such as the Kurzweil, which do the job of reading text from the printed page into the computer automatically, but at the present state of the art, inaccurately (so need a lot of checking). Some corpora of computerised text are already available of course (e.g. the London Oslo Bergen or LOB corpus for many varieties of everyday English, and the works of many literary authors), but these may not always contain the sort of texts that are appropriate to one's purpose. The *Oxford Text Archive* is the best source.

Also, what you want searched for has to be overtly marked. You can't at present ask OCP (Oxford Concordance Package) to pick out, say, all instances of verbs in the present continuous tense – only all words ending in *-ing* and sort through them! If you ask for *may* you are likely to get the month of *May* as well as the modal verb *may* in the list. This will be improved on if in future 'tagged' texts become more available – these being texts on computer with special symbols and code letters added between the words which identify the part of speech of the word, the types of phrases, and other syntactic information. At present this tagging is either done by a grammarian going through the text and doing it by hand, or by experimental computer programs which run through a text and automatically identify the part of speech of each word and so forth ('parsers') – not usually with complete accuracy (see Leech, 1986).

But perhaps the main point is that the computer, as we have seen often before, provides a stimulus or resource here. It can prompt valuable thought and discussion about language, but cannot monitor the nature or quality of that thought or discussion. This the teacher must still orchestrate.

3 Software designed for teaching linguistics

As yet there is not a great deal of software available that is designed directly to teach linguistics rather than language – what this author has christened dedicated 'CALingL' software (Scholfield, 1988). And what is available is mainly directed at higher education. However, some of it clearly has wider potential use in awareness heightening.

Actually a good many aspects of linguistics, e.g. many that are the subject of exercises in current basic textbooks, *could* involve new purpose-written programs along the lines to be described, if anyone has the time and inclination to pursue them. For example, L. Wright at UCNW has written a little program to deal with a particular aspect of the historical development of French (a sound change) which points to some of the potential of historical linguistics for computer-aided Language Awareness work (Wright, 1987). However, at present the dedicated CALingL software of which I am aware focuses mainly on teaching in two areas of the subject – phonetics/phonology and grammar/syntax, which I shall now look at.

In relation to the teaching of phonetics and phonology at least two areas are at present having purpose-written software. One set of programs, described by Fudge (1987), is for first-year undergraduate courses in acoustic and articulatory phonetics. Essentially the programs present on screen dynamic displays of sound waves, jaw movements, etc., associated with particular sounds, to accompany a lecture or to be used for individual study. The computer is thus primarily a visual aid which has certain advantages over pictures in a book or on an OHP (overhead projector) in what can be shown.

Another aspect of this area of language that lends itself to computerisation is transcription. Any basic awareness heightening about the sounds of language will inevitably lead to this: apart from the intrinsic value in forcing the user to think about the differences between the letters in which words are written in conventional orthography and the vowel and consonant *sounds* of which the words are composed, a recep-

tive competence in transcription is useful for a foreign language learner
to exploit the pronunciation information given in many dictionaries.

Here a number of programs are available in various institutions
which enable the student to practise this. My own program is *English
Phonemic Transcription Practice* (described more fully in Scholfield,
1988). It presents the user either with an English word or a short
sentence in orthography for him or her to try transcribing in the
conventions of Gimson, or with a word or sentence in transcribed
form to which he or she should apply the orthographic counterpart.
Various keys on the computer are rigged to enable phonetic symbols to
be typed, and the user is given several attempts to get the right answer,
with some degree of help provided about where he or she may have
gone wrong before being given the right answer (or the user may
initially elect just to look at transcriptions without trying to write them).
In fact the program allows for up to three 'right' transcriptions to be
entered for each word by the teacher, who of course supplies the
computer with whatever sentences and transcriptions are required.
The French and German departments at UCNW are using similar
transcription programs as part of undergraduate teaching of those
languages.

The program just described is limited to *phonemic* transcription of
RP (*received pronunciation*) pronunciation in the conventions of Gimson.
Obviously the ideal would handle narrower phonetic transcription too,
in any desired conventions, for any accent of English. Other desirables
would be the capability to treat longer stretches of text and, the real
challenge, to transcribe automatically the orthographic form entered
by a teacher or user, rather than needing someone to supply the
transcribed version. The ultimate program would enable the computer
to provide a really authentic synthesised rendition in actual sound as
well, but even with the present advances in speech synthesis research
this seems some way off.

Other programs of this sort that I am aware of have some of these
desirable features (and some less desirable ones). For example, a
program by Hawkins (Queen Margaret College, Edinburgh) deals
with transcription of single words only, and involves examples entirely
determined by the program (not entered by a teacher). However, it
has the extra features, compared to mine, of calculating a score,
and being designed to cover Scots as well as RP pronunciation of
every word included. A more ambitious program is that of Knowles
(University of Lancaster) which copes with text, and can automatically
switch between different transcription conventions (e.g. Gimson and
Jones' EPD (English Pronouncing Dictionary)). However, in the form

in which I have seen it described (Knowles, 1986), it does not appear to deal with alternative pronunciations or involve any detailed correction prompt to the user.

Programs of the above sort are more 'closed' than much of what has been discussed earlier; that is to say, the software provides a stimulus *and* handles the user's responses reasonably adequately, hence they lend themselves to individual self-access use for transcription practice by the user, without the need for the teacher to be present, though the initial presentation of the conventions and rationale of transcription would have to be done by the teacher. This kind of computer use has the advantage that learners can go at their own pace and that the teacher, having once entered the sentences and transcriptions, is saved a lot of paper and marking time thereafter. However, the activity does not have the 'learner-centred' properties of more 'open' activities in the sense that the computer is the clear arbiter of right and wrong and is in the driving seat of the activity, which is more 'computer-centred' (with computer replacing teacher).

The second major area of language that lends itself to CALingL computerised practice is grammatical analysis – really the grammatical equivalent of transcription in phonology. Any basic awareness heightening about language will inevitably involve getting used to the different grammatical classes to which words belong (the parts of speech) and the types of syntactic structure which occur – under whatever name this is done (as recognised by the Kingman Report (DES, 1988a: 21). Apart from the intrinsic value in forcing the user to think about the differences in behaviour between words and the distributional regularities of words in sentences, this is important for many other areas of discussion about language. Some basic understanding of the facts and some terminology in this area is needed in order to be able to talk sensibly *about* language and dialect grammatical differences, or grammatical errors, or children's syntax, etc.

I am aware of one or two programs which enable the user to practise this. My own experimental program is *Constituent Structure – Draw Your Own Tree* (described more fully in Scholfield, 1988). It presents the user with a sentence for which he or she has to try to label the part of speech of each word and build a tree diagram on screen showing the hierarchy of phrases and clauses, etc., with appropriate labels (or the user can initially elect just to look at correct examples). The labels and trees can be 'traditional grammar' ones (e.g. as reflected in Quirk *et al.*, 1986), or those specified by X-Bar syntactic theory (Radford, 1981) – though the latter would be unlikely to be used in school Language Awareness work! The user can build and correct labels and tree in any preferred order (top-down, bottom-up, a bit here then a bit there, etc.) till it is considered to be right and then call on a 'right' answer, pre-stored by the teacher, to make visual comparison. Though this is really just 'parsing' updated, it is perhaps just a bit more fun done this way than in the traditional written form. And the manner of entry has the beneficial effect of forcing the user to think of each constituent in terms of the actual words that represent it at the 'bottom'.

The program also has some possible uses outside syntax. Obviously, trees giving the structure of words in morphemes or of phonological strings in syllables and segments (if not requiring phonetic symbols) could be drawn, or indeed, at the semantic level, trees of complex propositions in terms of their component propositions. Furthermore, there is some scope for use where non-syntagmatic trees are relevant – e.g. one can use the program to construct a family tree of the Indo-European languages on a selection of modern languages as the base. Or hyponymy hierarchies in lexical semantics could be displayed, or indeed almost any kind of classification, limited only by the space available on screen.

Returning to the grammatical use, a more developed program of this sort would actually check the tree and labels supplied by the user and automatically show where he or she had gone wrong – even suggest 'tests' for the membership of parts of speech or for constituency that the user might have overlooked in his or her wrong decisions. Also it would allow the user to move constituents about. The ultimate would incorporate a parsing program so that the user could type in any sentence of English, make a suggestion as to the labels and tree, and be provided with the correct answer automatically, without the teacher having to enter all the correct trees beforehand.

I have seen something similar written as a spin-off from some IBM work on syntax of a more research nature, though I am not aware of it being used for teaching. There is also something related in use in Holland (Pijls *et al.*, 1987), more in a school teaching context in relation to awareness of first language Dutch. This latter differs from my software in that it involves a program that automatically does the parsing, and, consequently, runs on more powerful machines than the BBC. Also, though it allows users to put together sentences on screen, with all the facilities of entry via menus and a 'mouse', in fact the parser seems to do the work of building the trees, not the user. Thus the program simply tells if the user has tried to build an impossible sentence, which would be of more value to foreign learners than native speakers. And it *shows* trees, although it does not let the user build a tree, which is the real challenge. The nearest it gets is to allow the user to hide certain labels for phrases, etc., identified by the tree, and try to supply them again.

As with transcription practice programs, the grammatical ones just discussed lend themselves to self-access use, in the context of prior introduction and discussion of the principles led by the teacher.

4 Conclusion

Having all too sketchily reviewed some of the *sorts* of activity available, I must now gather the main points that seem to emerge about their use and usefulness.

Clearly, no claims can be made that computer work will take over the field of Language Awareness heightening. As yet the language topics for which useful computer-related activities are available are scattered, and the activities usually depend heavily on teacher involvement either in prior preparation or in monitoring and follow-up. This is crucial since in many cases it is *how* the program is used that is vital and makes it either a valuable part of a useful activity or a boring waste of time. Only the teacher can ensure that the best use is made. Further, a number of the activities described above can in fact be done almost identically without a computer – e.g. cloze exercise discussion and transcription practice. The computer serves to make the activity (arguably) more interesting, and perhaps saves the teacher some time.

However, if sensibly handled, I think occasional computer activities can be tremendously useful either in a thorough-going awareness course, or as awareness activities interspersed in a course primarily devoted to developing actual language competence and performance. Many of them offer great opportunities for learner-centred inductive learning, or at least self-paced learning. And if done by pairs or groups with the emphasis on off-computer discussion, experience suggests that motivating and awareness heightening effects may be high (though it must be admitted that properly researched empirical evidence is largely lacking as yet).

The author is only too aware (that word again!) that he has only touched on the range of computer-aided Language Awareness heightening activities that his audience may have developed or come across. He hopes that readers will help him by letting him know of interesting programs and uses of programs of this sort, so that he can build up a centralised store of information on the subject.

Section Five: Evaluation of Language Awareness

The four papers assembled in this section all address the bottom-line question: but do LA activities work? We ourselves expressed surprise in our introductory chapter about the whole educational system being asked to take LA on board 'on trust' by people in high places who have a gut-level 'feeling' that it *does* work. At that point we went in pursuit of work seriously addressing this question of evaluation. We discovered relatively little. We approached experts in testing and educational evaluation: they too were unable to direct us to any significant body of relevant studies or publications. The four papers we introduce here represent the best of recent evaluative work in the field.

First, the four papers give a cross-sectional survey, so to speak, of LA evaluation in the four main areas of language education: Heap, in Paper 18, deals with LA in the Mother Tongue English; Masny (Paper 21) with English as a second language in Francophone Canada, where English is used in the community as well as the school, so that an acquisition-rich learning environment is guaranteed; in Paper 19, Zhou Yan-Ping, by contrast, is operating in a clearly foreign language and acquisition-poor learning environment (a secondary school in Shanghai); Scott, in Paper 20, evaluates LA in a Brazilian English for Special Purposes setting. We see this as a first step towards identifying the specific types and special mixes of LA work that are likely to be required to give optimum results in these four sorts of environment.

At the same time we are of course cognisant of the fact that these environments, as described in this section, are idealisations. We do not wish to suggest that there are *four* standard types of teaching situation. In reality, there are innumerable learning environments that fall somewhere along a continuous scale between these ideals, so that every single situation will have to be described 'without prejudice' and not assigned to one of the four types we see described in this section.

Second, there are important differences in the research 'designs' adopted by each of the four contributors. Masny's is clearly a descriptive-correlational study, in that she undertakes no teaching and plots no changes resulting from this teaching in LA and/or language proficiency between a 'Time 1' and a 'Time 2'. She identifies changes by, so to speak, freezing time and looking at learners at different stages of learning under roughly the same conditions: hers is a cross-sectional study. It contrasts in these two respects (correlational and cross-sectional) with Zhou's study, which is experimental (in the sense that she uses a Control and an Experimental group, each of which receives different teaching input), and is (minimally) longitudinal, in the sense that she measures foreign language proficiency before and after a 'treatment' period of 18 lessons of 50 minutes duration each in order to see the effects it has brought about.

Heap's evaluation was in two phases: first, he undertook an informal evaluation that involved trying to explain why it happened that pupils in his own school who had been exposed to the LA materials showed 'disproportionately' high attainment in French, science and drama. These observations, and a wish to explain them, paved the way to a formal evaluation involving more schools and allowing him to set up control and experimental groups, each of which took a pre-test and an end-of-treatment test for purposes of comparison. Scott's research method was not experimental in that he did not isolate control and experimental groups and compare their achievements under differential treatments; his approach was observational, making use of a questionnaire (see Holmes and Ramos, Paper 15) that invited learners to identify and assess the LA-based procedures they had used in workshops. This approach to research reflects Scott's approach to teaching, apparently: *conscientização* in teaching involves knowing WHY something needs to be taught or learnt (e.g. finding good reasons for studying the passive voice); likewise the assessment of *conscientização* involves locating WHERE it positively helped, which in turn becomes a justification for having invoked it – proving WHY again. For Scott, LA is vindicated by the high positive correlation he found in his survey between users' high assessment of LA on the one hand and the gains these same learners made on the course: if the 'good' and satisfied learner-clients rated LA highly, then there must be value in it. In this stance he agrees with Heap, who likewise found that LA fostered a methodology that was learner-centred, with the result that the learners became more self-reliant and more prepared to undertake (even self-critical) self-appraisal. One might speculate that it was these positive effects on methodology and attitude that motivated Heap to look for justification for LA to show to his fellow teachers. He had long since become dissatisfied with 'preaching to the converted' the good news of LA and now wished instead to proselytise and win more converts – but now through appeal to fact rather than to faith.

A terminological distinction is in order here: while the three other studies sought to *evaluate* LA, Heap was intent on *validating* it.

We have moved to the third aspect of these evaluative studies: explanation. Why, when LA was shown to have positive effects on, or to correlate positively with enhanced attainment, should this have come about? And when not, why not? The reasons suggested by three of the writers at least show remarkable consensus on this. For Masny, the key to the high correlation between LA, as tested by judgement of grammaticality tests, and highly developed reading skills lies in the student's capacity for *decontextualisation*. By this she means 'detaching language from the here-and-now ... communicative proficiency in which background is not assumed to be shared (implicitly) by the sender and receiver'. Moreover, this capacity is 'related to successful language learning in the classroom'. Heap's explanation why LA works draws on the ideas derived from Bernstein by Mason (1986), particularly the notion that the key to success at school lies in the child's ability to learn and use the 'elaborated' code that is characterised by its *abstractness*. Scott in turn seems to be thinking along similar lines when he refers to the desirability of 'getting students to develop metaphors and analogies'... [which] .. 'in the light of the *conscientização* theory proposed here ... would be logical development'. There is something abstract about metaphor, as there is something detached about abstraction. That Zhou also sees LA in terms of detachment and a willingness to confront abstraction can be inferred from the kind of teaching input that her experimental group received but her control group did not (cf. her Figure 1). Explicit formal teaching in her study was characterised by the activity of Error Detection and Correction. Now this type of input is known as *negative evidence* (Chomsky, 1986: 55), and it is of the type that children acquiring their first language do not get and also the type of evidence that teachers have been reluctant to use in their language teaching, for fear of learners learning mistakes. Zhou's study suggests that it is not deleterious to learning, since it accomplishes that detachment from language we call LA. It would seem then that these four contributors have jointly stumbled on the same philosopher's stone: perhaps we have the key to LA if we view it as a learnable capacity to detach oneself from one's language and one's uses of language, to see oneself objectively from outside as the articulate mammal that man uniquely is.

Zhou then, like the other three, finds good cause for doing LA work in school: her study confirms that there is indeed an interface between conscious and unconscious knowledge, but the seepage from consciously learnt to unconsciously used language knowledge is not uniform but is determined by the specific structure involved. Her explanations are also interesting: for these she resorts to the native language of her Chinese learners, pointing out that the variable English tense marker is a *particular* problem for the Chinese learner: this could be the beginning, through LA, of a return to Contrastive Analysis and its prediction of learning difficulties.

But Zhou has another explanation for the observed failure to learn: how Chinese teachers tend to teach the structure in question: 'In the Chinese classroom, the foregrounding or focus function of the passive is seldom explained to the learner.' What is significant here is that you have to have been a teacher in a Chinese school to know that: such information cannot be found in books. Throughout Heap's paper we likewise have a sensation that somebody is addressing us who knows about schools and learners. And yet, Heap tells us that he would never have got his study off the ground had he not enjoyed cooperation and encouragement from universities. All this points to the need for there to be more trust and cooperation between universities (where one type of research gets preferred) and schools (where another sort needs to be undertaken). Toncheva, in Paper 11, has shown us how the perceptive teacher can spot learners making crucial decisions about their learning in the classroom with the result that LA is self-generating in the classroom: in these papers we see that the classroom is the place for the final evaluation of LA.

18 Evaluating the effectiveness of an LA course

Brian Heap

1 The Wigan language project

I was asked to evaluate Mary Mason's LA materials (which had come to be known as the Wigan Language Project (WLP)) during the academic year 1987–8. The project, which had been running for four years in Wigan LEA, mostly in my own school, Shevington High School, consists of a LA course in three parts to be covered in each of the first three years of secondary education. This course is now being published under the series title of *Illuminating English* by TRACE, Wigan. Book One: *Language Awareness*, is designed to widen students' general language knowledge, making their intuitive knowledge of language explicit and providing them with the chance of developing a model of concrete language, by looking at grammar, functions, varieties, roots. The picture of language structure they gain will affect study of their own language, other varieties of their own language, and other languages. Book Two: *Reading for Learning*, is designed to demystify academic English, the sorts of language used by teachers and textbooks, by building on the concrete model that the students have already gained and introducing a model of abstract language almost as if it were a foreign language. The two relevant models of language are described in Mason (1986, 1987). The course covers the vocabulary of abstract language by exploring the pervasive Greek and Latin influences. It unveils the metaphor recurrent in academic English, shows how morphology systematically alters word classes, and how short sentences enter into the construction of longer ones. This gives school students a chance to become familiar with the language of abstract thought before they become dependent on such language for their learning. The third book of the course, *Writing for Learning*, is based on Hoey's (1983) work on discourse organisation. This is intended to take students to the level of language 'above' the sentence, giving them an idea of organisation involved in whole texts. The course is designed to be followed independently by students of any ability who work through each unit 'tasting' as much as they can of each point.

The project had received some support within the Local Education Authority, including the approval of the Director of Education. The funding provided had enabled the trials to be carried out in schools. The WLP, however, was gaining acceptance very slowly and it was felt necessary to justify the course to others in terms that they would accept.

I include some of the history of the informal evaluation undertaken during the trials in the years previous to the formal evaluation exercise because I feel it is important as a background to the formal exercise, the main point of this paper.

The evidence that started to appear as a result of the pilot lessons led us to consider the course quite carefully and to start our own informal evaluation. The experience within schools laid the foundations for the formal evaluation exercise and pre-empted problems that could have occurred. Yet, I feel that the practical concerns and problems encountered are worth mentioning to anyone undertaking their own evaluation. I wish, therefore, to outline these aspects, hoping the information will be of use.

2 First steps towards evaluation

The evaluation exercise that I undertook in 1988 was a straightforward exercise leading to a report for the Wigan authority, not an academic paper. The first section of the report contains a review of relevant literature with the aim of providing a rationale for explicit language study in schools, and a look at Wigan's own curriculum framework, which showed a realisation of the need for LA, but no solution. Both were used to judge the face value of the WLP. The second section covers the practical elements of the evaluation exercise and the evidence gained with a view to providing hard evidence of the effect of the content and the style of working involved, leading to the conclusions drawn. The aim was to produce a document containing evidence that could be used to persuade other schools, heads, advisers, officers and councillors of the benefits of the WLP.

Many of the discussions about LA tend to involve preaching to the converted, but it is necessary to convince many others with a wide variety of views and experiences. This was the reason for the formal evaluation. It must again be stressed that the test results were to be used for justification to others. However, we need the evidence of effect on students' progress through school as the main focus.

In order to write a review of literature concerning LA in general and evaluation of LA materials in particular, I had to locate such literature.

This was where I encountered the problem of LA being a relatively recent term, receiving mention in a variety of writings but, as it was not an established area, it did not have the easily located plethora of literature that one expects of a long-standing compartmentalised subject. Fortunately, I was seconded to the Centre of Educational Research and Development at the University of Lancaster, where I received advice and support in the practical details of an evaluation exercise as well as gaining access to university staff. After several contacts I was led to the Department of Linguistics and Modern English Language where I made very fruitful contact which led to some extremely valuable information and support. This led to a relatively successful coverage of relevant literature.

3 Informal evaluation

The organisation of the evaluation exercise stemmed, in the main, from the informal evaluation we had undertaken in Shevington High School. One class had been the subject of pilot lessons for a year with the then head of English. By coincidence this class was noticed as being represented disproportionately in the top sets in French, firstly, and then in science even though all first-year classes (seven, mixed ability) had produced similar scores in the routine cognitive abilities testing earlier in the year. The pilot class had covered most of Book One of the WLP during their first year and I continued with Book One and some pilot lessons of Book Two in their second year, and a comprehension test using an academic text showed a noticeable difference between the scores obtained by the pilot class and those of another class chosen at random. It was then decided to put the evaluation on a more formal setting within the school, so the following year group was divided into an experimental and a control group. We were also looking for testing which would reflect that which is normally expected of school students. The Language Aptitude Test from York University had already shown itself to be a good discriminator, having been used to predict group performance in FL and we are, after all, concerned with potential here. In fact the major problem arose with a test for Book Two, which involves analysis of the features of abstract language of the academic world. Many English tests covered the literary, narrative text, but not the abstract impersonal, so eventually a text was chosen from an 'O' level home economics textbook and transformed into a cloze comprehension test (1 in 7 deletion). Because of the effects noticed in the experimental groups it was considered essential to ensure that every student would benefit from the course. This meant, therefore, that it was no longer possible to compare groups within the school. The time had come to evaluate the course in other schools within the authority to see if the results would be replicated.

It must be stressed that although the preoccupation seems to be with formal testing, that is not the case. There has always been a wish to gather evidence from the usual work undertaken in schools as a source of continuous evaluation. The problem, however, lies with people detecting what could be evidence of the effect of the course. One notable remark passed by the head of drama concerned his work on symbolism with third-year students. Some classes took much less time than others to understand the concept and he then realised that the quicker classes were following the LA course.

4 Formal evaluation

4.1 Method
I was seconded for one year to undertake the formal evaluation of the course, which by this time was being prepared for publication by Wigan College's publishing company, TRACE. Three other schools now volunteered their cooperation for the evaluation exercise. All three followed the first book of the WLP with a number of classes. Two of the schools (D and M) ran experimental and control groups for the purpose of the evaluation exercise, while the third school (C) did not feel able to commit itself to the formal testing, yet provided valuable comment.

The groups were organised as follows: at first-year level School D provided two classes (termed 'upper' and 'lower' band) as part of the experimental group covering the full ability range, apart from those receiving remedial attention and two classes from the same two bands for control purposes, while School M provided one class (termed 'the second set') as part of the experimental group and another class ('the third set') for control purposes. I have included the results for the whole first year at Shevington at the same time, for comparison. At second-year and third-year level the whole year group at Shevington was used as an experimental group while the equivalent year groups from School M were used for control purposes.

Each group was given its assigned pre-test at the beginning of the academic year and the post-test at the end of that year. The first-year groups were given the York University Language Aptitude Test of which there is only one version. The second-year groups were given the cloze comprehension of the home economics text about cheese production mentioned earlier. Book Three, the third-year work, was a pilot of the work about discourse organisation and the testing was therefore a pilot also. It was decided to use a writing assignment that would show an example of the students' organisation of a whole written piece. The students were asked, in the pre-test, to consider the future for young people and, in the post-test, to consider whether this country was the best place in which to live. Unlike the tests for the first two parts, there was no set marking scheme, so marks from one to five were awarded on the basis of holistic impression.

Throughout the testing, it was the group picture that was required, rather than individual scores, so as to minimise the effects of one-shot testing. The first point of note must be the remarkably similar pre-test scores for the groups in each year (see Table 1); the scores for the whole first year at Shevington differed because the full ability range was involved at Shevington and not at other schools. The increase in the mean scores for each group is expressed as a percentage increase for ease of comparison. Mary Mason's original intention was to introduce school students to the features of *Reading for Learning* (Book Two) and she provided Book One as a preparation. That Book One could be shown to have such a significant effect could be considered a bonus. The significant difference in progress as measured by the scores for tests relating to Book Two show how effective the course is. It must be mentioned also that the students involved had *not* been able to finish the trial version of Book Two inside one year so had not covered many of the features of the more complex sentence structure in *Reading for Learning*.

The tests for the first two year groups employed a completely objective marking scheme. The test for the third-year work did depend, however, on impression marking and evaluation concerning Book Three may need refinement, but I feel that the remarkable difference in progress as measured by the scores demanded attention.

As well as considering the effect of the content of the course of students' progress it was possible to consider the learning method adopted in the WLP which was intended as a learning package. Comments were passed by staff involved in the evaluation about greater self-reliance among many students, about students wanting to be left to work and realising when they needed help or when they had achieved their objective, many with obvious enjoyment and interest in the topics covered. I was concerned also with the effect of different teaching styles on the students' progress. The quantitative outcomes showed no evidence of effect of different styles.

The effects noticed at Shevington High School were in evidence

TABLE 1 Test results

Group	Pre-test		Post-test		Increase	
	Mean	S.D.	Mean	S.D.	Mean	%
Book 1: Language Aptitude Test						
Experimental	24.88	7.58	34.27	8.05	9.40	37.8
Control	25.65	7.67	32.85	8.31	7.21	27.8
Shevington (comparison)	19.54	10.82	26.54	12.16	7.00	35.8
Book 2: Academic English Comprehension Test						
Experimental	26.25	7.21	32.38	7.37	6.13	23.4
Control	26.24	8.34	30.23	9.11	3.99	15.2
Book 3: Academic Writing Test						
Experimental	2.76	0.96	3.20	0.96	0.44	15.94
Control	2.80	0.93	2.85	1.04	0.05	1.79

$p = 0.042$

$p = 0.003$

$p = 0.000$

again at these other schools within the authority. The test results were replicated, but once again I encountered the problem of interpretation of evidence. For example, ten students from the experimental group in School M were transferred into the set above with an explanation that this was not connected with the work they were doing in English lessons (LA) but with the work in all subjects – a similar picture to the pilot study.

5 Conclusions

Many people in schools would like to know about such evidence which could be used to persuade others such as their own senior management. We must take the evidence available and also let people know that it is available.

The evaluation exercise was very useful for me and I know that the Wigan authority will take the results of my work into account in future planning in schools. I hope also that others may find the evidence useful.

19 The effect of explicit instruction on the acquisition of English grammatical structures by Chinese learners[1]

Zhou Yan-Ping

1 Introduction

The role of formal instruction in second language acquisition (hereafter SLA) research has long been a controversial issue. Research findings from morpheme and 'relative utility' studies have led to a conflict of opinion among SLA researchers on the question whether there is any need to teach grammar. Some hold that given a 'natural order' in acquisition, grammar teaching is unnecessary (Terrell, 1981; Krashen, 1981, 1982). Others argue that raising learners' consciousness of grammatical properties may accelerate SLA. In the SL classroom, learners should be made aware of the grammatical properties of the target language (Sharwood Smith, 1981; Rutherford, 1987).

Out of this debate grew two conflicting theories. The monitor theory, postulated by Krashen, advocates that there is no interface between explicit and implicit knowledge; according to him, learning is independent of acquisition. Protagonists of the interface position represented by Bialystok, Sharwood Smith and McLaughlin argue, however, that there is an interface between explicit and implicit knowledge. One can be converted into the other by dint of practice. The teacher's task, therefore, is to sensitise the learners to specific linguistic properties and provide opportunities for them to practise the properties learnt. Empirical studies have been carried out in an attempt to find evidence in support of formal instruction. Owing to the methodological problems in their research design, the findings from these studies are ambiguous. While some are in favour of formal instruction and some show negative effects, others do not offer clear results. The ambiguity had something to do with the research method applied. Three problems will be identified:

1. *Some of the studies do not measure the absolute effect of formal instruction on the acquisition of specific grammatical properties, but examine the 'relative utility' of formal instruction.*

Long (1983) presents a comprehensive review of the relevant studies on the effect of formal instruction. These studies investigated the effect of formal instruction on L2 proficiency in relation to the effect of simple exposure to the L2 learner in naturalistic settings. The problem is that most of the investigations were carried out in acquisition-rich environments where English is the target language. In such environments, learners had access to L2 through both formal instruction and natural exposure.

Therefore, when analysing the results, it is difficult to separate the effects of instruction and exposure.

2. *Some of the studies looked at the combination effect of several features of formal instruction rather than a single feature.*

For example, in Van Elek and Oskarsson's study (1972), five grammatical properties were taught in the experimental lesson series. One hundred and twenty-five adult learners of English were assigned to two groups and treated with explicit and implicit methods, respectively. The results revealed that after 40 hours of instruction, both groups made some progress in the acquisition of the structures, but the explicit group made better progress than the implicit group. They concluded that the explicit method was more effective than the implicit method. However, the two methods adopted in their study differed not only in the feature of explicitness but also in other features such as the deductive/inductive presentation of the rules and different exercise types: pattern drills versus fill-in-the-blanks and translation task. When interpreting the data, it is difficult to identify which feature is the decisive factor that contributes to a better progress in learning.

3. *The duration of the experiment.*

To the best of our knowledge, only the small-scale, feature-focused research that was carried out by Seliger (1975) evaluates the inductive and deductive methods with regard to one aspect of syntax, i.e. the pre-nominal modifiers. The only difference between the two methods had to do with the point at which explanation was given in the lesson. Seliger observed that the deductive method was superior to the inductive method in respect of long-term retention, but in this study instruction took place for too short a period of time (only 65 minutes). No broad generalisations can be drawn from such a single limited-duration study.

It should also be noted that the majority of the studies on the effect of formal instruction have not been framed in terms of the theoretical notion of the interface position. Only two empirical studies related the findings to the interface debate (Van Baalen, 1983; Ellis, 1984). The findings from Van Baalen's study were in favour of the interface position: the explicit group outperformed the implicit group on the easy rules on spontaneous language production, lending support to the argument that explicit knowledge can be converted into implicit knowledge. Ellis' study confirms neither the interface nor the non-interface position, although some of the findings were compatible with Krashen's theory. Ellis maintains that more studies should be carried out before either the interface or the non-interface position can be confirmed.

From the above discussion, we can see that in order to gain a clearer picture on the effects of various kinds of formal instruction, more empirical studies should be carried out. These studies should incorporate the following characteristics:

(a) The experiment should be done in an acquisition-poor setting where learners have no target language exposure outside the classroom.
(b) It should focus on one feature of formal instruction.
(c) The formal instruction given to the students should last a reasonable period of time.

The present study represents an attempt to examine the absolute effect of formal instruction on SLA. The experiment, which has tried to incorporate the three features mentioned above, was conducted in one of the middle schools in Shanghai, China – an acquisition-poor setting. It took place over a period of three weeks and focused on just one feature: the explicitness of formal instruction.

2 Purpose of the study

The main objective of the present study was twofold. First, to investigate the role of formal instruction in SLA by comparing the effects of two methods, explicit formal instruction and implicit formal instruction, on Chinese adolescent learners of English. In this study, formal instruction denotes the kind of instruction that draws learners' attention to the formal characteristics of the grammatical features. Explicit formal instruction is defined as the method in which learners are required to work out and articulate the grammatical properties and rules if they can. The teacher provides explanations of the properties and rules with metalanguage within the students' grasp (mainly in their native language). Implicit formal instruction refers to the method whereby the learners are guided to make generalisations on their own. No explanations of the properties and rules are given. These two methods were compared with respect to the learners' acquisition of the three areas of grammar: the simple past tense, the present perfect and the passive construction. The second objective of the study was to ascertain if there existed an interface between explicit knowledge and implicit knowledge. The research hypotheses for the experimental survey were:

1. Formal instruction in general is conducive to the success of SLA. It helps L2 learners to improve their proficiency in the production of well-formed sentences in different learning tasks.
2. Explicit formal instruction (EFI) is more effective than implicit formal instruction (IFI) in accelerating the rate of SLA. The EFI group will make better progress than the IFI group in the performance of different tasks.
3. There is an interface between explicit and implicit knowledge. Through formal and functional practice, explicit knowledge can be converted into implicit knowledge.

3 The design of the study

3.1 The subjects
The sample used in this research consisted of forty Grade 8 students in Beihai Middle School in Shanghai. All of them volunteered to take part in this ESL programme. Table 1 presents the characteristics of the sample.

These subjects were randomly assigned to the two treatment groups on the basis of prior English proficiency level as reflected by their (a) test score on a cloze test, (b) average academic score, (c) pre-test score. One group received explicit formal instruction, the other received implicit formal instruction.

Table 2 provides data for a comparison of the two treatment groups with regard to their prior proficiency in English.

TABLE 1   Characteristics of the subjects

Number of subjects	40
Number of schools	1
Secondary level	2
Age range	14–15
Sex: Male	16
Female	24
Motivation	High
Target language exposure	Classroom only

TABLE 2   Comparison of the initial proficiency in English between the two treatment groups[2]

Test	Treatment group						
	EFI			IFI			
	N	$\bar{X}$ (%)	S	N	$\bar{X}$ (%)	S	2-tailed prob.
Pre-test	20	33.73	0.065	20	34.93	0.055	0.543
Cloze test	20	69.04	0.187	20	70.71	0.156	0.581
Academic score	20	90.16	0.082	20	90.12	0.103	0.354
Total		192.93			194.76		

As can be seen, there was no significant difference between the two groups in respect to their prior English proficiency. In terms of the total raw scores, the IFI group was slightly superior to the EFI group.

3.2 The experimental lesson series

The experimental lesson series consisted of eighteen 50-minute experimental lessons per method. In order not to interfere with the regular course, all the lessons were conducted after normal classes (from 3.00 to 5.00 p.m.). The investigator taught both EFI and IFI groups. Each group had two periods of classes on alternate days in which the eleven grammatical properties of the three structures were taught. The distributions of the eleven properties of the three structures are as follows:

(a) The simple past tense:
  – irregular versus regular verb morphology;
  – do-support for negative and interrogative constructions;
  – anaphoric use of the past tense.
(b) The present perfect:
  – perfect of persistent situation;
  – experiential perfect;
  – perfect of result;
  – difference between the simple past tense and the present perfect;
  – distinction between *since* and *for*.

(c) The passive construction:
  - morphological properties of the passive;
  - mapping of *AGENT* and *PATIENT* onto noun phrases;
  - focus function of the passive.

These properties were selected according to the following principles:

(a) They should be easy enough for the students at this level to learn (the low scores of the pre-test and the relatively high scores of the post-test suggest that the choice of the structures was appropriate).
(b) They should be structures that present special difficulties to Chinese learners and were found to be sources of errors in the classroom, presumably because of syntactic differences between the two languages.
(c) They should not have been dealt with in the regular course and were unknown to the subjects.[3]

Since the selected three structures are not equally complex, the proportion of time devoted to each structure varied. The schedule of all experimental activities is given in Table 3 (left hand column).

3.3 Methods compared

The two methods adopted in this study had much in common in terms of teaching techniques. The only difference between the two was related to the degree of explicitness in the explanation of the grammatical features. Figure 1 summarises the classroom activities carried out in the two groups.

It can be seen that in the first, second and fourth stages, the two groups performed the same activities. In the third stage, however, four types of hypothesis-testing activities were assigned to each group, three of which were the same (dialogue completion, sentence transformation, multiple choice). But the error detection and correction activity was only performed by the EFI group; the IFI group had the fill-in-the-blank exercise. It should be mentioned that although the exercise type differed, the contents of the exercise were exactly the same; that is to say, the same grammatical properties were practised. The assignment of the different tasks to different groups was dictated by the principle that, in the IFI group, grammar should be taught in an implicit/covert way, while in the EFI group, the learners should learn the grammar explicitly/overtly. The grammatical information should be openly presented and explicitly explained. Therefore, the learners in the EFI group were directly exposed to grammatical errors. It

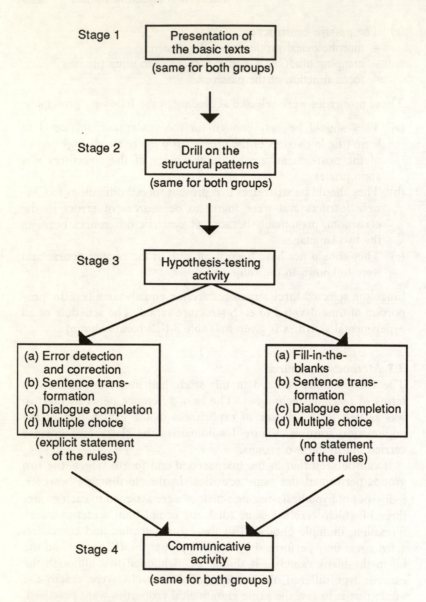

Stage 1 — Presentation of the basic texts (same for both groups)

Stage 2 — Drill on the structural patterns (same for both groups)

Stage 3 — Hypothesis-testing activity

(a) Error detection and correction
(b) Sentence transformation
(c) Dialogue completion
(d) Multiple choice

(explicit statement of the rules)

(a) Fill-in-the-blanks
(b) Sentence transformation
(c) Dialogue completion
(d) Multiple choice

(no statement of the rules)

Stage 4 — Communicative activity (same for both groups)

FIGURE 1   Teaching and learning activities in the classroom

was assumed that by drawing the learners' attention to such erroneous sentences, their consciousness of the grammatical properties would be better raised. This also accords with Rutherford's (1987) postulation that one of the instruments to raise learners' consciousness of aspects of the grammatical system could be error identification and correction.

In accordance with the principle set forth for the experiment, the learners in the EFI group were asked to articulate the regularities they had discovered; the teacher explained the rules when necessary. In the IFI group, no rule statement was given.

Two versions of a workbook comprising eighteen worksheets were compiled, one for each group. Most of the texts and exercises were selected from *Project English*, Volume II (Hutchinson, 1986). The book claims to adopt an analytical approach in which learners are treated as thinkers who are guided to work out the rules themselves. This principle is identical with the principle we laid down for the experiment. This book, therefore, serves the purpose of the present study very well, but we adapted the text to our experimental purpose, because each unit in the text contains many more exercises than can be covered in the experimental lesson. In order to control the teaching variable, the subjects were not allowed to take the workbook home. There was no homework. The teacher collected the workbooks after class.

3.4 Measurement instruments and data analyses

To investigate the efficacy of the two methods with respect to the eleven grammatical features of the three structures, an achievement test battery was designed and used both as pre- and post-tests to measure the subjects' progress. This was a written test with 246 grammar items representing eleven grammatical properties. The subjects were required to perform five tasks, namely, error detection, error correction, passage/dialogue completion, reading comprehension and spontaneous language production (see Appendices 1–5, test samples).

In the error detection and correction tasks, eighty grammar items were tested, half of which were correct (eight for each property, except the function of the passive). The first part of the judgement task was composed of twenty sentences. The learners were not told which structure was being investigated, but they were told some sentences contained errors. In the second part of the judgement test, some of the verbal forms were underlined and numbered. The learners were asked first to make judgements about the acceptability of the sentences and then make corrections if necessary.

The third task was an ordinary sentence completion test with forty-four grammar items, four for each property. The learners were required to answer the questions with the information given or fill in the blanks with proper verb forms (see Appendices 1 and 2).

The reading comprehension test was specially designed to examine the subjects' understanding of the temporal and aspectual properties of the simple past tense and the present perfect (see Appendix 3).

The last task was a spontaneous production test in which the subjects were required (i) to describe a series of actions the teacher performed and (ii) to describe the pictures with the words given (see Appendices 4 and 5). These two kinds of tests were formerly employed by Smith (1979) and Van Baalen (1983) in order to elicit the learners' internalised/acquired knowledge of the language. We assume along with Smith and Van Baalen that improved spontaneous performance indicates a high level of automatisation of the target language, and that the explicit knowledge which the subjects obtained during the course of instruction was transferred into implicit knowledge.

The test items in the spontaneous language production task covered all the three structures: part (i) was related to the different use of the simple past tense and the present perfect; part (ii) examined the use of the passive construction. In the first four tasks – namely, error detection, error correction, sentence completion, reading comprehension – no time limit was set, but a time limit was imposed on the last task. When the teacher was performing the actions, the subjects were required to write down simultaneously the appropriate sentences. Altogether 15 minutes were set for the last task. So the learners had no time to monitor their performance. It was assumed that the action/picture description would elicit natural, acquired knowledge.

The achievement test was administered both as a pre-test and a post-test, so that comparisons could be made to see whether there was any significant difference between the scores from the two tests.

All the test papers were scored by the investigator. Both binary and ternary scales were used for scoring. For example, in the error detection task, a binary scale was employed. If an error was discerned by the subject, 4 points would be given. If the subject failed to spot the error or took the right version for the wrong one, he received a '0'. In error correction, a ternary scale was adopted. If a correct version was supplied, the subject received 4 points. But if the verb form was partly right, a score ranging from 1 to 3 was given. For example, given the following erroneous sentence:

*All the cakes has ate by the guests.

If the subject changed the sentence to *All the cakes have been eaten by the guests*, 4 points would be given; the correction *All the cakes have been aten by the guests* would score 3 points; 2 points would be given to the answer *All the cakes have been ate by the guests*; and the subject would receive 1 point if the sentence was corrected as *All the cakes has aten by the guests*.

The ternary scale was also used in the sentence completion and action/picture description tasks. In the reading comprehension task, the binary scale was used. Any correct version of the test item received 4 points. The total score for the achievement test was 984 points (246 × 4).

The results from both pre- and post-tests were hand tabulated and numerically coded. They were then entered into a data file and were statistically analysed using the Statistical Package for the Social Science (SPSS). *t*-Tests and paired *t*-tests were utilized to determine if there was significant difference in the subjects' performance in the pre- and post-tests. The following section reports the results of the statistical analyses.

4 Results of statistical analyses

The results of the study can be summarised as follows:

(i) Positive findings were obtained which show the form-based classroom instruction is conducive to the success of SLA, be it implicit or explicit.

Paired *t*-tests were used to measure and compare statistically the results of the pre- and post-tests within each method to see if there is a significant gain on the post-test in each case. The figures for two-tailed probability indicate that both groups made marked progress in terms of overall performance on test items across task types and eleven linguistic properties. All of the pre- and post-test scores were found to be significantly different at the 0.01 level, suggesting that each method in itself (IFI, EFI) provided the students with a chance to improve considerably on language proficiency over the instruction period.

(ii) The second hypothesis is only partially confirmed by the statistical analyses. The available data indicate that the EFI group did significantly better than the IFI group in carrying out various learning tasks. The level of significance reached the 0.01 level. However, a different picture emerges when we compare the mean scores of the two groups across the eleven grammatical properties. Table 3 shows

TABLE 3   Comparison of the post-test results in terms of properties

Property		EFI Group			IFI Group			
		N	$\bar{X}$	S	N	$\bar{X}$	S	T	2-tail Prob.
PST	IR	20	87.00	0.109	20	81.92	0.110	1.46	0.151
	DS	20	77.56	0.178	20	60.87	0.230	2.57*	0.015
	AN	20	90.25	0.099	20	84.37	0.144	1.50	0.142
PP	EX	20	79.75	0.185	20	78.75	0.156	0.18	0.855
	RE	20	68.25	0.189	20	64.06	0.192	0.69	0.491
	PE	20	77.69	0.185	20	73.37	0.156	0.80	0.431
	DI	20	77.37	0.136	20	67.12	0.098	2.74*	0.010
	SF	20	71.87	0.238	20	68.15	0.190	0.55	0.587
PAS	AG	20	82.31	0.081	20	75.87	0.109	2.12*	0.042
	FO	20	83.56	0.090	20	78.06	0.068	2.18*	0.036
	FC	20	90.00	0.082	20	67.50	0.337	2.90*	0.009

*Statistical significance

the comparison of the post-test results in terms of those properties. Two observations can be made:

First, there is a clear statistical difference between the two groups in the passive construction. A significant difference can be discerned on all the three properties of the passive. The EFI group did conspicuously better than the IFI group in the use of the foregrounding (Focus) function of the passive (FC $p = 0.009$, raw score: 90/67%). In the other two properties, namely, the mapping of AGENT and PATIENT to the NP slots (AG) and the morphological properties of the passive (FO), significant differences at the level of 0.05 were found.

Second, the two groups showed no clear statistical difference on the acquisition of tense and aspect. Among the eight properties relating to tense and aspect, only two (do-support (DS) and the simple past/present perfect contrast (DI)) reached the level of significance. From the data available, we may claim that explicit formal instruction is more effective than implicit formal instruction in accelerating the rate of acquisition of the passive construction. However, this is not true of their learning of tense and aspect. As far as these two categories are concerned, explicit instruction is not superior to implicit instruction.

It is interesting that the result from the comparison of the gain scores of the two groups is identical to that of the comparison of the post-test scores of the two groups. The EFI group performed significantly better than the IFI group across task types. But with regard to the grammatical properties, the former did not outperform the latter, except on the passive construction.

The result of the spontaneous production test appears to be in favour of the interface position. The EFI group did significantly better than the IFI group in the picture and action description tasks ($p < 0.01$) This suggests that explicit knowledge can be converted into implicit knowledge through practice.

5 Discussion

The findings from this study suggest that formal instruction in general is conducive to the success of SLA. The scores obtained from the pre- and post-tests within each group have provided ample evidence to support the first hypothesis.

5.1 Marked improvement on test items across task types and properties in both groups

As we saw above, there was substantial overall progress in each group as a result of experimental lessons. The two methods functioned well and led to significant difference at the 0.01 level both across task types and properties. It was observed that the initial scores of the present perfect and the passive construction were very low, ranging from 0.94% to 46.87%. However, after the experimental treatment, all the scores exceeded 64%. The lowest group gain score was 3.12%, which appeared in the IFI group on the test items relating to the property of do-support for negative and interrogative constructions. The highest gain score reached 88.13% which was obtained by the EFI group on the foregrounding function of the passive. Although the initial scores of the simple past tense were already relatively high, ranging from 46.48% to 72.75%, noticeable progress can still be observed. Statistics show that both groups improved appreciably on the properties of the irregular past tense morphology (IR) and the anaphoric use of the past tense (AN). Figures 2 and 3 demonstrate,

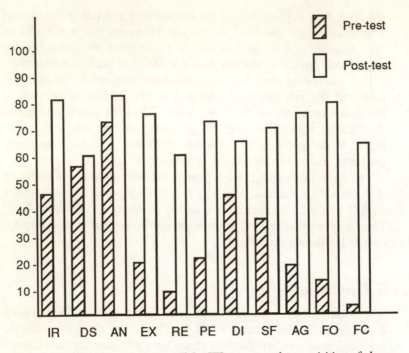

FIGURE 2   Overall improvement of the IFI group on the acquisition of eleven properties

respectively, the overall improvement of the IFI and EFI groups on the acquisition of the eleven grammatical properties:

The evidence indicates that focusing learners' attention on the formal characteristics of grammatical features facilitates the rate/success of SLA. As was stated in section 3.1, the subjects in this study did not have any target language exposure outside the classroom. Therefore, the conspicuous improvement the subjects made can only be related to the amount of formal instruction they received in the classroom. Thus the proposal that form-based classroom teaching of specific linguistic properties and structures contributes to the acquisition of L2 learners has been confirmed by the findings of the present study.

5.2 Evidence for the internalisation of grammatical knowledge

It must be emphasised that the learners' post-test performances are not simply an indication of their familiarity with the test items. No evidence has emerged pointing to a task bias in the post-test, and the better performance of the EFI group should not be ascribed to a

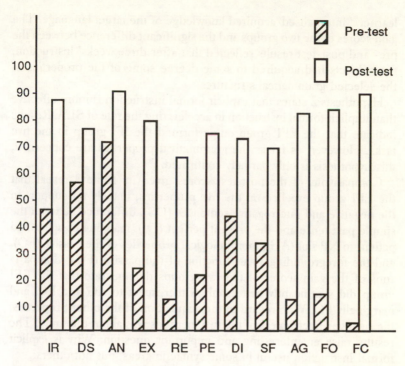

FIGURE 3 Overall improvement of the EFI group on the acquisition of the eleven properties

practice effect in the experimental lessons. Rather there is substantial evidence showing that the learners of both groups have internalised the linguistic properties and structures.

From the description of the task types in section 3.4 and the test papers in Appendices 1 to 5, we can see that most grammatical items in the achievement test were contextualised, involving the meaningful use of the target language. For example, in the sentence completion task, the subjects were required to finish the dialogue using non-verbal cues (cf. 'Tom's diary' in Appendix 1). In the same task, the subjects were asked to complete a passage with information given in the chart (cf. Appendix 2). In the reading comprehension task, the learners were provided with several dialogues and their understanding of the temporal and aspectual properties would be a prerequisite to the correct inference (cf. Appendix 3). The picture/action description task elicited the subjects' spontaneous use of the learnt structures (cf. Appendices 4 and 5). These tasks by and large examined the learners' internalised/acquired knowledge of the target language. The gain scores of the two groups and the significant difference between the pre- and post-test results reflected that after three weeks' instruction, the subjects had acquired to some degree some of the properties of the selected grammatical structures.

Hypothesis 2 states that explicit formal instruction is more effective than implicit formal instruction in accelerating the rate of SLA. Results indicate that the EFI group outperformed the IFI group in the five tasks. However, as far as the grammatical properties are concerned, this hypothesis is only partially confirmed.

Comparisons of the post-test scores given in Table 3 reveal that the EFI group excelled on the five properties, namely do-support in the negative and interrogative sentences (DS), difference between the simple past tense and the present perfect (DI), mapping of agent and patient to NP slot (AG), morphological properties of the passive (FO), and the foregrounding/focus function of the passive (FC). Comparisons of the gain scores of the two groups demonstrate that the EFI group did significantly better only with respect to AG and FC, and marginally FO. With regard to the acquisition of the other properties, the relative effectiveness of the two methods was about the same. The results raise an interesting and important question: Why is explicit formal instruction useful in some syntactic areas, but not others?

5.3 Morphological complexity of tense marking in English

In English, tense marking is morphologically complex, because it is not always suffixed to the verb stem. Sometimes it is suffixed to modals; at other times, it appears on aspectual elements or dummy DO, e.g.

> I could not go.
> He had gone before I arrived.
> I did not see him.

The regularities of tense marking in English can be summarised as follows:

(i) In a declarative/affirmative sentence, tense marking appears on the first verbal element of the clause, whatever that is. It can be a main verb or an auxiliary verb, e.g.

> John left the classroom (main verb is inflected).
> John could draw well when he was only five (inflection on the modal auxiliary).
> John had turned off the light before he went to bed (inflection on the aspectual element).

(ii) In negative and interrogative sentences, tense marking appears on the first auxiliary element if there is one (including modal and aspectual morpheme). If there is no auxiliary element, tense marking appears on a dummy DO, e.g.

> John was not singing.
> Was John singing?
> John did not pass the mid-term examination.
> Did John pass the mid-term examination?

The variable positioning of the tense marker may present a serious problem for learners whose first language is Chinese, a language generally considered to be morphologically impoverished.

5.4 Lexical idiosyncrasy of irregular morphology
Another aspect of past tense morphology that poses problems for Chinese learners is the existence of irregular past tense forms. Irregular verbs, unlike regular ones, are not inflected with the -ed morpheme. Although some patterns can be found in how the past tense of the irregular verbs is formed, which verbs take irregular tense morphology are entirely idiosyncratic. The learner has to identify the verbs that take on irregular morphology and this is no easy task. Past tense marking is morphologically complex, but is governed by regularities such as the conditions for the tense marking of dummy DO. Given the poor language environment, it would be difficult for the Chinese learners to induce some complex rules on their own from a limited amount of exposure. It is in this context that explicit instruction may be useful. In the EFI group, the above-mentioned regularities were explicitly explained to the learners who may benefit from clear statement of the regularities on the part of the teacher. Our results indeed suggest that the EFI group benefited from the explicit statement of the tense marking regularities.

5.5 Semantic complexity of the present perfect
Results from this study reveal that there was no significant difference between the two groups with respect to the acquisition of the five properties of the present perfect.[4] A possible explanation for this finding is that the concept of aspect is semantically complex and abstract. On the one hand, the present perfect bears the core meaning of current relevance of a prior event; on the other hand, it carries shades of peripheral meanings (cf. Comrie, 1976, 1985). In our study, besides the core meaning of the present relevance, we explained to the EFI group the peripheral meanings. However, as indicated in

Table 3, the EFI group did not surpass the IFI group with regard to their performance on these properties, suggesting that the explicit explanation of the peripheral meanings of the present perfect did not generate better application of the present perfect in appropriate situations.

The second noticeable point is that, with limited exposure to the norms governing the use of the present perfect in English, it is difficult for the Chinese learners to derive the core meaning of the present relevance by implicit instruction alone. The expression of the current relevance is very subjective and abstract. Without explicit explanation of such meaning, the learners will find it extremely difficult to distinguish correctly between the past tense and the present perfect. This claim is confirmed by the low score of the IFI group in the post-test (cf. Table 3, DI: 67.12%). We should also mention that, although the EFI group performed significantly better than the IFI group in the post-test, the comparison of the gain scores between the two groups did not show any significant difference, giving further evidence to the idea that the core meaning of the present perfect is one of the evasive areas for Chinese learners.

5.6 Explicit instruction accelerates the acquisition of the passive construction

In this study, the EFI group achieved outstanding performance on the passive construction. Significant differences can be discerned between the two groups in all the three properties of the passive construction, either in the comparison of the post-test scores or the gain scores. A possible explanation is that the selected properties of the passive construction are less complex than those of tense and aspect with respect to their structure and meanings.

5.6.1 Mapping of semantic roles to NP slots

This property only involves a syntactic operation, that is, the interchange of the subject and object noun phrases. An explicit statement of the mapping of the agent and patient to different NP slots greatly facilitates the acquisition of the property of AG. Notice that, in the pre-test, the IFI group significantly outperformed the EFI group (p = 0.031). However, after the experimental treatment, the EFI group did significantly better than the EFI group (cf. Table 3).

5.6.2 Passive morphology is simpler than past tense morphology

The following schema shows that the passive morpheme, unlike that of the past tense, is attached to a fixed position. The passive 'be' is always located between the auxiliary and the verb,[5] and the passive -en always appears suffixed to the verb:

NP$_1$	AUX		V		NP$_2$
NP$_2$	AUX	be	V+en	by	NP$_1$

In our experimental lesson, the position of the passive morpheme – as well as two common errors related to the passive morphology: subject/verb concord and insertion of dummy DO – were directly explained to the EFI group. The results of the spontaneous production task (a picture description task) reveal that the subjects in the EFI group had performed significantly better than the IFI group, suggesting that they had internalised the morphological rules involved in passive formation.

5.6.3 The foregrounding function of the English passive

In English, the passive construction is used when one wants to foreground or draw attention to the result or the patient. This has to do with the fact that the subject position is considered to be a salient position in the sentence. The subject of the passive structure, where the patient NP is located, is therefore highlighted or emphasised in some sense (cf. Keenan, 1985).

In the Chinese classroom, the foregrounding or focus function of the passive is seldom explained to the learner. The common practice in the teaching of the passive structure is sentence transformation. The learners are asked to convert active sentences into passive ones, or vice versa. The consequence is that the learners do not know when to use the passive structure. Again, given a relatively impoverished learning environment, it is difficult for the learners to induce this function from the teachers' limited use of the passive structures by mere exposure. Given this context, it seems plausible that explicit description of the foregrounding function of the passive will facilitate its acquisition. In our experiment, the explicit explanation of this property to the EFI group proved to be an aid to the learners. The results of the picture description test indicate that the EFI group did conspicuously better than the IFI group.

Findings from this study appear to be in favour of the interface position. The action/picture description task of this study, which required an internalised knowledge of the three selected structures, allows us to examine the interface position on a small scale. Results of the learners' performance on this task reveal that the EFI group significantly outperformed the IFI group in spontaneous language production, lending support to the possibility of transfer of explicit linguistic knowledge into the learners' competence. Krashen's theory seems incapable of handling the superiority of the EFI group over the IFI group.

6 Conclusions

In this study, we examined the absolute effect of formal instruction on the acquisition of the three grammatical structures by Chinese adolescent learners of English. The overall results seem to support the general conclusion that form-based classroom instruction facilitates SLA. However, our findings do not suggest that explicit instruction is always a better means of accelerating the rate of acquisition. Rather, they indicate that explicit instruction is more effective in teaching the less complex properties and structures such as the mapping of agent and patient to NP slots and the morphological properties of the passive construction. With respect to the more complex properties such as the semantic meanings of the present perfect, explicit instruction does not show any superiority to implicit instruction. This finding is compatible with that of Van Baalen (1983).[6] A tentative conclusion can be drawn that explicit instruction is effective with simple rules but not with complex ones. Results from this study appear to be in favour of the interface position, but because of the small size of the sample and limited number of test items, no conclusion can yet be drawn about the existence of the interface. More empirical studies are necessary to explore why explicit knowledge can be transferred into implicit knowledge and which method is most effective to accelerate this transference. This might be a profitable line for future enquiry.

Notes

1. This article is based on a portion of the author's MPhil thesis prepared under the supervision of Dr Thomas Lee at the Chinese University of Hong Kong. I wish to thank Professor William Rutherford and Rod Ellis for their helpful comments on an earlier version of this paper presented at the International Conference on Syntactic Acquisition, CUHK, 1989. Special thanks are due also to Miss Lao Zhi-xiu of Beihai Middle School and her lovely students who made this project possible. I am indebted to the Lingnan Foundation, the United Board of High Christian Education in Asia and the Weixin Group of Hong Kong for financial support, without which the study would not have been successfully completed.

2. The average academic score was obtained on the basis of two scores: the score on the mid-term examination and the average score of a series of quizzes held in their regular English course.

3. Owing to a communication failure between the investigator and the teacher of English in Beihai Middle School, the past tense had been taught before the experiment. But based on the mean scores of each group in the pre-test, we may claim that, before the experiment, the subjects had not acquired the selected grammatical properties. Note the following pre-test mean scores for the three areas under investigation:

Past tense		Present perfect		Passive	
EFI	IFI	EFI	IFI	EFI	IFI
58.59	59.65	29.36	28.83	33.73	34.93

×
(percentile)

4. A significant difference was found in the post-test with respect to the property of DI. However, the comparison of the gain scores of the two groups did not show any significant difference ($p = 0.109$).
5. Adverbs are excluded from the discussion here.
6. In Van Baalen's study, it was found that the pupils who received explicit instruction equal those pupils who were exposed to more implicit procedure in the case of more complex structures (do-support and -ing form), while with less complex structures (SVO-order and 3rd person-s), the explicit group outperformed the implicit group.

Appendix 1: Sample of sentence completion task A

This is Tom's diary. Answer the questions with the information you get from the diary.

下面那段材料是汤姆的日记. 根据日记内容 回答问题

Monday, 9.00	Meet Mr Ford at the Guest House 宾馆
11.00	Fly to Beijing
Tuesday	Not feel well, catch cold, stay at the hotel
Wednesday morning	Visit Qinghua University, interview some students and teachers
afternoon	Write a report, send it back to Xinmin Evening Newspaper (新民晚报) by telex 电传
evening	Phone Sam Jones, invite him to the concert
Thursday	Leave Beijing, go to Chang chun by train
Friday	Visit Jilin University, meet some friends

Questions: 1. When did Tom fly to Beijing?

He ....

2. Did he do anything on Tuesday? Why?

....

3. What did he do on Wednesday?

....

4. Did he invite Sam to visit the friends?

....

5. Did he leave Beijing during the weekend?

....

(Complete answers are required)

请用完整句子回答

Appendix 2: Sample of sentence completion task B

Look at the chart below and fill in the blanks according to the information you get from the chart.

看下面的图表 根据图表内容填空

Beijing is in the north of China. It often snows in winter. The following chart is the record of the weather forecast.

Monday:	cloudy
Tuesday:	rain and snow
Wednesday:	snow
Thursday:	heavy snow
Friday:	rain and snow
Saturday:	snow

It is Sunday today. Xiao Fang is at home. She .... (stay) at home since ...., because it began to snow that day. She telephoned Li Hua early in the morning. Li Hua said, 'I will come before 10 o'clock.' So Xiao Fang began to wait for her. It is three o'clock in the afternoon, but Li Hua is still not here. Xiao Fang .... (wait) for Li Hua for ....

Appendix 3: Sample of reading comprehension task

Read the following English and Chinese sentences. Indicate which Chinese sentence gives the correct inference of the English sentence.

读下面的中英文句子. 指出哪句中文句子最正确
地表达了英文句子的意思

1. *Jane*: Have you received any letter from John?
   Bob: No. But he has come to Shanghai.

   (a) 约翰现在在上海

   (b) 约翰现在不在上海

   (c) 约翰现在是否在上海不清楚

2. *Jane*: Have you received any letter from John?
   Bob: No. But he came to Shanghai the other day.

   (a) 约翰现在在上海

   (b) 约翰现在不在上海

   (c) 约翰现在是否在上海不清楚

3. Dr Guan is watching the football match on TV. His student is talking to him.
   Student: Dr Guan, you like to play football, don't you?
   Dr Guan: Yes, indeed. I watch football match on TV every weekend. I played football when I was young.

   (a) 关博士现在还踢足球

   (b) 关博士年轻时踢足球, 现在不踢了

   (c) 关博士现在还踢不踢足球不清楚

Appendix 4: Sample of action description task

Look at the teacher's performance and use the following words to describe the series of actions that the teacher carries out. Pay attention to the tense you use.

看老师的动作用下面的词和词组描述老师
所做的一系列动作.

1. show, put on, take off, give
2. take out, open, take out, close
3. put on, take off, put on, go out
4. hide, take out, read, throw
5. fall down, sit on, stand up with pain, go out

The action description task was based on Carlota S. Smith's (1979) experiment on the L1 acquisition of tense and aspect in which the subjects were asked to describe actions performed by the experimenter. It was assumed that action description elicited acquired knowledge of the language. The following section illustrates a series of actions performed by the investigator of the present study:

The investigator put on a white coat, took it off, put on a red coat and then went out.

The following description will count as a correct answer: *The teacher put on a white coat. She took it off. She put on a red coat. She has gone out.* The first three sentences should not have current relevance and should have the simple past tense; while the last sentence should appear in the present perfect.

Appendix 5: Sample of picture description task

(a) Look at the pictures and fill in the blanks according to the information you get from each picture.

看下面的图画. 根据图画里的内容填空

1. ....have been caught by.............................

2. ....has been found by.............................at last.

3. ....was invited by.............................to go to the concert.

4. ....was taken care of by.............................

(b)   Make up a sentence to describe what is happening in each picture, using the word given.

用所给的词造句, 说明图画里的内容. 每个词造一句句子.

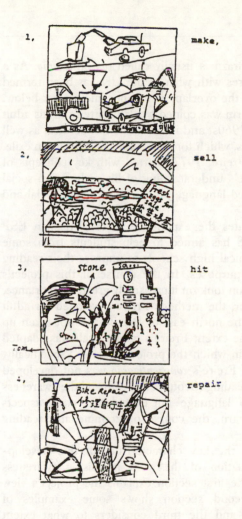

20 A Brazilian view of LA

Mike Scott

Language Awareness in Brazil is usually called *conscientização*. As a term it shares some features with what in the UK has been termed Language Awareness, but the overlap, as will become clearer below, is far from perfect. The term was coined by Paulo Freire in his adult literacy work in the early 1960s, and in his usage has political as well as educational connotations, which for many years kept Freire in exile. His adult literacy work (Freire, 1972) started with key concepts of importance to the illiterate's understanding of his or her own social condition, and thus reached language proficiency through social and political awareness.

The present paper relates the experience of the Brazilian ESP Project, which since 1978 has aimed to help students from some fifty universities and technical high schools to improve their reading in English for academic purposes. In the course of this project's development, Freire's notion took on increasingly greater importance, from about 1983. However, the methods Freire developed for adult literacy with the poor in the north-east of Brazil were not taken up by the project, and to some extent Freire's notion itself was adapted to the specific conditions in which the project operates. Specifically, the political dimension of Freire's *conscientização* was not developed except in terms of critical reading (Scott *et al.*, 1988) and the awareness has not been restricted to 'language' but extended to cover aspects of reading, learning to learn, the course programme and reading strategies.

I shall relate some of the key characteristics of this development, and refer to evaluation of the work in raising awareness through *conscientização*. The first section explains the project's view of *conscientização*; the second section shows some examples of '*conscientização* in action'; and the third considers to what extent and with what success it is applied in the classrooms of Brazil's universities and technical high schools.

1 *Conscientização* in ESP theory

The project developed, in terms of theory, through a number of stages.

In broad outline they can be described thus:

(i)   From 1978 to 1980, a fairly traditional approach involving the writing of subject-specific materials which aimed to teach learners the 'basic' elements of grammar and vocabulary which would be relevant to their needs.

(ii) From 1980 to about 1983, emphasis was placed on the importance of appropriate reading strategies, so that grammar and vocabulary were very much suppressed. At this time some of the techniques were developed, which are described below as characteristic of Brazilian *conscientização*, but they were not used in the full sense of *conscientização* as defined in Scott (1986). These techniques were used as Language Awareness devices in training teachers of Language for Special Purposes (LSP). Not only teachers of English were involved: teachers of Portuguese as a native language, Spanish, French and German have been involved to varying extent in the work of the ESP Project in Brazil, the major aim of the project from about 1980 onwards, but were not systematically or fully implemented in classes with ESP students.

(iii) From 1984 to the present, *conscientização* was implemented, to varying degrees, by the teachers involved in the project, in their classes with technical school or undergraduate or postgraduate students.

This historical perspective will perhaps become more meaningful when related to Figure 1. The idea is that *conscientização* can be viewed as a pyramid, where the uppermost layers are the most superficial (and traditional). The 'deeper' we can get, the better. But first it is useful to present the definition from Scott (1986:2), which has been fairly central to Brazilian ESP work on *conscientização*:

> . . . ensuring students understand, with their hearts as well as their
> heads, why they are learning and practising the skills being taught,
> how they individually do so, and to what extent proposed strategies are
> effective, and what the reading process involves.

This definition attempts to encapsulate several important distinctions. *Conscientização* is seen as involving why something is to be taught or learnt. Any reasonable explanation of this will necessarily mean explaining about the reading process (in a context where the specific purpose in ESP has largely meant reading), and offering suggestions as to how reading can be done more effectively. To what extent the whole approach works well or badly will be a subject for discussion in class, as we shall see in relation to Figure 1. And at the same time, awareness is not just rational understanding, in the sense that we understand that the French Revolution started in 1789, but involves 'feeling the fact'. In the case of history it is hard to 'feel' the French Revolution except through empathy – in reading EAP one 'feels' the effectiveness of certain strategies by trying them out. Knowing about strategies is prior to feeling the 'click of realisation' that they really work, and in our experience this 'click' comes weeks or months after the initial level of knowledge has been attained.

TASK

TASK + LABEL

TASK + LABEL + REASON explained

TASK + LABEL + REASON discussed

TASK + LABEL + REASON + SELF-OBSERVATION

TASK + LABEL + REASON + GROUP OBSERVATION + DISCUSSION

FIGURE 1   The pyramid of *conscientização*

The first level is exemplified in traditional materials by the phrase 'Exercise 13'. Students do not yet know what the task is, as it is merely labelled by its position in the course. If the exercise states 'Exercise 13: the Passive Voice', we are at Level 2. Students still don't know why the passive voice is important.

Hardly any course books get beyond Level 2. Presumably the materials writer hopes that the teacher will explain this in class. (Usually the materials writer has no contact at all with the teacher, and little chance of evaluating how the materials are being used, so this may well be a forlorn hope.) The 'Notes for Teachers' might provide some justification, but this is clearly not the same as providing reasons to students.

The next two levels of *conscientização* provide the reason for the passive voice: by this I do not mean the reason why the passive voice has come into existence in English, but the reason for studying it, though the latter reason may include the former. Reasons might be: it's a frequent structure; it's difficult to understand unless we provide you with systematic practice of it; it's not quite the same structure as in your L1; it's in the required syllabus; it'll come in handy when you're writing, etc. The passive voice is merely used for illustration. In fact, Castaños (1978) has shown that some at least of these reasons are not really applicable in the case of this structure for Latin American university students.

These reasons can (in Level 3) be simply presented to students or (Level 4) discussed with them. Whether teachers prefer to operate at Level 3 or Level 4 will be likely to correlate with their own perceived role. Freire (1972: 45–6) puts it like this:

> Education thus becomes an act of depositing, in which the students are the depositories and the teacher is the depositor. Instead of communicating, the teacher issues communiqués and 'makes deposits' which the students patiently receive, memorize, and repeat.

The 'bank deposit' view of the teacher's role will thus be likely to go with merely telling students why they have to study the passive voice.

The next levels go deeper. In Level 5 we include self-observation: that is, students observe to what extent the claimed reasons and justifications apply. After understanding why they should (or should not) study the passive voice explicitly, they will individually 'notice' (self-observation) whether they still have problems with passive voice constructions and how they individually coped with learning it. If they go so far as to compare notes with classmates (group observation), they are very likely to find out that certain structures are useful to some students and not to others, that some colleagues have good strategies for learning them while others have not, and so on. The deepest level of *conscientização*, then, is when time is set aside for discussion on the effectiveness and the detail of how students are performing.

It is true that this happens to some slight extent in many classrooms anyway. No teacher is, in Freire's terms, at all times a simple bank depositor in the students' accounts. However, the proposal is that a small amount of time be systematically devoted to ensuring that students are fully aware (with their hearts as well as their heads, as in the definition above) about what is going on in their language-learning classroom. To meet this view of *conscientização*, teachers need to plan for '*conscientização* experiences' as an integral part of the class work. The teacher, as manager of the learning environment, should be organising the awareness as well as the seating arrangements!

2 *Conscientização* in action

In the heady days of 1980 and 1981, the Brazilian ESP Project was coming to grips with a new way of working. The process of materials-writing, perceived by teachers as their most urgent need at the time, underwent twin changes in emphasis: first, a new view of the relative importance of language items as subordinate to reading strategies, and second a project decision not to produce a set of materials written by 'experts' but instead to train teachers to do the materials-writing themselves. A series of local, regional and national meetings took place, and workshops concentrating on teacher-*conscientização*, materials preparation and related issues took place. It was at this time that some of the first *conscientização* materials were developed and used.

Early issues of *The ESPecialist* devoted considerable space to the following methodological issues of principle:

- Establishing a three-level concept of comprehension ('general', 'main points' and 'detailed' as opposed to either 'intensive' versus 'extensive' or no division at all, which is tantamount to 'detailed').
- Relegation of grammar and vocabulary to the second ESP Division, placing reading strategies in the first.
- Development of the concept of 'coping' strategies (dealing with text despite the problems).
- Use of 'authentic' text (neither written nor adapted for EFL or ESP purposes, but written for communication of ideas, and preferably photocopied, not typed).
- 'Field of knowledge' principles of text selection not necessarily in line with subject specialisms but in terms of student interests, background knowledge and subject-related fields.
- Minimal discourse grammar (grammar above the sentence, leading towards text structure).
- Psycho-linguistic principles of text processing (the role of short-term memory, mental set, saccades and fixations, skipping over words, background knowledge and schemata, etc.).

These principles were discussed in the workshops in the early 1980s (and ever since), and illustrated with a number of pieces of evidence. To that extent, teacher-*conscientização* was happening.

However, it was not yet a major part of project thinking to suggest that these ideas should be shared in any detail with students. Our own awareness about awareness-raising was limited!

There were, it is true, explanations in the early materials about the three levels of comprehension and some of the psycho-linguistic principles of text processing, for example the University of Santa Catarina Self-Access materials included from 1981 on a four-page 'awareness' statement for the student covering the following items:

(i)   Different levels of comprehension
(ii) Different ways of reading

(iii) Some psycho-linguistic aspects of the reading process
(iv) How to handle texts in English. (The original was in Portuguese.)

The UFSC *Self-Access Project Report* is in the CEPRIL archive. Besides this report there is an article in the April 1984 issue of *English Language Teaching Journal* on 'Using a "Standard Exercise" in Teaching Reading Comprehension'. Nevertheless, the emphasis in the early phase of the project was on getting teachers to understand why these methodological principles were important and getting them to teach their own students less grammar and vocabulary and more reading strategies. Many teachers were thus teaching their students to use appropriate strategies but not yet raising their awareness much about why this might be desirable.

In my view, it was not until 1983 that a serious and full-blooded attempt was made to incorporate *conscientização* – to the extent proposed in Scott 1986 – with ESP students. This was the work of Carvalho, with her students in the Federal University of Piaui (Carvalho, 1984). She developed experimental materials and incorporated a think-aloud technique in handling the texts in pairs. She made constant reference both in class and in the photocopied teaching and testing materials to awareness of strategies used and commentary as to their effectiveness or otherwise. Since then a number of teachers in many of the participating institutions have followed this lead.

Whatever the extent of 'full' student *conscientização* in the Brazilian ESP Project, to be discussed in the following section, there are some techniques and materials which have gained wide popularity and will give the flavour of the project's attempts at awareness-raising. For example, almost all the teachers involved in the project have used the following text from *Resource Package* No. 1, CEPRIL (Pontifícia Universidade de São Paulo) with their students. The text was written in Portuguese by the present author in 1980. The version presented here, it is important to note, is a translation by the same and present author; the original title is *Problema na Clamba*, and the text as well as the subsequent discussion is in Portuguese – of a sort.

A PROBLEM AT THE CLAMBA

That day, after plomating, I went down to see dran Joe wanted to go down to the clamba with me. I decided to grull him. But as I was grulling the token, I saw him going by with his golisett – so I realised that he had other plans for the day.
So I decided to go in the pod. Everything was straight-forward till I got to the clamba. I parked the zulp pretty nack, put the key in my

pocket, and ran down to enjoy sim chint all that lovely sunshine and the pli sulapent sea.

It seemed there was not a single galp on the clamba. I took off my grisps, and put on my bangole. It was pli quiet there that it even saltipated me. But I soon forgot my saltiplations in the pleasure of swimming in the pod, and as a matter of fact I took off my bangole so as to feel more at ease. I don't know how long I stayed there swimming, silting, corristing, even stepating in the sea.

It was in the pod later, when I got back to the clamba, that I saw that neither my grisps nor my bangole were where I had left them. What to do next?

Teachers use this text in one of their first classes with a new group. They usually do not tell their students why they are showing them a typed text in Portuguese (courses are 90 per cent photocopies of 'authentic' texts in English in the rest of the course), but instead, after students have read the text, ask them why they've struggled through such a weird text. The discussion is *conscientização*.

Students become aware that (a) they can understand the text without knowing all the words, (b) that some words are easy to infer (e.g. *clamba*) and others (in the *pod*, *grull*) are harder, (c) that a rough idea is good enough for many (e.g. *plomating*) and (d) that it is one's background knowledge of the world and knowledge of text relations (grammar, morphology, text structure, etc.) which makes it possible to know what happened in the narrative. Some teachers ask whether the narrator is a man or a woman (everyone presumes it's a man though the text does not make that clear in English or in Portuguese).

The text is of course within the tradition of *Jabberwocky*, of *Clockwork Orange*, John Lennon's *In His Own Write*, of works by Cortazar in Spanish and no doubt authors in every language. Our students, however, have usually never seen this kind of thing, and the resulting discussion is most valuable.

A similar exercise uses a text in a foreign language which students can be guaranteed not to know, accompanied by a set of questions in Portuguese. In the project we have used several texts in Albanian and Serbo-Croat, provided by our expert on languages used in Yugoslavia, John Holmes.

Another 'text' which has been widely used in student *conscientização* is the following:

IL	UNA	PARIS
Y A	PIEDRA	IN THE
TROP DE	EN EL	THE SPRING
DE GENS ICI	EL CAMINO	

with discussion as to why one tends not to spot the repeated words. When appropriate, this discussion may lead into such concepts as chunking, and short-term memory features, which discourage excessively slow reading.

One of the most useful of the *conscientização* devices that has been widely used relies upon a metaphor. Figure 2 shows the forest and the trees (and incidentally illustrates the English saying 'You can't see the wood for the trees' though the existence of this saying is not of much interest in itself). Once the concept has been explained, it becomes natural for students to make such reports as 'I'm still too near to the forest. I'm having difficulty breaking my habit of detailed reading and worrying about all the unknown "twigs".'

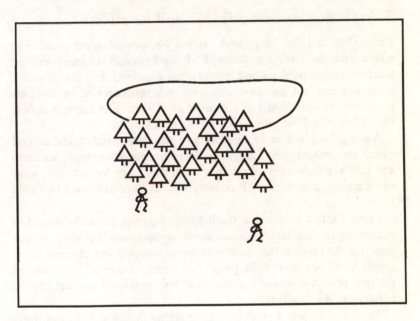

FIGURE 2   The wood and the trees

The message discussed is that the stick-figure who is near the trees cannot see the forest, while the one who is farther away can see the overall shape of the forest and may be able to spot that behind it there is a lake, though he cannot see the tiny details of each branch and twig (for that matter the one who is near cannot see such detail except on the nearest trees).

This metaphor work has been extended in numerous teacher workshops in recent years, and the range of metaphors and analogies has grown to include such ideas as – reading as mountain-climbing or swimming, the dictionary as a bottle of medicine, levels of comprehension as differing scales in maps, cognates as old friends at a party, and so on. However, to my knowledge there has not yet been any work done in getting students to develop metaphors or analogies, and in the light of the *conscientização* theory proposed here, that would be a logical development.

This leads me to the final section, in which I shall consider evidence as to whether *conscientização* has or has not taken hold in the Brazilian ESP Project.

3 Assessing *conscientização* and its effects

From 1986 to 1988 the project carried out an evaluation exercise in which students, former students, ESP teachers and subject-specialist teachers at the participating universities answered a series of questionnaires and took part in discussions on a vast range of topics. This evaluation was published in Celani *et al.* (1988). The findings reflect the situation in 1986 when data were collected.

Among the plethora of questions in this large study were several which give insights into Language Awareness. For example, students and ESP teachers were asked, in a multiple-choice format item, what items appeared in their ESP course. Results were as shown in Table 1.

From Table 1 we see that the interested parties generally agreed in perceiving reading strategies as course components, but that 'awareness' (in the original the word was *conscientização*) was claimed to be taught by 87 per cent of the project-oriented teachers, 71 per cent of the non-project-oriented teachers, but only perceived as taught by 45 per cent of the students.

Another item asked students 'After taking this course do you think your English has: improved a lot / improved a little / stayed the same / got worse?'. The results of this question can be used as a tally, cross-tabulated with several items in the student questionnaire, to give an idea of the importance or otherwise of *conscientização*. Table 2 shows this. Note that fourteen (out of over two thousand) students who thought their English had 'got worse' have been disregarded in the cross-tabulation as percentages of fourteen people are quite misleading. All the chi-square relations are significant at better than the 1 per cent level.

TABLE 1   Awareness of items taught

What items appear(ed) in your course?

	ESP Teachers*		Students
	Proj.	Non-proj.	
Reading strategies	99%	85%	83%
Awareness of reading processes	87%	71%	45%
Translation into Portuguese	25%	41%	55%
Explanation and practice of grammar	27%	44%	33%
Text functions	61%	50%	26%
Critical reading	75%	62%	31%
Use of the dictionary	71%	65%	49%
Exercises for increasing vocabulary	54%	41%	43%
Work on connectives	71%	47%	53%
Text structure	96%	79%	77%
Word formation (prefixes, suffixes)	87%	71%	65%
Other	5%	3%	†
N (number of students)	84%	34%	2041

*Proj[ect] ESP teachers were those who reported being 'active' members of the ESP Project, in contrast with non-Proj[ect] ESP teachers.
†Did not appear in the questionnaire.

What Table 2 suggests is that the 'satisfied customers' had very different views on some items in the questionnaire when compared with those who had not perceived any improvement (in a 45 hour ESP course). Thus, the items marked with an asterisk (where there is at least a 10 per cent difference between the three types of student in their statement on the various items) seem to show greater value to the more satisfied students. It is very likely that those who thought their English had improved 'a lot' tended to be more supportive of the various questionnaire items throughout. 'Reading strategies taught' refers to the item already shown in Table 1. It seems that almost all students were taught reading strategies, whether they felt benefit from that or not. ('Learned reading strategies' refers to a different item, where students were asked 'You think as a result of this course you manage to:. . .?')

It is clear that *conscientização*, and related items such as 'developed own reading mode', or 'awareness of the programme', do not distinguish as much between the 'satisfied' and the 'dissatisfied' as some of the other items.

TABLE 2   Apparent value of items taught

	Improved a lot	Improved a little	Stayed same	
English reading changed	66%	47%	22%	*
Learned to get gist	90%	80%	56%	*
Learned to scan	51%	33%	16%	*
Learned to summarise	44%	27%	12%	*
Learned reading strategies	67%	54%	35%	*
Developed own reading mode	38%	26%	16%	*
Awareness of programme	45%	32%	21%	*
Reading strategies taught	82%	82%	77%	
Conscientização taught	65%	43%	35%	
Grammar taught	43%	32%	24%	
Text functions taught	35%	25%	21%	
Critical reading taught	47%	30%	17%	*
Dictionary use taught	55%	49%	47%	
Vocab. increase taught	60%	43%	33%	*
Connectives taught	62%	51%	41%	*
Text structure taught	86%	75%	71%	
Affixes taught	75%	65%	50%	*
N (number of students)	333	1371	325	

This finding matches that of Orlando who, in a study on the same data sources concentrating on awareness of course objectives, concluded:

> ... there is not much difference between those students who mentioned 'conscientização' and those who did not, in terms of their awareness of the objectives of the ESP course. (Celani *et al.*, 1988: 152).

Zimbarg, who looked into students' claims of a 'changed mode of reading', also using the same set of data sources, however, found that:

> Students who mentioned having 'conscientização' (awareness) in their courses also tended to change their mode of reading. Thus, becoming aware of the processes involved in the reading activity seems to contribute to changing one's mode of reading. In comparison with the teaching of reading strategies, *conscientização* seems to have had more effect. (Celani *et al*, 1988: 165)

Overall, the data from the sizeable project evaluation carried out in 1986 seems to suggest on the one hand that reading strategies and *conscientização* were being implemented in the project's ESP courses, but that some teachers were not engaged in *conscientização* as explained in this paper, and perhaps about half the students were not aware of what their teachers intended to be awareness-raising!

This conclusion need not be too dispiriting. If *conscientização* were something swift and overwhelming, like St Paul's experience on the road to Damascus, it would be a teacher's magic wand, and there are no magic wands in education.

The evidence, then, suggests that *conscientização* in the Brazilian context is, as one would expect, incomplete. The theory as well as the practice will no doubt develop in the coming years, and, we hope, continue to benefit those needing to read English for their academic purposes.

21 Language learning and Linguistic Awareness: the relationship between proficiency and acceptability judgements in L2[1]

Diana Masny

Linguistic Awareness can be defined as individuals' ability to reflect on, and match, intuitively spoken and written utterances with their knowledge of the language. This tacit knowledge can be made explicit through outward expression ranging from spontaneous self-correction to explicit reflection on the production of utterances. This means that individuals are able to abstract themselves from the normal use of language and focus their attention on the properties of the language *per se* (e.g. vocabulary, syntax and phonology). An important feature of Linguistic Awareness is that it is an aspect of language competence in which individual differences have been observed both in children and in adults.[2]

A review of second language research on Linguistic Awareness (Chaudron, 1983) suggests that, first, the ability to detect deviance is considered to be a reliable correlate of developing second language competence (d'Anglejan and Renaud, 1985; Masny and d'Anglejan, 1985); second, Linguistic Awareness is said to facilitate second language development (Gass, 1983); third, the transfer of linguistic abilities across languages (reading in L1 and in L2) has been shown to influence second language Linguistic Awareness (Cummins, 1983). More recently, Bialystok and Ryan (1985b) have examined the interrelationship of language and cognition in the growth of metalinguistic skills in terms of developed analysed knowledge of language and cognitive control. In their model, bilingualism is considered to promote higher levels of cognitive control while literacy is said to develop analysed knowledge of language. Metalinguistic abilities are related to other language skills to the extent that both call on analysed knowledge and cognitive control.

The present second language research is designed to examine which specific aspects of language competence are related to Linguistic Awareness and to establish the strength of that relationship and the conditions in which such a relationship might hold. In first language research, several variables (e.g. language knowledge, age, cognitive development) may be said to influence individuals' ability in performing different types of metalinguistic tasks. This second language study centres on the role of language knowledge in making judgements of acceptability. In other words, what language abilities are tapped when second language learners at various stages of language proficiency make judgements of acceptability?

1 The study

1.1 Subjects

Seventy-eight subjects (45 females, 33 males) were enrolled in three different courses in English as a second language (ESL) at a French college in Montreal: 24 at the intermediate level, 34 at the inter-mediate-advanced, and 20 at the advanced. The mean age was 18 years old. Of the 78 subjects, 55 (70.5%) claimed French to be their mother tongue. Although the mother tongue of the remaining 23 subjects was not French, all had received their secondary schooling in French in Quebec and had followed the regular five-year programme in ESL. According to information provided on a language background questionnaire, the subjects' first contact with English was generally at school at age 9. The mean number of years studying ESL was 7.

1.2 Materials

For purposes of concurrent validation, two complementary measures were chosen for each language ability.

Listening: A dictation containing three unrelated paragraphs with increasing levels of difficulty was administered and then scored in the standard manner. A dictation was used since it is an auditory task requiring discourse processing skills involving the integration and conceptualisation of knowledge. The second listening task was the listening comprehension subtest of the CELT (Comprehensive English Language Test) designed to assess subjects' ability to comprehend statements, questions and dialogues. This test correlated significantly with the dictation task ($r=0.71$, $p=0.001$).

Reading: A multiple-choice (M-C) reading match test from Oller and Perkins (1980) was composed of three different passages. For each underlined word, phrase or clause, subjects had to refer to the multiple-choice item that went with it and select an appropriate synonym or paraphrase. The CELT-V vocabulary subtest was used as a complementary measure designed to assess subjects' understanding of vocabulary. A significant correlation with the reading match test was established ($r=0.66$, $p=0.001$).

Speaking: An FSI (Foreign Service Institute) type oral interview was

TABLE 1 Descriptive statistics

	Group 1, N=24			Group 2, N=34			Group 3, N=20			Max. score
	Mean	S.D.	Var.	Mean	S.D.	Var.	Mean	S.D.	Var.	
FSI interview	53.0	5.3	28.1	58.4	8.6	74.0	67.7	10.3	106.1	99
Oral cloze	16.2	5.9	34.3	22.6	9.1	83.2	30.4	6.2	38.5	49
M-C writing	55.0	10.5	111.1	65.3	12.8	165.2	86.2	9.0	81.3	108
Essay	20.8	2.2	4.8	20.7	4.2	17.5	25.5	4.8	22.6	36
CELT-LC	30.5	5.9	34.8	35.9	7.7	59.1	46.6	3.2	10.1	50
M-C reading	25.5	2.7	7.4	27.1	3.9	15.1	32.4	2.2	4.7	36
CELT-Vocab	26.1	6.8	46.5	35.6	11.3	127.7	56.3	8.0	63.9	75
Dictation	123.4	14.6	212.7	135.2	18.9	356.1	160.1	10.4	108.3	174
LA	180.0	9.7	94.0	183.9	12.6	158.1	198.0	12.7	162.3	250

used to measure subjects' oral proficiency. The interviewer recorded the conversations which were later evaluated by two English language teachers trained on the evaluation to be used with the FSI oral interview. Inter-rater reliability was established at $r=0.65$, $p=0.001$. A second measure, the oral cloze test (Oller and Perkins, 1980), consisted of five different texts ranging from easy to difficult (ten blanks per text, every seventh word deleted). This task, according to Oller (1979), is considered a measure of oral production in which it is necessary to draw on inferences and generate expectancies while requiring knowledge of discourse constraints. Results were scored using the 'acceptable' method. Correlation between subjects' scores on the oral interview and the oral cloze was $r=0.55$, $p=0.001$.

Writing: The first task, multiple-choice writing (Oller and Perkins, 1980) consisted of three subtests each containing three passages in increasing order of difficulty (a total of nine passages). The first subtest required subjects to select an appropriate word, phrase or clause to continue the story. The second subtest required editing errors while the third required correct ordering of words, phrases or clauses. In the second task, subjects wrote an essay about an accident they had witnessed. They had to say who was involved, who was at fault, whether there were any injured persons. Subjects' essays were evaluated for the following categories: compositional organisation, appropriate vocabulary, control over English structures, and quality of writing. Each category contained a six-point scale (Mullen, 1980). Two persons received training prior to rating the essays. Inter-rater reliability was $r=0.69$, $p=0.001$. Moreover, subjects' scores on the multiple-choice writing task correlated significantly with the essay ratings: $r=0.61$, $p=0.001$.

Linguistic Awareness: An acceptability judgement task was devised to assess subjects' intuitions concerning several aspects of grammatical knowledge: word order, passive, dative alternation, aspect. Fifty sentences were both written and played simultaneously on tape. Subjects could listen as well as follow on paper. Upon hearing and reading each item, subjects had to refer to a five-point scale and select a point on the scale ranging from the sentence being completely acceptable to not acceptable at all. An earlier pilot study with native English speakers ($n=10$) as benchmark data allowed us to design and choose the items for the task. Then, with advanced ESL subjects ($n=38$), a reliability coefficient (Kuder-Richardson 20) was established at 0.98.

The rationale for this choice of task was to measure language learners' sensitivity to syntactic and lexical organisation of the language, to assess their knowledge of structural forms and relationships based on the expectancy of specific linguistic elements co-occurring in predictable ways according to the underlying rule system and transitional probabilities of the language. This task can be said to probe what second language learners know intuitively and not what they are frequently taught in classrooms.

In each group, two test forms were distributed. The items were identical in both; however, in the second form, the order of the items was reversed to counterbalance any order effects. Half of each group received one form, the other half, the other form.

1.3 Results

An exploratory examination (boxplots, and stem-and-leaf designs: Hull and Nie, 1981) of the distribution of the values for each test showed them to have a normal distribution. Another preliminary statistical procedure, a multivariate analysis of variance (Hull and Nie, 1981) revealed significant differences between the three proficiency groups tested on all tasks ($F=7.007$, $df=22/128$, $p=0.001$). Table 1 presents a descriptive analysis of the data. Moreover, the relationship among subjects' scores on the different tasks was examined by means of a Spearman correlation. (See Tables 2A, 2B & 2C.)

Since this study was designed to examine the relationship of Linguistic Awareness to specific aspects of second language competence, the two tasks measuring subjects' performance on each of the language abilities were combined as a composite score prior to analysis. Accordingly, the independent variables were reading (Reading match test/CELT-V), listening (CELT-LC/dictation), speaking (FSI-type interview/oral cloze), and writing (multiple-choice writing test/essay). The dependent variable was the language judgement task.

The question being addressed is whether second language learners at various stages of second language development draw on similar or different language abilities to make judgements of grammaticality. A multiple regression analysis was computed for each group to determine the relationship among the different language abilities (independent variables) and individual variation in the ability to make judgements of acceptability. Concerning the first group from the intermediate level, the overall regression was non-significant: $F=2.65$, $df=4/24$, $p=0.12$. The results showed that the relationship between individual variation in the ability to make judgements of acceptability and subjects' scores on the different language variables (reading, writing, listening and speaking) was non-significant (Table 3A). On the other hand, in Group 2 (intermediate-advanced level) with the judgement

TABLE 2A Spearman correlation coefficient (Group 1)

N=24	FSI	OC	MCW	Essay	CLC	MCR	CV	D	LA
FSI interview		0.39*	0.08	0.18	0.50**	0.30	0.34*	0.30	0.16
Oral cloze			0.21	0.32	0.66**	0.51**	0.32	0.64**	0.26
M-C writing				0.16	0.39*	0.47*	0.60**	0.26	0.29
Essay					0.19	-0.12	0.31	0.62**	-0.18
CELT-Listening						0.61**	0.45*	0.59**	0.19
M-C reading							0.29	0.29	0.60**
CELT-Vocab								0.63**	-0.02
Dictation									-0.05

*$p<0.05$ **$p<0.005$

TABLE 2B Spearman correlation coefficient (Group 2)

N=34	FSI	OC	MCW	Essay	CLC	MCR	CV	D	LA
FSI interview		0.24	0.35*	0.39*	0.36*	0.01	0.55**	0.19	0.30
Oral cloze			0.36*	0.15	0.69***	0.33*	0.59***	0.22	0.30
M-C writing				0.58**	0.46***	0.53**	0.63***	0.70**	0.65**
Essay					0.23	0.14	0.54***	0.56**	0.25
CELT-Listening						0.31*	0.56**	0.45**	0.53**
M-C reading							0.29*	0.67**	0.40*
CELT-Vocab								0.54**	0.65**
Dictation									0.42**

*$p<0.05$ **$p<0.005$

TABLE 2C Spearman correlation coefficient (Group 3)

N=20	FSI	OC	MCW	Essay	CLC	MCR	CV	D	LA
FSI interview		0.47*	0.35	0.20	0.59***	0.01	0.76**	0.53**	0.68**
Oral cloze			0.55**	0.23	0.64***	0.55***	0.68**	0.60**	0.18
M-C writing				0.37*	0.43*	0.73***	0.71***	0.71***	0.19
Essay					−0.11	0.35	0.22	0.20	−0.04
CELT-Listening						0.19	0.68**	0.52**	0.35
M-C reading							0.32	0.58**	0.16
CELT-Vocab								0.72**	0.62**
Dictation									0.24

$*p < 0.05$ $**p < 0.005$

task as the criterion variable, the overall regression was significant: $F=22.2$, $df=4/34$, $p=0.001$. According to the results, the predictor variable, reading, was significantly related to subjects' judgements of acceptability (Table 3B). In the third group (advanced level) the overall regression was significant: $F=11.3$, $df=4/20$, $p=0.003$. Individual variation on the ability to make judgements of acceptability was significantly related to speaking (Table 3C).

TABLE 3A   Multiple regression: effect of independent variables on the ability to make judgements of acceptability (Group 1)

	R	R^2	r	Beta	F	Significance
Speaking	0.33	0.11	0.33	0.47	2.65	0.12
Listening	0.35	0.12	0.15	−0.34	1.45	0.57
Reading	0.39	0.15	0.22	0.22	1.19	0.41
Writing	0.39	0.15	0.12	0.03	0.85	0.91

TABLE 3B   Multiple regression: effect of independent variables on the ability to make judgements of acceptability (Group 2)

	R	R^2	r	Beta	F	Significance
Reading	0.64	0.41	0.64	0.45	22.15	0.001
Writing	0.66	0.43	0.59	0.30	1.07	0.31
Listening	0.66	0.44	0.43	−0.15	0.54	0.47
Speaking	0.67	0.44	0.51	0.08	0.14	0.71

TABLE 3C   Multiple regression: effect of independent variables on the ability to make judgements of acceptability (Group 3)

	R	R^2	r	Beta	F	Significance
Speaking	0.62	0.39	0.62	0.54	11.3	0.005
Writing	0.64	0.40	0.23	−0.27	0.5	0.48
Reading	0.66	0.44	0.53	0.37	0.9	0.37
Listening	0.66	0.44	0.41	−0.07	0.04	0.85

2 Discussion

The discussion is constrained to the data and results obtained in this study. In Group 3 (the most proficient subjects), the results revealed that subjects' ability to make judgements of acceptability was significantly related to speaking, measured by the FSI-type oral interview and the oral cloze task (Table 3C). These results can be explained in the light of subjects' ability to decontextualise language and the presence of literate features in oral language related to classroom discourse practices often found in formal contexts of language learning.

Decontextualisation refers to detaching language from the here-and-now context (context-bound), bringing one's experience under the control of language alone without a supportive context. Decontextualisation can be defined as an aspect of communicative proficiency in which background knowledge is not assumed to be shared (implicitly) by the sender and receiver. It is incumbent on the sender to make that knowledge explicit through elaborate use of the linguistic code with minimal recourse to paralinguistic cues or non-verbal behaviour. Examples of communicative exchange that call for decontextualised language skills include describing orally how to repair defective equipment, reading a manual, explaining how to assemble a bicycle, writing a formal letter requesting an interview for a job.

In first language research, Tannen (1982) identified certain decontextualised characteristics of oral discourse: distance between sender and receiver, explicitness of reference, complexity of syntactic structures, permanency of information. Michaels and Collins (1984) referred to a literate discourse style in their study comparing Grade 4 children's speech and writing. They observed that children who talk 'in a lexically and grammatically' explicit manner using a variety of lexical and syntactic devices characteristic of discursive prose had less difficulty in making the transition to the written mode than other children in their study who relied on paralinguistic cues to signal the same discursive functions. These findings seem to suggest that interpersonal communicative exchanges characterised by features of contextualisation do not appear to be related to discourse practices required in school.

In second language research, the relationship between contextualised and literate uses of language revealed low correlations (Cummins, 1983). Snow *et al.* (in press) demonstrated that in children learning a second language, contextualised language skills required for conversational styles are not related to decontextualised language skills.

In the present study, the oral cloze task used as one measure of speaking is said to be linked to Linguistic Awareness since the cloze and the judgement tasks call on subjects' linguistic knowledge (lexical and syntactic constraints).[3] Moreover, the FSI-type oral interview, the second measure, required subjects to talk, for example, about an interesting person they know, an important person in their life, or having three wishes. Under these conditions, subjects were responding in a decontextualised manner in which background information is not assumed to be shared by sender and receiver. In addition, the presence of a distant audience, the interviewer, creates a sense of objective detachment to the message being conveyed.

It is not surprising perhaps to find a significant relationship between Linguistic Awareness and speaking in this study since subjects were responding to the formal nature of the linguistic exchange (interview) that often characterises classroom second language learning. Snow (1987) found similar results in 8-year-old children learning French as a second language. In her study, the more academically successful subjects in an interview were more specific, provided more information and less knowledge was assumed to be shared. Snow uses the term 'imperial decontextualisation' to refer to formal responses of the subjects to an interview in the context of the classroom. In a more recent French second language study on grade-school children, Snow *et al.* (in press) suggested that oral decontextualised language tasks might be related to successful language learning in the classroom.

In Group 2, the statistical analyses revealed that subjects' scores in reading measured by the CELT-V and a multiple-choice reading task, were significantly related to their ability in making acceptability judgements. First language studies have demonstrated empirically that vocabulary is related to Linguistic Awareness (Saywitz and Wilkinson in S. Kuczaj (ed.), 1982; Smith and Tager-Flusberg, 1982). In the present study, the CELT-vocabulary subtest correlated significantly with the judgement task (Table 2B).

First language research on Linguistic Awareness and reading points out the important interactive relationship between these two variables (Downing and Valtin, 1984; Downing, 1987; Ryan, 1980; Yaden and Templeton, 1986). In developing reading competence, the learner must focus attention on language and become aware of the rearrangements of phonological and syntactic components; to do so entails making phonological and syntactic judgements. Skilled readers are those most apt at performing metalinguistic tasks related to sentence structure (Ryan and Ledger, 1984).

Second language research on reading reveals that awareness of structural relationships is vital and subject to individual variation. Various studies (Anthony, 1984; Guerra, 1984; Masny, 1987) demonstrated that reading competence in L1 and in L2 is related to Linguistic Awareness in L2. More recently, Bialystok and Ryan (1985b) proposed that reading competence is linked to subjects' analysed (explicit) knowledge of the language, a major component contributing to subjects' metalinguistic abilities.

In the present study, the subjects in Group 2 demonstrated that the better readers are also those most apt at making judgements of acceptability. The ability to read, however, is not *per se* sufficient to carry out the judgement task. Their level of proficiency in the second language and information-processing capacities affect subjects' ability to read and to perform metalinguistic tasks. According to Daneman and Carpenter (1980), individual variation in reading is related to subjects' differential capacity for storing and maintaining information, recoding concepts and relations into single chunks so as to reduce the information-processing load in short-term memory. The ability to process efficiently is further enhanced by the individual's knowledge of lexical and syntactic constraints of the language. Similarly, with regard to Linguistic Awareness, individual differences in processing information in reading are characteristic of individual variation in subjects' ability to perform metalinguistic tasks.

In Group 1, subjects' scores on the judgement task were not significantly related to any of the language abilities. While 18-year-old college-level subjects are able to read, write or speak English, the results might be explained in the light of the following: knowledge of the second language (lexical, syntactic and discourse constraints) and information-processing capacity in a second language.

In first language research, the ability to deal with complex syntax is considered a reliable predictor of reading competence (Torrance and Olson, 1984).[4] Moreover, adult-like acceptability judgements are related to subjects' mastery of the grammatical constraints of the language (Hakes, 1982). With regard to the subjects in Group 1, the indications are that a certain level of proficiency in the second language must be attained before being able to perform different types of metalinguistic tasks. Such conclusions were also reached by Galambos and Hakuta (1988) in their bilingual study.

A second explanation is related to subjects' ability to process information in L2, automatic and controlled processes. As the level of language competence increases and becomes associated with automatic processing, greater opportunities arise for controlled processes to operate in tasks involving problem-solving, including Linguistic Awareness. Language learners at less proficient stages of second language development are said to call on controlled processing in comprehension and production, thus loading memory capacity and creating difficulties in processing information efficiently (Dornic,

1977). With increased fluency, automatic processing takes over as a result of improved comprehension and production strategies. The competent learner's appeal to controlled processing is considerably reduced. Consequently, the limited capacity of the controlled processes is able to deal with analytic tasks such as reading or Linguistic Awareness.[5] Bialystok and Ryan (1985a) proposed that controlled processing is an important aspect of metalinguistic ability. They suggest that the more bilingual subjects are, the better they can put controlled processes to work in their ability to perform metalinguistic tasks.

3 Conclusion

The findings of this study revealed that as learners become proficient in the second language, they draw on different language abilities in making judgements of acceptability. It was found, however, that the first group might not have reached a significant level of proficiency in the second language to handle the metalinguistic task. Meanwhile for the other second language learners, the ability to make judgements of acceptability was related to reading (Group 2) and to speaking (Group 3).

For these two groups, knowledge of the second language and information-processing capacity in reading and in speaking[6] can be said to assist these learners in performing the judgement task. Second language learners have knowledge of the constraints (syntactic, lexical, discourse) of the language and process information efficiently allowing learners to tap controlled cognitive processes to reflect on language.

I have suggested, moreover, that oral decontextualised language ability can play a role in relation to Linguistic Awareness. Decontextualisation is a more generalised ability that can be applied to other aspects of language competence such as reading. Snow *et al.* (in press) have concluded from their research on second language learning that decontextualised language skill becomes increasingly important to reading in older children. Although this hypothesis was not tested in this study, I am proposing that in addition to decontextualised oral language, decontextualised reading may help explain the importance of reading competence to Linguistic Awareness in L2 with adolescent subjects. Finally, present research in L1 proposes that oral tasks that promote decontextualisation or Linguistic Awareness lead to reading and writing development in children. In this study, with adolescent subjects, the reverse has been noted. Reading was important to the less proficient subjects while speaking to the more proficient. The progression observed in children is said to be related in large part to age, cognitive and language development. However, in this study, the subjects are much older learners exposed to classroom second language learning and contact with the English language to promote oral expression is limited. Reading may be more important to the second group of subjects since they are more likely to rely on reading activities inside and outside the classroom and on transfer of reading abilities from L1.[7] The more proficient third group has greater oral language abilities that they put to use in the formal context of the second language classroom. The latter can be said to promote second language oral decontextualisation, an aspect of communicative proficiency considered to be linked to Linguistic Awareness.

In conclusion, current research on Linguistic Awareness reveals its increasing importance to second language development. The present study examined the strength of that relationship and the condition which determines this relationship. The context of second language learning in the classroom with adolescent subjects demonstrates that Linguistic Awareness is significantly related to different aspects of second language competence thereby affording language learners the opportunity to gain control over language to meet their communicative needs.

Notes

1. This research was supported by a grant from the Quebec Ministry of Education (FCAR) and a travel grant to the BAAL Language Awareness seminar was provided by the Faculty of Education, University of Ottawa.

2. Questions arise as to the distinction to be drawn between the role of linguistic awareness in second language learning and Krashen's Monitor model. Linguistic Awareness constitutes an integral feature of second language development since learners' implicit knowledge can be tapped in their ability to reflect on language. In the Monitor model, learners' appeal to explicit and conscious knowledge of the grammar is relevant to learning only and could never contribute anything to the acquisition of a second language. Krashen proposes moreover that learners rely on explicit knowledge and specifically, conscious representation of the rules of the grammar to monitor, edit and correct second language performance. My view is that Linguistic Awareness leads to greater control over reading, writing and speaking competence in varied settings and for different purposes.

3. Ryan and Ledger (1984) administered the oral cloze task in L1 to children as a measure of linguistic awareness.

4. In the present study, the CELT-structure subtest was also administered. The findings reveal that in Group 2, knowledge of structure correlated significantly with reading ($r=0.40$, $p=0.01$) and with the judgement task ($r=0.31$, $p=0.01$).

5. Hakes (1982) suggested that controlled information processing is a major component in developing metalinguistic abilities.
6. The oral cloze task, according to Oller (1979), requires knowledge of discourse constraints. Moreover, the oral cloze taxes short-term memory thus influencing information-processing capacity.
7. The linguistic questionnaire administered to the learners revealed that subjects in Group 2 read more in French than subjects in Group 3. Moreover, subjects in Group 2 claim to make greater efforts at learning English and French vocabulary than subjects in Group 3. Subjects in Group 3, however, did more in English overall (speaking, reading, writing and watching television) than the subjects in the other two groups.

Section Six: Conclusion

In our final paper (Paper 22), we return to the great need for increased communication and collaboration between teachers and tertiary level institutions and consider the role of the Consortium of Language Awareness Centres in forging a way ahead.

22 Language Awareness: a way ahead

Peter Garrett and Carl James

The papers collected in this volume represent a largely retrospective *record* of work in LA research and development that their authors have undertaken. Some of this work has been practice- and problem-driven, initiated by practitioners who, dissatisfied with some features of their teaching, have looked about them for 'new ways to do old things better' (Corder, 1978: 80). By contrast, other work reported is clearly theory-driven: broader theories of learner-centred humanistic education, often incorporated into some specific theory of language education have been the sources of inspiration, suggesting 'new things to do' (Corder, 1978:80).

This concluding paper is different in being prospective: it looks *ahead* and tries to identify some of the areas that need attention. Why is such speculation needed? Our answer is that there are large numbers of people, at all levels ranging from the solitary teacher to the government committee, who have invested considerable time and money in the LA field. The momentum must be maintained, for unless it is, we fear that LA either will be stillborn, or will stagnate and wither away in the same way that other promising educational innovations have been allowed to in the past, either by apathy, scepticism or even straightforward underfunding.

First, however, we must anticipate a possible misapprehension: we are in no way claiming to have identified and to be able to chart in detail *the* way forward for LA as a language-educational enterprise. Rather we hope to underline the importance of looking further ahead and thinking in terms of the dissemination, implementation and development of LA work, as well as its definition and justification.

Our focus here is primarily on LA in the sense of educational programmes of the sort we see developing in the UK (without wishing to appear ethnocentric or parochial). We also consider LA more generally, in the sense of making implicit knowledge explicit. Throughout we use the word 'student' to include learners of all types, including primary school pupils.

1 Promoting LA: Two Apparent Paradoxes

In our introductory paper, we drew attention to the fact that the recommendations in the Kingman Report (DES, 1988a) for implementing some form of LA in British schools were only founded on intuition, in the absence of prior evaluation. We are, in fact, calling simultaneously for the promotion of LA and for its evaluation. We do not see any necessary inconsistency in this, as some might, arguing that educational innovations, like drugs, should not be tried until they have been thoroughly tested. Historically, hunches, intuitions and even 'inspiration' have been the starting point for many new successes (like the discovery of the laws of gravity!). Criticism is warranted, however, when such hunches are taken as sufficient justification for the validity of an idea: there must be adequate follow-up and testing of these hunches. We see the promotion and the evaluation of LA as compatible and complementary. Indeed, educational innovations can only be properly evaluated in the long (or at least medium) term, in the everyday prevailing conditions in which education operates.

A second apparent paradox is that LA may be promoted through negative as much as positive evaluation, that is, by being found wanting as well as being warranted. Negative evaluation may provide important pointers as to how to improve LA activities. It may do this at two levels. First, it may show us that some of WHAT we include in our LA work is not helping us to achieve our goals. This, in a conspicuously ill-defined, even over-extended, field seems crucial at this juncture in particular. Second, it may reveal that HOW we are implementing LA is not sufficiently effective, and lead us to improve our methods.

True, consistently negative evaluation might, in the end, lead us to the conclusion that LA work in general fails to produce any of the educational benefits we hoped for or expected from it, or any other significant gains. This, quite simply, is a prospect which, if we want to lay claim to being professionals, we must be prepared to face.

2 Promotion and propaganda

We are mindful of the statements by Heap (Paper 18) and Wright (Paper 5) that a major benefit of positive evaluation of LA work will be to provide the proof with which to convince sceptical colleagues of its value. A recent development in LA in the UK has been the establishment of a National Consortium of Centres for Language Awareness, each to promote and develop LA within its locality. Hopefully, such regional centres will be able to involve themselves in informing local teachers and 'key' people about developments in LA, and convincing them of its value, even assisting them in implementation. Convincing them entails dispelling misgivings, and evaluation would appear to be very much an integral part of such work. Perhaps, though, it would be as well for the consortium to take stock of what other misgivings or barriers are likely to be encountered 'on the ground'. LA in British education is very much a grassroots movement, as has been repeatedly stressed. So for the future promotion of LA, priority must be given to the task of identifying, cataloguing and, hopefully, being better prepared to overcome the common misgivings about LA. This then will open the way ahead.

3 Misgivings galore?

Individual experience alone provides a reasonable basis for beginning the task of setting out these misgivings here. There would seem, at this stage, to be two main types.

3.1 Definition again

Many people, who would like and feel they ought to, still do not know what the legitimate remit of LA is. We have earlier pointed to its capacity for self-diversification. Doubtless, some will find the term itself off-putting. Language Awareness? Is that one of those fashionable subjects where you spend most of the time learning *about* language instead of actually getting on with learning it? This suspicion surrounding LA is likely to be especially damaging to its image in our present age of 'skills-promotion'. If LA does not manifestly produce usable 'skills', what is the point of it? This is a comment which must be taken seriously. After all, the same criticism discredited the firmly entrenched Grammar Translation Method in FL teaching half a century ago. The Cognitive Code approach, which shares many of the attributes and assumptions of LA work, actually succumbed to such criticism in the late 1960s. Need history repeat itself?

Similarly, there is the *déjà-vu* response: we've seen this all before. We tried 'it' and 'it' didn't work then. Why should 'it' work now? In response, we need to be able to convince them that the entity of the last generation is not the same 'it' as LA.

Or is LA just another refuge, a soft option for the weaker learner, a recipe therefore for the progressive erosion of standards in our schools and in society at large? Hardly so, considering the Kingman Committee had such (albeit intuitive) faith in it.

3.2 'We have no resources'

Having received answers to their misgivings about the nature of LA, and possibly even impressed by the enthusiasm, materials and syllabuses we have shown them, teachers, directors, advisers may remind us of the constraints they are subjected to by their inadequate resourcing. When they are clamouring for more resources to enable them to satisfy the basic requirements of the curriculum, how can we persuade them to earmark *extra* resources for LA? There is a shortage of teachers. In-service training will be required to provide the necessary expertise (see, for example, Chandler *et al.*, 1988). And where does LA feature in the National Curriculum? There is no room for it on the timetable. Perhaps they will explain that since nowadays everything is taught 'thematically', such separate areas as LA are out of the question.

Again, these are misgivings that we ought to look closely at in order to have satisfactory answers ready. Certainly, it must be emphasised that LA is NOT another subject we are trying to add to the already cluttered timetable; on the contrary, LA cuts through the traditional barriers on that timetable and in the curriculum it represents (see Anderson, Paper 10). It can readily be accommodated into a thematic context. Why not heighten awareness of the language of science while one is actually 'doing' science? What better context? Indeed, we would even go as far as to argue that the less LA is integrated into the curriculum, the greater the danger that LA becomes marginalised. We oppose this tendency to reification of LA. While having a legitimate claim to curricular time, LA will not be well served by being timetabled. Furthermore, the potential for marginalisation is heightened by the tendency of publishers hitherto to produce 'packaged' LA materials as if LA is a separate entity or an appendage. Perhaps the greatest risk of misrepresentation would come from evaluating LA input that has itself been distorted, even devalued, by marginalisation.

Whatever misgivings are voiced, in some cases, we may find ourselves pondering at times whether there is, after all, some other underlying personal resistance (conscious or unconscious) that bars the way more than situational (e.g. resource) constraints. Such tendencies in the way we try to explain other people's behaviour should not come unexpectedly (Lalljee, 1987; Nisbett *et al.*, 1973), and indeed this whole area of 'causal attribution' could itself be usefully included in LA courses (see below). Suffice it to say, the above-mentioned National Consortium of Centres for Language Awareness, working hand in hand with teachers and educationists within their localities, could examine and anticipate such misgivings and obstacles, so as to more effectively promote and implement LA.

4 Evaluation of LA

Above, we have argued strongly the case for evaluation of LA, in broad terms. Our focus now turns towards considering this evaluation in terms of the five (not independent) LA domains (affective, social, power, cognitive and performance) which we set out in the introductory paper of this volume (Paper 1). Let us first remind our reader of the main aims within each of the five domains.

Affective: to form attitudes and to awake and develop attention, sensitivity, curiosity, interest and aesthetic response (Donmall, 1985).
Social: to foster better relations among all ethnic groups (Donmall, 1985).
Power: to give the individual control over language and language learning for the achievement and expression of, as well as sensitivity to, identity and purpose.
Cognitive: to improve intellectual functioning.
Performance: to improve proficiency.

5 Cognitive domain

Widdowson (1983) draws a distinction between 'pure' education and training. So when we speak about the effects of LA on foreign language learning, for example, or writing skills, we are concerned with training, which falls within the domain of performance (see below). Discussions of cognitive gain, however, are about education. Education is concerned with the liberal notion of knowledge for its own sake, which requires no external justification in terms of direct skills enhancement. We should not assume that education has no practical applications, however. There is a need to engage a wide range of cognitive abilities in decision-making in any situation. Education fostering such abilities is of unquestionable value in everyday life.

This point is brought out by Walmsley (1984), who reviews some research undertaken with the express purpose of seeing whether teaching grammar pays dividends by leading to an increase in writing proficiency, as would be expected if 'transfer of training' occurs. There was, it was found, no evident boost to writing skills. We do not, in mentioning this, wish to imply that LA is about the teaching of grammar, but to highlight Walmsley's point that learning grammar, or doing linguistics or LA work, is not merely to be 'measured against a purely materialist yardstick' (Walmsley, 1984:15). LA work, as enquiry by the child into the nature of his or her linguistic environment, brings with it its own intrinsic, or cognitive, justification. After all, 'we do not measure the success of geography lessons primarily in terms of whether a student can find his or her way round the town or not' (Walmsley, 1984:15).

Evaluation of cognitive gains from LA is, it would seem, bound to be rather imprecise and difficult to quantify. Yet if cognitive claims are made for LA, it seems important to see how far they are justified. For the child entering primary school needing to learn about the world through language at a rate more rapid than spontaneity will allow, will or can LA work of some description bring qualitative improvements to the current language provision? In Paper 1 we drew attention to Mason's resubstantiation of the language deficit identified by Bernstein among 'disadvantaged' children. It is pertinent to ask whether, if such handicaps to cognitive development exist, LA work at school can make up for them (Mason, 1986).

There have been various attempts to assess the cognitive impact of bilingualism and bilingual education. Numerous limitations and criticisms of this research have been voiced: e.g. Is the relationship between bilingualism and cognitive development a chicken and egg problem? How representative are the samples in the studies? How long lasting are any of the gains? Nevertheless, it is fair to say that the vast majority of the research judgements have tended to be positive (Baker, 1988: 44).

Even if we go to the extreme of unquestioningly asserting that bilingualism brings cognitive advantages, such as divergent thinking, field independence, or an analytical orientation towards languages, it is an enormous leap to simply assume that LA courses will therefore likewise give the same advantages. It may be, for example, that LA brings no identifiable cognitive gains. It may be that it brings cognitive gains which differ in type and/or quantity from those claimed in some of the studies into bilingualism.

6 Performance domain

Just as there has been research into the impact of bilingualism and bilingual education on performance, there is a need to evaluate LA along the same dimension. An important issue here, of course, is what performance will be evaluated, and this is likely to depend on the particular type of LA and its goals. Some of the work carried out under the LA rubric, for example, consists of 'taster courses' (DES,

1990), which give students a chance to try out foreign languages over a period of weeks, with the aim of increasing interest and improving performance in a subsequent modern language course. In such cases, assessment of the impact of LA work might compare the subsequent performance in the modern language of comparable groups of students who have done such a course with others who have not, measured by standardised language tests. Studying and comparing students' perceptions of their own abilities in the second language may also be revealing (see Lambert and Tucker, 1972).

We have argued, as far as UK-type LA programmes are concerned, for an integrated 'LA across the curriculum'. This would require a somewhat different approach to the assessment of effect on performance, since one would, needless to say, be looking at performance throughout the curriculum, including, for example, biology and chemistry. Nevertheless, where opportunities arise, the same principle might be applied of measuring and comparing the performance of comparable groups of 'LA and non-LA' (= experimental and control) students, preferably taught by the same teacher. Such evaluation could be conducted by teachers as researchers most effectively. Alternatively – again, if possibilities exist – evaluation might proceed by measuring the performance of LA students against some kind of wider (e.g. national) norm (see Swain and Lapkin, 1982).

7 Affective domain

A great deal of research has been conducted into the relations of various types of attitude and motivation to second language achievement (Gardner and Lambert, 1972; Gardner, 1985). Despite argument about the importance of attitude and motivation relative to aptitude in classroom-based second language learning (Krashen and Terrell, 1983: 39), there is considerable evidence that these factors play a significant role in second language acquisition. With the integrated approach to LA that we are suggesting, however, we would set our sights wider than second language classrooms to classrooms in general, when examining the affective impact of LA.

How to go about measuring attitudes is a well-documented area (see, for example, Henerson *et al.*, 1987). The attitudes on which to focus will obviously depend upon the particular type of LA, and its goals or the claims made for it. Possibilities include attitudes towards school and lessons in the various school subjects, attitudes towards language learning, attitudes towards ethnic groups, etc.

Why measure attitudes, though? Are we not more interested in the *effects* of any change in attitude? Even if LA leads to attitudinal benefits, what will students then be able to *do* better? Quite apart from what has been said above about attitudes and second language acquisition, it has been said that attitudes have three distinct components: cognitive, affective and action (Triandis, 1971), and that this explains why a clear or strong relationship is often not found between attitudes and behaviour (e.g. Garrett et al. 1990). So, in the end, even if, by our measurement, there is some positive attitude change accruing from LA work, there may be no tangible, visible benefits.

Affective claims are made for LA, however. How then is one to respond to these? There appear to be two alternatives. Either we ask if affective benefits are sufficient in themselves if they do not affect behaviour in any significantly positive way. Or we look for some evidence in students' classroom behaviour that LA has awakened and developed attention, interest, etc. The latter seems the only rational course to take if we are to attempt to evaluate LA in relation to the claims that are made in its favour. Many may feel that the affective dimension is of minor importance compared to performance. After all, performance gains are what will lead to examination success, and, for the majority, this is the most important outcome of all. Against this, however, must be measured the possibility that a positive attitude may be longer-lasting than knowledge acquired for examinations (Baker, 1988).

Changes in the level of interest and attention in students might be discovered from direct questioning of students and teachers themselves through questionnaires and interviews, or from changes in the patterns and content of teacher–student and student–student interaction in the classroom. Classroom features suggesting a higher level of interest among learners might include, for example, a higher proportion of on-task to off-task talk, an increase in responsiveness or in the amount of initiating behaviour, such as hand-raising, question asking, etc. (See Chaudron, 1988, for a review of such studies in the field of second language classrooms.) Clearly, differences which LA work might bring with it (e.g. task-type) would need to be considered (see below for further discussion). Cultural differences, it must be stated, may also play a significant role in such areas of behaviour (Chaudron, 1988), and are indeed themselves in need of further research.

8 Social and power domains

The social domain relates primarily to LA as an educational programme about language, rather than to the implicit/explicit instruction divide in second and foreign language learning, and is of particular concern to LA used in bi- or multicultural settings with a focus on the improvement of inter-ethnic relations. A distinction needs to be made here between assimilation and free social interaction. The first of these may be a sign or result of better relations, but may equally be an unhappy, politically enforced state of affairs; the second, however, we would define as the free and self-determined movement across community boundaries in a non-threatening environment where ethnic identity requirements are satisfied.

One suggestion for researching such relations is work focusing on social networks. This research approach, which examines the types and degree of contact in communities, has been widely employed in the social sciences for some time, and during the last decade has also found its place in socio-linguistic study (see, for example, Milroy and Milroy, 1978; Milroy, 1980; Cheshire, 1982a, 1982b). By mapping out social networks over time, it may be possible to detect changes in inter-ethnic interaction.

Such research might be directed at linguistic factors. Speech Accommodation Theory (Giles and Smith, 1979; James, forthcoming) suggests that better inter-ethnic relations could display themselves through a narrowing of linguistic differences. In other words, the different groups would come to share more linguistic features, perhaps taking on, as their common stock, particular lexical items, idioms, grammatical features, etc.

We are clearly not suggesting here that a year or two of LA work in one or two local classrooms might change networks in whole communities, even if this is undoubtedly a long-term aim for the proponents of LA directed at making gains in this domain. Rather we suggest that such signs might be sought close to the teacher and the school itself, looking for changes in the patterns of interaction and friendship between students from different ethnic groups.

Even before any evaluation has been conducted in relation to this domain, however, we would like to put forward a suggestion which we intuitively feel will aid LA programmes in their goal of achieving significant improvements in the field of inter-ethnic relations. We would argue, like Little and Singleton (Paper 9), the need for a broadening of LA into other areas concerned with communication, areas which will be of as much value to LA with a 'monolingual' or 'monocultural' focus, as it will be to LA with a multilingual, cross-cultural one. One example would be the above-mentioned area of causal attribution (the reasons given for behaviour). In addition, Merchant (Paper 4) suggests including an exploration of attitudes to language. It is also important in social relations, again whether they are within a particular (e.g. social, regional, ethnic) group or between or among such groups, that people's intentions are correctly understood. To take a cross-cultural example, Thomas (1983) shows how the frequently perfectly reasonable transfer of the Russian speaker's 'konešno' to English 'of course', when used with equivalent frequency, might, instead of conveying enthusiasm to the addressee, sound dismissive or insulting; an effect that has clear interpersonal and social implications.

The 'konešno' example is an instance of Thomas' (1983) 'pragma-linguistic failure' (as opposed to 'socio-pragmatic failure' – see below). This pragma-linguistic area is easily incorporated into the 'Language' nature of LA. Others to consider include the power and solidarity connotations in the selection of pronouns (Banks, 1989; Fairclough, 1989), initiating and changing topics in conversation (West and Zimmerman, 1985), interruptions in conversation (Zimmerman and West, 1975), and suitable strategies of politeness, which vary from culture to culture (Davies, 1986; Oleksy, 1989; Thomas, 1983). Some areas are concerned with broader dimensions of communication than specific linguistic features. For example, there are significant and interesting cross-cultural differences in styles of persuasion (Al-Jubouri, 1984; Johnstone, 1989). Similarly, Scollon and Scollon (1983) provide some illuminating examples of how cross-cultural differences in communicative styles (e.g. showing deference; looking for common ground) in 'gatekeeping encounters' (e.g. job interviews, legal trials) can have disastrous consequences. Ways of speaking, body movements, even cross-cultural differences in the use of silence, or 'non-talk' (see, for example, Enninger, 1987; Scollon and Scollon, 1981) may all lead to a muddled or erroneous interpretation of intended meanings. Also, at the socio-pragmatic level, there may be failings in judgements of the size of an imposition that the speaker is making on the listener (Goffman, 1967) and of what is and what is not other people's business (Lakoff, 1974). There is a point, then, where LA goes beyond *Language* Awareness to *Communication* Awareness. Learning about the languages of different groups is only part of learning about communication and miscommunication between them.

It is commonly argued that such areas as this must be considered as the 'icing on the cake'; that attention to details such as these must come at later levels of (e.g. language) learning (see, for example, Prabhu, 1987, discussing his particular teaching context). With these social and power domains in mind, however, we echo the opposite viewpoint, expressed *inter alia* by Davies (1986) and Thomas (1983) that their effects can be cumulatively quite strong. They can have considerable implications at both the individual and cultural levels. At the former level, miscommunication may lead to irritation (Johansson, 1973) and a withdrawal of further interpersonal cooperation; at the latter level, it is quite possible that such cross-cultural misunderstandings generate and perpetuate some extremely negative ethnic stereotyping. Young learners in school classrooms also have much to gain from awareness work at these levels.

9 Theoretical models as sources of wider insights

Research into and evaluation of LA will be not only of direct value to the development of LA itself, but will hopefully also provide some valuable data to contribute to our understanding of broader areas such as ethnic relations, or second language acquisition. In relation to the latter specifically, a number of models have in recent years been evolving in the social psychology of second language acquisition: e.g. the Social Context Model (Clement, 1980); the Socio-Educational Model (Gardner, 1985); the Inter-Group Model (Giles and Byrne, 1982; Garrett *et al.*, 1989); the Acculturation Model (Schumann, 1986). All respond in various ways to the role of attitudinal and motivational factors in second language acquisition. Giles and Byrne (1982), for example, identify the degree of hardness/softness of inter-group boundaries as one important variable in their Inter-Group Model of second language acquisition. As it stands at present, then, this model would predict that if LA work results in softer inter-group boundaries, second language acquisition will be promoted. In so far as the LA performance domain concerns, for some, the improvement of second language proficiency, there are clearly areas of mutual interest here too.

10 The implicit and explicit side of LA

Whichever domains LA work is aimed at, there are choices to be made about how to go about things. As stated at the outset, we are not only concerned with *what* to include in our LA work, but how to go about it, what methods and techniques to use in our implementation of the syllabus. Wright (Paper 5) notes that LA tends to be bound up with an inductive methodology. In fact, it seems reasonable to claim that, for many, such a discovery approach to teaching and learning about language is what makes LA so interesting, more than the content itself. Thus Zhou Yan-Ping (Paper 19) compares the effectiveness of inductive versus deductive (explicit) instruction. As we have seen, the explicit/implicit approaches feature not only in the giving and getting of knowledge (Zhou Yan-Ping), but also in knowledge itself: becoming aware of what you already know or your (and others') learning strategies, so as to give you more power and control over your own learning (e.g. Hedge and Gosden, Paper 14).

These assumptions too require evaluation. Does heightening awareness of how one learns and how others learn help in all domains? Zhou Yan-Ping (Paper 19) seeks evidence as to whether explicit teaching, or a combination of introspection, observation and discovery is more effective for language performance. Others (e.g. Abraham, 1985) have wondered whether the answer to this question will vary according to the individual's cognitive style. In any event, this is a question which has important implications for other models of second language acquisition (e.g. Bialystok, 1978; Krashen, 1981; Sharwood Smith, 1981). The same question could be asked in relation to the other domains. How, for example, can we best raise students' awareness of communicative styles or socio-pragmatic ground rules: through explicit instruction, or perhaps through conscious reflection and discussion of video-recorded incidents (see, for example, Roberts and Sayers, 1987)?

Considerations of inductive and deductive methodology have brought us back to the point of delivery, to LA in the classroom. It is not only how LA is defined inside and outside the classroom that is crucial to any evaluation, but also how it is 'delivered'. One complication here of course is that there is no necessary 1 : 1 relationship between method and content. Can one attach the term LA to a specific content-focus? Can it be attached to a specific methodology? Are the content and methodology attached to each other and therefore mutually determining?

As far as language teaching is concerned, inductive method is not the monopoly of LA, for example; it is as much an integral part of audio-lingualism. Similarly, nor does group work 'belong to' LA, even if many favour it, for example, as a route to more talk about language. It seems, then, that a way forward is to ensure that we also evaluate our methods according to our LA goals. We may even discover that our findings have implications elsewhere. For example, if group work can lead to gains in the social domain through improvement in positive feelings between group members (Aronson, 1975), teachers may decide to employ it more in other (non-LA) schoolwork, thus hopefully increasing the momentum towards the goals of LA.

11 Conclusion

Within UK education, LA programmes have always been proposed as a solution to problems, from Hawkins' (1981) initial interest in the modern languages problem in British education, to subsequent interest from multicultural education, to Kingman's focus on English proficiency. Doubtless this, along with the lack of teacher training (Chandler *et al.*, 1988; DES, 1990) accounts for much of the diversity of LA, and the concomitant difficulties of evaluation. Perhaps with more collaboration and integration regarding LA in UK schools, along with the LINC teacher training programme at Nottingham University to implement the recommendations of the Kingman Report (DES, 1988a), and the establishment of the National Consortium of Centres for Language Awareness, greater clarity will now be brought to LA. In the meantime, there is a continuing need, identified by Mitchell and Hooper (Paper 3) and underlined by the HMI Report on LA (DES, 1990), to observe and evaluate what actually happens with LA in classrooms; to see what teachers actually do, and what pupils actually get; to see what characterises LA as it evolves, and to find more effective ways to deliver its content and achieve its goals.

Note

We are grateful to Phil Scholfield and Nikolas Coupland for reading and commenting on an earlier version of this paper.

Composite Bibliography

Abbott, G. 1981. Encouraging communication in English: A paradox. *English Language Teaching Seminar*, **35**, 228–30.

Abraham, R.A. 1985. Field independence-dependence and the teaching of grammar. *TESOL Quarterly*, **20**(4), 689–702.

Alatis, J.A., Stern, H.H. and Strevens, P. (eds). 1983. *Applied Linguistics and the Preparation of Second Language Teachers*. Georgetown University Press, Washington, DC.

Alexander, L. 1976. Where do we go from here? A reconsideration of some basic assumptions affecting course design. *English Language Teaching Journal*, **30**(2), 89–103.

Al-Jubouri, A.J.R. 1984. The role of repetition in Arabic argumentative discourse. In Swales, J. and Mustafa, H. (eds) *English for Specific Purposes in the Arab World*. University of Aston, Birmingham.

Allen, D. 1988. English, whose English? *National Association of Teachers of English, for National Association of Advisers in English*.

Allwright, R. 1982. Perceiving and pursuing learners' needs. In Geddes, M. and Sturtridge, G. (eds) *Individualisation*. Modern English Publications, pp. 24–31.

Anthony, R. 1984. Metalinguistic awareness and reading in bilingual education: Implications of a Chilcotin/English study. Unpublished PhD dissertation, University of Toronto.

Aronson, R. 1975. The jigsaw route to learning and liking. *Psychology Today*, **8**(9), 43–50.

Atkins, M.J. 1984. Practitioner as researcher: some techniques for analysing semi-structured data in small scale research. *British Journal Ed. Studies*, **32**(3), 75–82.

Baker, C. 1988. *Key Issues in Bilingualism and Bilingual Education*. Multilingual Matters, Clevedon.

Banks, S.P. 1989. Power pronouns and the language of intercultural understanding. In Ting-Toomey, S. and Korzenny, F. (eds) *Language, Communication and Culture: Current Directions*. Sage, pp. 180–98.

Barrs, M. 1988. Blanks in teaching. In Mills, C. and Timson, L. (eds) *Looking at Language in the Primary School*. National Association for the Teaching of English.

Beach, R and Bridwell, L. 1984. *New Directions in Composition Research*. Guilford Press.

Bell, L.A. 1979. Methodological and pedagogical problems in the teaching of language and area studies degree courses. *Quinquereme*, **2**(2).

Ben-Zeev, S. 1977. Mechanisms by which child bilingualism affects understanding of language and cognitive structures. In Hornby, P.A. (ed.) *Bilingualism: Psychological, Social and Educational Implications*. Academic Press, New York, pp. 29–57.

Bergson, H. 1911. *Creative Evolution*. Macmillan.

Bernstein, B. 1959. A public language: some sociological implications of a linguistic form. *Journal of Sociology*, **10**, 311–26.

Bertoldi, E., Kollar, J. and Ricard, E. 1988. Learning how to learn English: from awareness to action. *English Language Teaching Journal*, **42**(3), 157–64.

Bialystock, E. 1978. A theoretical model of second language learning. *Language Learning*, **28**, 69–84.

Bialystok, E. and Ryan, E.B. 1985a. A metacognitive framework for the development of first and second language skills. In Forrest-Presley, D.L., Mackinnon, G.E. and Waller, T.G. (eds) *Meta-cognition, Cognition, and Human Performance*. Academic Press, New York, pp. 102–28.

Bialystok, E. and Ryan, E.B. 1985b. Toward a definition of metalinguistic skill. *Merrill-Palmer Quarterly*, **31**(3), 229–51.

Bloor, T. 1986. What do language students know about grammar? *British Journal of Language Teaching*, **24**(3), 157–60.

Bolinger, D. 1980. *Language, the Loaded Weapon: The Use and Abuse of Language Today*. Longman.

Bolitho, R. and Tomlinson, B. 1980. *Discover English*. Heinemann.

Bourne, J. 1989. *Moving into the Mainstream: LEA Provision for Bilingual Pupils*. NFER–Nelson.

Bowers, R., Bamber, B., Straker Cook, R. and Thomas, A. 1987. *Talking about Grammar*. Longman.

Brami-Mouling, M.A. 1977. Notes sur l'adaptation de l'expression verbale de l'enfant en fonction de l'âge de son interlocuteur. *Archives de Psychologie*, **45**, 225–34.

Bravo Magaña, J.C. 1986. Naturalistic acquisition of English by three Mexican Spanish-speaking children – a longitudinal study. Unpublished PhD thesis, University of Reading.

Breach, R. and Bridwell, L. (eds). 1984. *New Directions in Composition Research*. Guilford Press, New York.

Brédart, S. 1980. Un problème de métalinguistique: l'explication des échecs de communication chez l'enfant de 8 à 12 ans. *Archives de Psychologie*, **48**, 303–21.

Brédart, S. and Rondal, J.A. 1982. *L'analyse du language chez l'enfant*. Pierre Mardaga, Bruxelles.

Breen, M.P. 1987. Contemporary paradigms in syllabus design. *Language Teaching*, **20**(2 & 3).

Brent-Palmer, C.A. (1979). Sociolinguistic assessment of the notion 'im/migrant semilingualism' from a social conflict perspective. *Working Papers on Bilingualism*, **7**, 135–80.

Bresnan, J. (ed.). 1982. *The Mental Representation of Grammatical Relations*. MIT Press, Cambridge, Mass.

Brindley, G.P. 1984. *Needs Analysis and Objective Setting in the Adult Migrant Education Program*. Adult Migrant Education Service, Sydney.

Brown, D. 1980. *Principles of Language Teaching and Learning*. Prentice-Hall, Englewood Cliffs, N.J.

Brumfit, C.J. 1981. Teaching the general student. In Johnson, K. and Morrow, K. (eds) *Communication in the Classroom*. Longman.

Brumfit, C.J. (ed.). 1988. *Language in Teacher Education*. National Congress on Languages in Education, Brighton.

Brumfit, C.J. and Mitchell, R. (forthcoming). The language knowledge of trainee teachers. University of Southampton, mimeo.

Byram, M.S. 1982. Where is the 16+ leading us? *British Journal of Language Teaching*, **20**(3), 145–8.

Cahm, E. 1980. Some problems in the teaching of Area Studies: the Portsmouth experience. *Journal of Area Studies*, **1**.

Campbell, R.N. *et al.* 1985. Foreign language learning in the elementary schools: a comparison of three language programs. *Modern Language Journal*, **69**, 44–54.

Canale, M. and Barker, G. 1986. How creative language teachers are using microcomputers. *TESOL Newsletter* **20**(1), Supp 3 (CALL), 1–3.

Canale, M. and Swain, M. 1980. Theoretical bases of communicative approaches to language teaching. *Applied Linguistics*, **1**(1).

Candlin, C.N. 1978. Editorial to Mackay, R. and Mountford, A. *English for Specific Purposes*. Longman.

Carter, R. (ed.). 1982. *Linguistics and the Teacher*, Routledge and Kegan Paul.

Carvalho, Lina Rosa L.R.G. de. 1984. Reading strategies in English as a foreign language. Unpublished MA dissertation, University of Santa Catarina.

Castaños, F. 1978. Paper presented at Mextesol Convention, Oaxaca (exact title unknown).

Cazden, C. 1975. Play with language and metalinguistic awareness: One dimension of language experience. In Bruner, J.S., Jolly, A. and Sylva, K. (eds) *Play: Its Role in Evolution and Development*. Penguin, pp. 603–8.

Celani, M.A.A., Holmes, J.L., Ramos R.G. de and Scott, M.R. 1988. *The Brazilian ESP Project – an Evaluation*. Pontificia Universidade Catolica, São Paulo.

Chambers, F. 1980. A reevaluation of needs analysis in ESP. *ESP Journal*, **1**(1), 25–33.

Chamot, A.U., O'Malley, J.M., Kupper, L. and Impink-Hernandez, M.V. 1987. *A Study of Learning Strategies in Foreign Language Instruction*. First Year Report. InterAmerica Research Associates, Rosslyn, Va.

Chandler, P., Robinson, W.P. and Noyes, P. 1988. The level of linguistic knowledge and awareness amongst students training to be primary teachers. *Language and Education*, **2**(3), 161–73.

Chandler, R. 1988. Unreproductive busywork. *English in Education*, **22**(3), 20–28.

Chaudron, C. 1983. Research on metalinguistic judgements: a review of theory, methods and results. *Language Learning*, **33**, 343–77.

Chaudron, C. 1988. *Second Language Classrooms: Research on Teaching and Learning*. Cambridge University Press.

Cheshire, J. 1982a. *Variation in an English Dialect*. Cambridge University Press.

Cheshire, J. 1982b. Linguistic variation and social function. In Romaine, S.

(ed.) *Sociolinguistic Variation in Speech Communities.* Edward Arnold, pp.
153–66.

Chesters, G. and Gardner, N. (eds). 1987. *STISS Special Publication: The
Use of Computers in the Teaching of Language and Languages.* Computers in
Teaching Initiative Support Service.

Chomsky, N. 1957. *Syntactic Structures.* Mouton, The Hague.

Chomsky, N. 1959. Review of Skinner, B.F.'s verbal behaviour. *Language*,
35, 26–58.

Chomsky, N. 1965. *Aspects of the Theory of Syntax.* MIT Press, Cambridge,
Mass.

Chomsky, N. 1968. *Language and Mind.* Harcourt Brace Jovanovich, New
York.

Chryshochoos, N. 1988a. Needs identification and learner awareness: an
experiment in the North-East. Mimeo, University of Durham.

Chryshochoos, N. 1988b. The fragile syllabus. Paper presented at the XXII
IATEFL Conference, Edinburgh, April 1988.

Chryshochoos, N. 1989. The hierarchy of needs: a solution. Paper presented
at the XXIII IATEFL Conference, University of Warwick, March–April
1989.

Chryshochoos, N. (in preparation). Establishing a hierarchy of needs.
Unpublished research for PhD thesis, University of Durham.

Clark, J.L. 1979. The syllabus. What should the learner learn? *AVLA Journal*,
17(2), 99–108.

Clark, R., Fairclough, N., Martin-Jones, M. and Ivanič, R. 1987. Critical
language awareness. *Centre for Language in Social Life Working Papers* 1.
Lancaster University, Department of Linguistics.

Clarke, P. 1988. Examining the 'silent period'. Paper presented at the 1988
Annual Congress of the Applied Linguistics Association of Australia.

Clahsen, H., Meisel, J. M. and Pienemann, M. 1983. *Deutsch als Zweitsprache:
der Spracherwerb Ausländischer Arbeiter.* Günter Narr Verlag, Tübingen.

Clement, R. 1980. Ethnicity, contact and communicative competence in a
second language. In: H. Giles, W.P. Robinson and P.M. Smith (eds).
Language: Social Psychological Perspectives. Pergamon.

Clyne, M. (ed.). 1986. *An Early Start: Second Language at Primary School.*
River Seine Press, Melbourne.

Cohen, L. and Manion, L. 1986. *Research Methods in Education.* Croom
Helm.

Collins COBUILD. 1987. *English Language Dictionary.* Collins.

Collins COBUILD. 1988. *Essential English Dictionary.* Collins.

Comrie, B. 1976. *Aspect.* Cambridge University Press.

Comrie, B. 1985. *Tense.* Cambridge University Press.

Cook, V.J. 1988. *Chomsky's Universal Grammar. An Introduction.* Blackwell.

Cook, V.J. 1989. Linguists' grammars and the language teacher. Paper
presented at the Third National Modern Languages Convention, NIHE,
Dublin, January 1989.

Cooper, C. 1985. Aspects of article introductions in IEEE publications.
Unpublished MA dissertation, University of Aston.

Corder, S.P. 1978. Pure and applied research in linguistics: is the difference
merely one of motivation? *Studies in Second Language Acquisition*, 1(2),
77–90.

Craft, M. 1982. Education for diversity – the challenge of cultural pluralism. Unpublished occasional paper. University of Nottingham.
Crookes, G. 1986. Towards a validated analysis of scientific text structure. *Applied Linguistics*, **7**, 57–70.
Crystal, D. 1988. *Rediscover Grammar*. Longman.
Cummins, J. 1978. Bilingualism and the development of metalinguistic awareness. *Journal of Cross Cultural Psychology*, **9**, 131–49.
Cummins, J. 1983. Language proficiency and academic achievement. In Oller, J.W. Jr (ed.) *Issues in Language Testing Research*. Newbury House, Rowley, Mass., pp. 118–30.

Daneman, M. and Carpenter, P.A. 1980. Working memory and reading. *Journal of Verbal Learning and Verbal Behavior*, **19**, 450–66.
d'Anglejan, A. and Renaud, C. 1985. Learner characteristics and second language acquisition: a multivariate study of adult learners and some thoughts on methodology. *Language Learning*, **35**, 1–19.
Davies, E.E. 1983. Language awareness as an alternative to foreign language study. *British Journal of Language Teaching*, **21**(2), 71–5.
Davies, E.E. 1986. Politeness and the foreign language learner. *Anglo-American Studies* **6**(2), 117–30.
Davies, F.I. 1988. Designing a writing syllabus in English for academic purposes: process and product. In Robinson, P.O. (ed.) *ELT Document No. 129.*
Davies, G. and Higgins, J. 1982. *Using Computers in Language Learning: a Teacher's Guide*. Centre for Information on Language Teaching, London.
Dennison, A. 1989. Language in initial teacher education. Unpublished MA education dissertation, University of Southampton.
Department of Education and Science (DES). 1975. *A Language for Life. Report of a Committee of Enquiry under the Chairmanship of Sir Alan Bullock.* HMSO.
Department of Education and Science (DES). 1985. *Education for All. Report of Committee of Inquiry into the Education of Children from Ethnic Minority Groups under the Chairmanship of Lord Swann.* HMSO.
Department of Education and Science (DES). 1987. *Quality in Schools: the Initial Training of Teachers, an HMI Survey*. HMSO.
Department of Education and Science (DES). 1988a. *Report of the Committee of Inquiry into the Teaching of English Language*. HMSO.
Department of Education and Science (DES). 1988b. *A Statement of Policy. Modern Languages in the School Curriculum*. HMSO.
Department of Education and Science (DES). 1989a. *The Education Reform Act 1988: Modern Foreign Languages in the National Curriculum.* HMSO.
Department of Education and Science (DES). 1989b. *English for Ages 5 to 16: Proposals of the Secretary of State for Education and Science and the Secretary of State for Wales. Under the Chairmanship of Professor C.B. Cox.* HMSO.
Department of Education and Science (DES). 1990. *A Survey of Language Awareness and Foreign Language Taster Courses: A Report by HM Inspectorate.* DES.
Devitt, S.M. 1986. Learning a foreign language through the media. *CLCS Occasional Paper No 18.* Trinity College, Centre for Language and Communication Studies, Dublin.

Dhingra, S. 1989. LDIP course evaluation summary. University of Nottingham.

Donmall, B.G. (ed.). 1985. *Language Awareness: NCLE Reports and Papers*, 6. CILT, London.

Dornic, S. 1977. *Information Processing and Bilingualism*. University of Stockholm, Psychology Department, Report 510.

Doughty, P., Pearce, J. and Thornton, G. 1971. *Language in Use*. Edward Arnold.

Downing, J. 1987. Comparative perspectives on literacy. In Wagner, D. (ed.) *The Future of Literacy in a Changing World*. Pergamon Press, pp. 27–47.

Downing, J. and Valtin, R. (eds). 1984. *Linguistic Awareness and Learning to Read*. Springer-Verlag, Berlin.

Dubin, F. and Olshtain, E. 1987. *Building on Purpose: Building Cognitive Skills for Intermediate Learners*. Addison-Wesley.

Dulany, D.E., Carlson, R.A. and Dewey, G.I. 1985. A case of syntactical learning and judgement: How conscious and how abstract? *Journal of Experimental Psychology: General*, 113(4), 541–54.

Edge, J. 1988. Applying linguistics in English language teacher training for speakers of other languages. *English Language Teaching Journal*, 42(1).

Ehrman, M. and Oxford, R.C. (1989). Effects of sex differences, career choice, and psychological type on adults' language learning strategies. *Modern Language Journal*, 73, 1–13.

Ellis, G. and Sinclair, B. 1989. *Learning How to Learn English*. Cambridge University Press.

Ellis, R. 1984. Can syntax be taught? A study of the effects of formal instruction on the acquisition of WH questions by children. *Applied Linguistics*, 5(2), 138–52.

Ellis, R. 1985. *Understanding Second Language Acquisition*. Oxford University Press.

Enninger, W. 1987. What interactants do with non-talk across cultures. In Knapp, K., Enninger, W. and Knapp-Potthoff, A. (eds) *Analyzing Intercultural Communication*. Mouton de Gruyter, New York, pp. 269–302.

Entwistle, N. and Ramsden, P. 1983. *Understanding Student Learning*. Croom Helm.

Faerch, C. and Kasper, C. 1984. Two ways of defining communication strategies. *Language Learning*, 34(1).

Faerch, C. and Kasper, G. 1987. *Introspection in Second Language Research*. Multilingual Matters, Clevedon.

Faern, S. and Shillaw, J. 1986. Unpublished report on needs analysis of science students in English. Mimeo. Language Centre, University of Hong Kong.

Fairclough, N. 1989. *Language and Power*. Longman.

Fairclough, N.L. (ed.). 1990. *Critical Language Awareness*. Longman.

Fanselow, J.F. 1987. Foreword in Wenden, A. and Rubin, J. (eds), pp. ix–x.

Findlay, P.G.A. 1980. Literature, language and society: on the place of literary study in Area Studies courses. *Journal of Area Studies*, 2.

Fletcher, P. and Garman, M. 1988. Normal language development and language impairment: syntax and beyond. *Clinical Linguistics and Phonetics*, 2(2), 97–113.

Flower, L. and Hayes, J.R. 1980. The dynamics of composing: making plans and juggling constraints. In Gregg, L.W. and Steinberg, E.R. (eds) *Cognitive Processes in Writing*. Lawrence Erlbaum, Hillsdale, N.J.

Flower, L. and Hayes, J. 1981. A cognitive process theory of writing. *College Composition and Communication*, 62(4), 365–87.

Foldberg, E. 1977. Why? When? What? How? A plea to think more of the language-learners. *English Language Teaching Journal*, 32(1), 15–23.

Frank, C. and Rinvolucri, M. 1983. *Grammar in Action: Awareness Activities for Language Learning*. Prentice-Hall, Englewood Cliffs, N.J.

Freire, P. 1972. *Pedagogy of the Oppressed*. Penguin.

Fudge, E. 1987. Using the computer in teaching phonetics. In Chesters, G. and Gardner, N. (eds), pp. 139–42.

Gairns, R. and Redman, S. 1986. *A Guide to Teaching and Learning Vocabulary: Working with Words*. Cambridge University Press.

Galambos, S.J. and Hakuta, K. 1988. Subject-specific and task-specific characteristics of metalinguistic awareness in children. *Applied Psycholinguistics*, 9, 141–62.

Gardner, K. 1968. The state of reading. In Smart, N. (ed.) *Crisis in the Classroom: an Enquiry into State Education Policy*. Hamlyn (out of print).

Gardner, R.C. 1985. *Social Psychology and Second Language Learning: The Role of Attitudes and Motivation*, Edward Arnold.

Gardner, R.C. and Lambert, W.E. 1972. *Attitudes and Motivation is Second Language Learning*. Newbury House, Rowley, Mass.

Garrett, P., Giles, H. and Coupland, N. 1989. The contexts of language learning: extending the intergroup model of second language acquisition. In Ting-Toomey, S. and Korzenny, F. (eds) *Language, Communication and Culture: Current Directions*. Sage.

Garrett, P., Griffiths, Y., James, C., and Scholfield, P.J. 1990. The language of pre-writing activity and the attitudes and writing of bilingual U.K. schoolchildren. Paper read to BAAL Annual Conference *Language and Nation*, Swansea University.

Gass, S. 1983. The development of L2 intuitions. *TESOL Quarterly*, 17, 272–93.

Giles, H. (ed.). 1977. *Language, Ethnicity and Intergroup Relations*. Academic Press.

Giles, H. and Byrne, J. 1982. An intergroup approach to second language acquisition. *Journal of Multilingual and Multicultural Development*, 3(1), 17–40.

Giles, H. and Smith, P. 1979. Accommodation theory: optimal levels of convergence. In Giles, H. and Sinclair, R.N. (eds) *Language and Social Psychology*. Blackwell, pp. 45–65.

Gleitman, H. and Gleitman, L. 1979. Language use and language judgement. In Fillmore, C.W., Kempler, D. and Wang, W.S. (eds) *Individual Differences in Language Ability and Language Behaviour*. Academic Press, New York, pp. 103–26.

Goffman, E. 1967. *Interaction Ritual: Essays on Face to Face Behaviour*. Doubleday, Garden City, New York.

Golebiowska, A. 1984. Motivating those who know it all. *English Language Teaching Journal*, 38(4).

Gosden, H. 1988. Consciousness-raising and the ESL learner: three case studies. Unpublished MA dissertation. UCNW, Bangor.

Grotjahn, R. 1987. On the methodological basis of introspective methods. In Faerch, C. and Kasper, C. Ch. 2.

Guerra, V. 1984. Predictors of second language learners' error judgements in written English. PhD dissertation, University of Texas (Austin).

Hakes, D.T. 1982. The development of metalinguistic abilities: What develops? In Kucaj, S. (ed.) *Language Development; Language, Thought, and Culture*. Lawrence Erlbaum, Hillsdale, N.J., pp. 163–210.

Hakes, D.T., Evans, J.S. and Tunmer, W.E. 1980. *The Development of Metalinguistic Abilities in Children*. Springer-Verlag, Berlin.

Halliday, M.A.K. 1975. *Learning How to Mean; Explorations in the Development of Language*. Edward Arnold.

Halliday, M.A.K. 1985. *An Introduction to Functional Grammar*. Edward Arnold.

Hampshire Modern Languages Skills Development Programme (HMLSDP). 1988. *French Level One*. Hampshire County Council Education Department.

Harding, A., Page, B. and Rowell, S. 1980. *Graded Objectives in Modern Languages* Centre for Information in Language Teaching, London.

Harley, B. 1986. *Age in Second Language Acquisition*. Multilingual Matters, Clevedon.

Harley, B. *et al.* (eds). 1987. *Development of Bilingual Proficiency: Final Report*. Modern Language Centre OISE, Toronto.

Harris, R. 1987. *The Language Machine*. Duckworth.

Hatch, E.M. 1983. *Psycholinguistics: A Second Language Perspective*. Newbury House, Rowley, Mass.

Hawkins, E.W. 1979. Language as a curriculum study. In *The Mother Tongue and Other Languages in Education. NCLE Papers and Reports* 2, 61–70. Centre for Information and Language Teaching.

Hawkins, E. 1981. *Modern Languages in the Curriculum*. Cambridge University Press.

Hawkins, E. 1984. *Awareness of Language. An Introduction*. Cambridge University Press.

Heap, B. 1988a. Teach English proper. *Link*, 9(1), 1–2, 8.

Heap, B. 1988b. Wigan language project – Evaluation of language awareness course. *Illuminating English*. Wigan Education Office.

Henerson, M.E., Morris, L.L. and Fitz-Gibbon, C.T. 1987. *How to Measure Attitudes*. Sage.

Higgs, T. and Cifford, R. 1983. The push toward communication. In Higgs, R. (ed.) *Teaching for Proficiency: The Organizing Principle*. National Textbook Company, Lincolnwood, IL.

Her Majesty's Inspectorate. 1977. *Matters for Discussion 3: Modern Languages in Comprehensive Schools*. HMSO.

HMSO. 1985. *The National Criteria. French.*

Hoey, M. 1983. *On the Surface of Discourse*. George Allen & Unwin.

Holec, H. 1980. Learner-centred communicative language teaching: needs analysis revisited. *Studies in Second Language Acquisition*, 3(1), 26–33.

Holmes, J. 1986. Snarks, quarks and cognates: an elusive fundamental particle in reading comprehension. *The ESPecialist*, 15, 13–40. CEPRIL, São Paulo, Brazil.

Holmes, J.L. 1988. Nine products in search of a process: the use of summaries in EAP. *The ESPecialist*, 9. CEPRIL, São Paulo, Brazil.

Holmes, J.L. 1989. Feedback: a systems approach to course design and evaluation. Working Paper 21. CEPRIL, São Paulo, Brazil.

Holmes, J.L., Ramos, R. de C.G. 1990. Tuning an evaluation instrument: validating a summary writing task for testing EAP reading comprehension. Paper given at AILA World Congress, Thessaloniki, April 1990.

Hornby, P.A. 1977. *Bilingualism: Psychological, Social and Educational Implications*. Academic Press, New York.

Horwitz, E.K. 1987. Surveying student beliefs about language learning. In Wenden, A. and Rubin, J. (eds).

Houghton, D., Long, C. and Fanning, P. 1988. Autonomy and individualization in language learning: The role and responsibility of the EAP tutor. In *ELT Documents 131: Individualization and Autonomy in Language Learning*.

Houlton, D. 1985. *All our Languages*. Edward Arnold.

Houlton, D. and Willey, R. 1983. *Why Support Children's Bilingualism?* Longman.

Hubbard, P., Jones, H., Thornton, B. and Wheeler, R. 1983. *A Training Course for TEFL*. Oxford University Press.

Hudson, R. 1984. *Word Grammar*. Blackwell.

Hull, C.H. and Nie, N. 1981. *SPSS Update 7–9*. McGraw-Hill, New York.

Hutchinson, T. 1986. *Project English*, Vol. II. Oxford University Press.

Hutchinson, T. and Waters, A. 1987. *English for Specific Purposes: A Learning-Centred Approach*. Cambridge University Press.

Ivanič, R. 1988. Critical language awareness in action. *Language Issues*, 2(2), 2–7.

Jackson, L. 1983. Linguistics on a degree course. *Quinquereme*, 6, 88–94.

James, C. (forthcoming). Accommodation in crosslanguage encounters in foreign language learning contexts. *Papers and Studies in Contrastive Linguistics*.

Johansson, S. 1973. The identification and evaluation of errors in foreign languages: a functional approach. In Svartvik, J. (ed.) *Errata*. CWK Gleerup, Lund, pp. 102–14.

Johnstone, B. 1989. Linguistic strategies and cultural styles for persuasive discourse. In Ting-Toomey, S. and Korzenny, F. (eds). *Language, Communication and Culture: Current Directions*. Sage, pp. 139–56.

Kaplan, R. 1984. Cultural thought patterns in inter-cultural education. In McKay, S. (ed.).

Karmiloff-Smith, A. 1979. *A Functional Approach to Child Language: a Study of Determiners and Reference*. Cambridge University Press.

Keenan, E. 1985. Passive in the world's languages. In Shopen, T. (ed.)

Language Typology and Syntactic Description, Vol I. Cambridge University Press.

Khan, V.S. 1980. The 'mother tongue' of linguistic minorities in multicultural England. *Journal of Multilingual and Multicultural Development*, 1(1).

Klein, W. 1986. *Second Language Acquisition*. Cambridge University Press.

Knapp, K., Enninger, W. and Knapp-Potthoff, A. (eds). 1987. *Analyzing Intercultural Communication*. Mouton de Gruyter, New York, pp. 37–49.

Knowles, G. 1986. The role of the computer in the teaching of phonetics. In Leech, G. and Candlin, C.N. (eds), pp. 133–48.

Krashen, S.D. 1981. *Second Language Acquisition and Second Language Learning*. Pergamon.

Krashen, S. 1982. *Principles and Practice in Second Language Acquisition*. Pergamon.

Krashen, S.D. and Terrell, T.D. 1983. *The Natural Approach: Language Acquisition in the Classroom*. Pergamon.

Kuhn, T. 1962. *The Structure of Scientific Revolutions*. Chicago University Press.

Labov, W. 1966. *The Social Stratification of English in New York City*. Urban Language Series 1. Center for Applied Linguistics, Washington, DC.

Lakoff, R. 1974. What you can do with words: politeness, pragmatics and performatives. *Berkeley Studies in Syntax and Semantics*. Benjamins, Amsterdam.

Lalljee, M. 1987. Attribution theory and intercultural communication. In Knapp, K., Enninger, W. and Knapp-Potthoff, A. (eds) *Analyzing Intercultural Communication*. Mouton de Gruyter, New York, pp. 37–49.

Lambert, W.E. and Tucker, G.R. 1972. *Bilingual Education of Children*. Newbury House, Rowley, Mass.

Lee, W.R. 1969. Some points about ways and means in the foreign-language course. *English Language Teaching Journal*, 23(2), 100–7.

Leech, G. 1986. Automatic grammatical analysis and its educational applications. In Leech, G. and Candlin, C.N. (eds), pp. 205–14.

Leech, G. and Candlin, C.N. (eds). 1986. *Computers in English Language Teaching and Research*. Longman.

Levelt, W., Sinclair, A. and Javella, R.J. 1978. Causes and functions of linguistic awareness in language acquisition: some introductory remarks. In Sinclair, A., Jarvella, R. and Levelt, W. (eds) *The Child's Conception of Language*. Springer, Berlin, pp. 1–14.

Lewin, M. 1979. *Understanding Psychological Research*. Wiley & Sons.

Little, D., Devitt, S. and Singleton, D. 1988. *Authentic Texts in Foreign Language Teaching: Theory and Practice*. Authentik, Dublin.

Little, D., Devitt, S. and Singleton, D. 1989. *Learning Foreign Languages from Authentic Texts: Theory and Practice*. Authentik, Dublin, in association with Centre for Information on Language Teaching (London).

Little, D. and Singleton, G.D.M. 1988. Authentic materials and the role of fixed support in language teaching: towards a manual for language learners. *CLCS Occasional Paper No. 20*. Dublin, Trinity College, Centre for Language and Communication Studies.

Liu Guo Qang. 1988. Interactive behaviour and interlanguage development.

Paper presented at the 1988 Annual Congress of the Applied Linguistics Association of Australia.

Long, M. 1983. Does second language instruction make a difference? A review of the research. *TESOL Quarterly*, **17**(3), 359–82.

Long, M.H. 1988. Maturational constraints on language development. *University of Hawaii Working Papers in ESL*, **7**(1), 1–53.

Marland, M. 1986. Towards a curriculum policy for a multilingual world. *British Journal of Language Teaching*, **24**(3), 123–38.

Martin, J.R. 1989. *Factual Writing: Exploring and Challenging Social Reality*. Oxford University Press.

Masny, D. (in press) Linguistic awareness and second language learning. *ITL: Review of Applied Linguistics*.

Masny, D. 1987. The role of language and cognition in L2 linguistic awareness. In Lantolf, J.P. and Labarca, A. (eds) *Research in Second Language Learning: Focus on the Classroom*. Ablex, Norwood, N.J., pp. 55–71.

Masny, D. and d'Anglejan, A. 1985. Language, cognition and second language grammaticality judgements. *Journal of Psycholinguistic Research*, **14**, 175–97.

Mason, M. 1986. The deficit hypothesis revisited (or Basil Bernstein, you were right first time!). *Educational Studies*, **12**(3), 279–89.

Mason, M. 1987. The linguistic mechanisms of abstract thought: a model and supporting stylistic analysis. *ITL Review of Applied Linguistics*, **75**, 1–35.

McDonald, P.F. and Sagar, J.C. 1975. Beyond contextual studies. *ITL Review of Applied Linguistics*, **13**(1), 19–34.

McGroarty, M. 1987. Patterns of persistent second language learners: elementary Spanish. Paper presented at the Annual Meeting of Teachers of English to Speakers of Other Languages, Miami, FL.

McKay, S. (ed.) 1984. *Composing in a Second Language*. Newbury House, Rowley, Mass.

Meisel, J.M. 1987. Strategies of second language acquisition: more than one kind of simplification! In Andersen, R.W. (ed.) *Pidginization and Creolization as Language Acquisition*. Newbury House, Rowley, Mass, pp. 12–157.

Meisel, J., Clahsen, H. and Pienemann, M. 1981. On determining developmental sequences in natural second language acquisition. *Studies in Second Language Acquisition*, **3**(1), 109–35.

Michaels, S. and Collins, J. 1984. Oral discourse styles: Classroom interaction and the acquisition of literacy. In Tannen, D. (ed.) *Advances in Discourse Processes: Coherence in Spoken and Written Discourse*. Ablex, Norwood, N.J., pp. 219–44.

Milroy, J. and Milroy, L. 1978. Belfast: change and variation in an urban vernacular. In Trudgill, P. (ed.) *Sociolinguistic Patterns in British English*. Edward Arnold, pp. 19–36.

Milroy, L. 1980. *Language and Social Networks*. Blackwell.

Mitchell, R. 1988. *Communicative Language Teaching in Practice*. CILT, London.

Mullen, K.A. 1980. Evaluating writing proficiency in ESL. In Oller, J.W. Jr and Perkins, K. (eds) *Research in Language Testing*. Newbury House, Rowley, Mass. pp. 160–70.

Naiman, N., Frohlich, M. and Todesco, A. 1975. The good second language learner. *TESL Talk*, (6), 58–75.
Naiman, N., Frohlich, M., Stern, H.H. and Todesco, A. 1978. *The Good Language Learner*. OISE Publications, Toronto.
National Association for the Teaching of English (NATE). 1987. *Evidence to the Committee of Inquiry into the Teaching of English Language*. Mimeo.
National Writing Project. 1986, 1987. *About Writing*, Nos 2 and 6. Newsletter of the National Writing Project.
NCC. March 1988. *National Curriculum: Draft Key Stage Order 1 for English*.
Nemoianu, A.M. 1980. *The Boat's Gonna Leave: A Study of Children Learning a Second Language from Conversations with Other Children*. Benjamins, Amsterdam.
Nevo, N. (forthcoming) Test-taking strategies on a multiple-choice test of reading comprehension. To appear in *Language Testing*.
Nicholas, H.R. 1987. A comparative study of the acquisition of German as a first and as a second language. Unpublished PhD thesis, Monash University.
Nisbett, R.E., Caputo, C., Legant, P. and Maracek, J. 1973. Behaviour as seen by the actor and as seen by the observer. *Journal of Personality and Social Psychology*, **27**, 154–64.

Oleksy, W. (ed.) 1989. *Contrastive Pragmatics*. Benjamins, Amsterdam.
Oller, J.W. Jr 1979. *Language Tests at School*. Longman.
Oller, J.W. Jr and Perkins, K. (eds). 1980. *Research in Language Testing*. Newbury House, Rowley, Mass.
O'Malley, J.M., Chamot, A.U., Stewner-Manzanarez, R. Russo, R.P. and Kupper, L. 1985. Learning strategy application with students of English as a second language. *TESOL Quarterly*, **19**(3), 557–84.
Oxford, R.L. 1989. The use of language learning strategies: a synthesis of studies with implications for strategy training. *System*, **17**(2), 235–47.
Oxford, R.L. 1990. *Language Learning Strategies. What Every Teacher Should Know*. Newbury House, New York.

Page, B. and Hewitt, D. 1987. *Languages Step by Step: Graded Objectives in the UK*. CILT, London.
Peck, A.J. 1988. *Language Teachers at Work*. Prentice-Hall, Englewood Cliffs, N.J.
Pijls, F., Daelemens, W. and Kempen, G. 1987. Artificial intelligence tools for grammar and spelling instruction. *Instructional Science*, **16**, 319–36.
Politzer, R.L. and McGroaty, M. 1985. An exploratory study of learning behaviours and their relationship to gains in linguistic and communicative competence. *TESOL Quarterly*, **19**(1), 103–24.
Porcher, L. 1983. Migrant workers learning French in France: a practical experiment. In Richterich, R. (ed.), pp. 14–23.
Prabhu, N. 1987. *Second Language Pedagogy*. Oxford University Press.

Quirk, R. and Svartvik, J. 1966. *Investigating Linguistic Acceptability*. Mouton, The Hague.

Quirk, R., Greenbaum, S., Leech, G. and Svartvik, J. 1986. *A Comprehensive Grammar of the English Language*. Longman.

Radford, A. 1981. *Transformational Syntax*. Cambridge University Press.

Ramesden, P. (ed.). 1988. *Improving Learning: New Perspectives*. Kogan Page.

Ramos, R.G. 1988. Estrategias Usadas por Falsos Principiantes na Leitura de Textos Academicos em Ingles. Unpublished MA thesis, Pontificia Universidade Catolica de São Paulo, São Paulo, Brazil.

Read, C. 1978. Children's awareness of language, with emphasis on sound systems. In Sinclair, A. *et al.* (eds), pp. 65–82.

Reber, A.S. and Allen, R. 1985. Syntactical learning and judgement, still unconscious and still abstract: Comment on Dulany, Carlson and Dewey. *Journal of Experimental Psychology: General*, 114, 17–24.

Reid, J.M. 1987. The learning style preferences of ESL students. *TESOL Quarterly*, 21(1), 87–111.

Richards, J. 1985. *The Context of Language Teaching*. Cambridge University Press.

Richterich, R. 1975. The analysis of language needs: illusion–pretext–necessity. *Modern Language Learning by Adults: Education and Culture*, 28, 9–14.

Richterich, R. 1983. *Case Studies in Identifying Language Needs*. Pergamon.

Richterich, R. 1984. Identifying language needs as a means of determining educational objectives with the learners. In van Ek, J.A. and Trim, J.L.M. (eds) *Across the Threshold*. Council of Europe, Pergamon, pp. 29–32.

Richterich, R. and Chancerel, J.L. 1978. *Identifying the Needs of Adults Learning a Foreign Language*. Council of Europe. Pergamon.

Rinvolucri, M. 1984. *Grammar Games: Cognitive, Affective, and Drama Activation for EFL Students*. Cambridge University Press.

Rivers, W. 1983. *Communicating Naturally in a Second Language*. Cambridge University Press.

Roberts, C. and Sayers, P. 1987. Keeping the gate: how judgements are made in interethnic interviews. In Knapp, K., Enninger, W. and Knapp-Potthoff, A. (eds) *Analyzing Intercultural Communication*. Mouton de Gruyter, New York, pp. 111–35.

Robinson, P.O. (ed.). 1988. *Academic Writing Process and Product*. ELT Document No. 129. Modern English Publications and the British Council.

Robinson, R. 1980. *ESP: English for Specific Purposes*. Pergamon.

Rogers, J. 1982. The world for sick proper. *English Language Teaching Journal*, 36(3), 144–51.

Rommetveit, R. 1988. On literacy and the myth of literal meaning. In Saljo, R. (ed.), pp. 117–126

Rose, M. (ed.). 1985. *When a Writer Can't Write: Studies in Writer's Block and other Composing Process Problems*. Guilford Press, New York.

Rothery, J. 1989. Learning about language. In Hasan, R. and Martin, J.R. (eds) *Language Development: Learning Language, Learning Culture. Meaning and Choice in Language. Studies for Michael Halliday*. Ablex, Norwood, N.J. pp. 199–286.

Rousson, M. 1975. The concept of need. In Chancerel, J.L. *et al.* (eds) *Adult Education 'Needs' – Methods of Identifying Them*. Council for Europe, Strasbourg, Mimeo *CCC/EES*, 75(20), 3.

Rubin, J. 1975. What the 'good language learner' can teach us. *TESOL Quarterly*, 9(1), 41–51.

Rubin, J. 1987. Learner strategies: theoretical assumptions, research, history and typology. In Wenden, A. and Rubin, J. (eds) *Learner Strategies in Language Learning*. Prentice-Hall, Englewood Cliffs, N.J.

Rutherford, W. 1987. *Second Language Grammar: Learning and Teaching*. Longman.

Ryan, E.B. 1980. Metalinguistic awareness and reading. In Waterhouse, H., Fischer, K.M. and Ryan, E.B. (eds) *Linguistic Awareness and Reading*. Del, International Reading Association, Newark, pp. 193–206.

Ryan, E.B. and Ledger, G.W. 1984. Learning to attend to sentence structure: links between metalinguistic development and reading. In Downing, J. and Valtin, R. (eds), pp. 149–71.

Sager, J.C. and Geake, P.M. 1981. The role of modern languages in degree course in European studies. *Journal of Area Studies*, 4.

Saljo, R. (ed.). 1988. *The Written World*. Springer-Verlag, Berlin.

Sanderson, D. 1983. *Modern Language Teachers in Action*. Language Materials Development Unit, York University.

Saywitz, K.C. and Wilkinson, L.C. 1982. Age-related differences in metalinguistic awareness. In Kuczaj, S. (ed.) *Language Development: Language, Thought, and Culture*. Lawrence Erlbaum, Hillsdale, N.J., pp. 129–50.

Schank, R.C. and Abelson, R.P. 1977. Scripts, plans and knowledge. In Johnson-Laird, P.N. and Wason, P.C. (eds) *Thinking: Readings in Cognitive Science*. Cambridge University Press.

Scholfield, P.J. 1988. Towards CALingL: Computer Assisted Linguistics Learning. *Bangor Teaching Resource Materials in Linguistics*, 1, 20–33.

Schumann, J.H. 1975. Affective factors and the problem of age in second language acquisition. *Language Learning*, 25(2), 209–35.

Schumann, J.H. 1986. Research on the acculturation model for second language acquisition. *Journal of Multilingual and Multicultural Development*, 7, 379–92.

Scollon, R. and Scollon, B.K. 1981. *Narrative, Literacy and Face in Interethnic Communication*. Ablex, Norwood, N.J.

Scollon, R. and Scollon, B.K. 1983. Face in interethnic communication. In Richards, J.C. and Schmidt, R.W. (eds) *Language and Communication*. Longman.

Scott, M. 1986. *Conscientização*. Working Paper No. 19. CEPRIL, PUC-SP, São Paulo.

Scott, M., Oliveira, N.A. de, Dias, R. and Pimenta, S.D. de O. 1988. *Teaching Critical Reading through Set Theory*. Working Paper No. 20. CEPRIL Pontificia Universidade Catolica, São Paulo.

Seliger, H. 1975. Inductive method and deductive method in language teaching: a re-examination. *ITL Review of Applied Linguistics*, 13(1), 1–18.

Sharwood Smith, M. 1981. Consciousness raising and the second language learner. *Applied Linguistics*, 11(2).

Shaw, P.A. 1982. Ad hoc needs analysis. *Modern English Teacher*, 10(1).

Sinclair, A., Jarvella, R.V. and Levelt, W.J.M. 1978. *The Child's Conception of Language*. Springer-Verlag, Berlin.

Smith, C. 1979. The acquisition of time talk: relations between child and adult grammars. *Journal of Child Language*, 7, 263–78.

Smith, C. L. and Tager-Flusberg, H. 1982. Metalinguistic awareness and language development. *Journal of Experimental Child Psychology*, 34, 449–68.

Smith, M.S. 1981. Consciousness-raising and the second language learner. *Applied Linguistics*, 2(2).

Snow, C.E. 1976. Semantic primacy in first and second language acquisition. *ISB Utrecht*, 1(2, 3), 137–61.

Snow, C.E. 1987. Beyond conversations: second language learners' acquisition of description and explanation. In Lantolf, J.P. and Labarca, A. (eds) *Research in Second Language Learning: Focus on the Classroom*. Ablex, Norwood, N.J., pp. 3–16.

Snow, C.E., Cancino, H., Gonzalez, P. and Shriberg, E. (in press). Second language learners' formal definitions: an oral language correlate of school literacy. In Bloome, D. (ed.) *Literacy in Functional Settings*. Ablex, Norwood, N.J.

Sorace, A. 1985. Metalinguistic knowledge and language use in acquisition-poor environments. *Applied Linguistics*, 6(3), 239–54.

Statutory Instruments. 1989. The Education (National Curriculum) (Modern Languages) Order.

Stephens, C. 1989. Metalanguage Set in Context. Unpublished MA (Education) dissertation, University of Southampton.

Stern, H. H. 1975. What can we learn from the good language learner? *Canadian Modern Language Review*, 34, 304–18.

Stern, H. H. 1983. *Fundamental Concepts in Language Teaching*. Oxford University Press.

Stevick, E.W. 1976. *Memory, Meaning and Method*. Newbury House, Rowley, Mass.

Stevick, E.W. 1980. *Teaching Languages: A Way and Ways*. Newbury House, Rowley, Mass.

Stock, H.L. 1977. The age barrier in second language acquisition: postwar German migrants in South Australia. MS thesis, Monash University.

Stubbs, M.W. 1976. *Language, Schools and Classrooms*. Methuen.

Stubbs, M.W. 1986. *Educational Linguistics*. Blackwell.

Swain, M. and Lapkin, S. 1982. *Evaluating Bilingual Education: A Canadian Case Study*. Multilingual Matters, Clevedon.

Swales, J. 1981. *Aspects of Article Introductions*. Aston ESP Research Reports No. 1.

Swales, J. 1985. A genre-based approach to language across the curriculum. Paper delivered to 1985 RELC Conference, Singapore.

Swales, J. 1986. The experimental research article: an applied genre analysis. Paper presented at the Conference on College Composition and Communication, New Orleans.

Swales, J. 1987. Utilizing the literatures in teaching the research paper. *TESOL Quarterly*, 21(1), March.

Tannen, D. 1982. Oral and literate strategies in spoken and written narratives. *Language*, 58, 1–22.

Tansley, P. 1986. *Community Languages in the Primary School*. NFER–Nelson.

Tarantino, M. 1988. Italian In-field EST users self-assess their macro- and micro-level needs: a case study. *ESP Journal*, 7(1), 33–53.

Terrell, T. 1981. The natural approach in bilingual education. In California State Department of Education (ed.) *Schooling and Language Minority Students: A Theoretical Framework*. Los Angeles, California, EDAC, CSULA, pp. 117–46.

Thomas, J. 1983. Cross-cultural pragmatic failure. *Applied Linguistics*, 4, 91–112.

Thomas, J. 1988. The role played by metalinguistic awareness in second and third language learning. *Journal of Multilingual and Multicultural Development*, 9(3), 235–46.

Tibble, J.W. (ed.). 1966. *The Study of Education*. Routledge and Kegan Paul.

Ting-Toomey, S. and Korzenny, F. (eds). 1989. *Language, Communication and Culture: Current Direction*. Sage.

Tinkel, A.J. 1979. A proposal for the teaching of linguistics at the secondary school level. *Midland Association for Linguistic Studies Journal*, 4, 79–100.

Tinkel, A.J. 1980. *The Relationship between the Study of Language and the Teaching of Languages*. National Congress on Languages in Education Working Paper B4. CILT, London.

Tinkel, A.J. 1981a. The relationship between the study of language and the teaching of languages. In *Issues in Language Education* NCLE Papers and Reports 3. CILT, London.

Tinkel, A.J. 1981b. Language study in the sixth form. *Nottingham Linguistic Circular*, 10(2), 186–92.

Tinkel, A.J. 1985. Contributions to *Language Awareness*. National Congress on Languages in Education Papers and Reports, Vol. 6, Donmall B.G. (ed.), CILT, London: Methodology related to language awareness work, pp. 37–45; Evaluation and assessment: formal examinations, pp. 85–89; Reports of courses and initiatives in core schools: The Oratory School, Reading, pp. 145–70.

Tinkel, A.J. 1986. Language awareness in the sixth form. *Modern Grammar Studies*, 3, 33–52.

Tinkel, A.J. 1988. *Explorations in Language*. Cambridge University Press.

Torrance, N. and Olson, D.R. 1984. Oral language competence and the acquisition of literacy. In Pellegrini, A.D. and Yawkey, T.D. (eds) *Advances in Discourse Processes: The Development of Oral and Written Language in Social Contexts*, Vol. 13. Ablex, Norwood, N.J., pp. 167–84.

Triandis, H.C. 1971. *Attitude and Attitude Change*. Wiley, New York.

Tribble, C. 1988. Lexical patterns in native and nonnative speaker writing: a preliminary corpus-based study of procedural lexis. Paper to the AGM of the British Association for Applied Linguistics, Exeter.

Trim, J.L.M. 1988. Foreword to Tinkel, A.J., *Explorations in Language*, p. vii.

Trudgill, P. 1975. *Accent, Dialect and the School*. Edward Arnold.

Tudor, I. 1988. Translation – between learning and acquisition. *Die neueren Sprachen*, 87(4), 360–71.

Tunmer, W.E., Pratt, C. and Herriman, M.L. (eds). 1984. *Metalinguistic Awareness in Children: Theory, Research and Implications*. Springer-Verlag, Berlin.

Tyacke, M. and Mendelsohn, D. 1986. Student needs: cognitive as well as communicative. *TESL Canada Journal*, **1**, 171–83.

Ullmann, R. and Geva, E. 1984. Approaches to observation in second language classes. In Allen, P. and Swain, M. (eds) *Language Issues and Education Policies*. ELT Document No. 119. Pergamon.

Ur, P. 1988. *Grammar Practice Activities*. Cambridge University Press.

Van Baalen, T. 1983. Giving learners rules: a study into the effect of grammatical instruction with varying degrees of explicitness. *Interlanguage Studies Bulletin*, **7**(1), 71–97.

Van Elek, T. and Oskarsson, M. 1972. An experiment assessing the relative effectiveness of two methods of teaching grammatical structures to adults. *ITL Review of Applied Linguistics* **X**(1), 60–72.

Walmsley, J. 1984. *The Uselessness of 'Formal Grammar'*. Committee for Linguistics in Education Occasional Paper, University College, London.

Weir, C. 1988. Academic writing – can we please all the people all the time? In ELT Document No. 129. Pergamon.

Wenden, A. 1986a. Helping language learners think about learning. *English Language Teaching Journal* **40**(1), 3–12.

Wenden, A. 1986b. What do second language learners know about their language learning? A second look at retrospective accounts. *Applied Linguistics*, **7**, 186–205.

Wenden, A. 1987. Conceptual background and utility. In Wenden, A. and Rubin, J. (eds) *Learner Strategies in Language Learning*. Prentice-Hall, Englewood Cliffs, N.J., pp. 3–13.

Wenden, A. and Rubin, J. (eds). 1987. *Learner Strategies in Language Learning*. Prentice-Hall International, Englewood Cliffs, N.J.

West, C. and Zimmerman, D. 1985. Gender, language and discourse. In van Dijk, T. (ed.) *Handbook of Discourse Analysis*: Vol. 4: *Discourse Analysis in Society*. Academic Press, New York.

Widdowson, H.G. 1983. *Learning Purpose and Language Use*. Oxford University Press.

WIDA. 1989. *Software Catalogue*. Wida Software Ltd, 2 Nicholas Gardens, London W5 5HY.

Wilkins, D. 1983. Some issues in communicative language teaching and their relevance to the teaching of languages in secondary schools. In Johnson, K. and Porter, D. (eds) *Perspectives in Communicative Language Teaching*. Academic Press, pp. 23–37.

Wright, L. 1987. APICALE: the teaching of French phonetic transcription and Romance philology. In Chesters, G. and Gardner, N. (eds), pp. 107–13.

Wright, T. 1990. Understanding classroom role relationships. In Richards, J.C. and Nunan, D. (eds) *Second Language Teacher Education*. Cambridge University Press.

Yaden, D.B. Jr and Templeton, S. (eds). 1986. *Metalinguistic Awareness and Beginning Literacy*. Heinemann.

Zimmerman, D. and West, C. 1975. Sex roles, interruptions and silence in conversations. In Thorne, B. and Henley, N. (eds) *Language and Sex: Difference and Dominance*. Newbury House, Rowley, Mass.

Zobl, H. 1983. L1 acquisition, age of L2 acquisition and the learning of word order. In Gass, S. and Selinker, L. (eds) *Language Transfer in Language Learning*. Newbury House, Rowley, Mass., pp. 205–21.

Index